D0060129

NO LONGER
PROPERTY OF PPLD

THE
HYPER-SOCIAL
ORGANIZATION

ECLIPSE YOUR
COMPETITION
BY LEVERAGING
SOCIAL MEDIA

FRANCOIS GOSSIEAUX

EDWARD K. MORAN

New York Chicago San Francisco Lisbon London
Madrid Mexico City Milan New Delhi San Juan
Seoul Singapore Sydney Toronto

The **McGraw·Hill** Companies

Copyright © 2010 by Francois Gossieaux and Edward K. Moran. All rights reserved. Printed in the United States of America. Except as permitted under the United States Copyright Act of 1976, no part of this publication may be reproduced or distributed in any form or by any means, or stored in a database or retrieval system, without the prior written permission of the publisher.

1 2 3 4 5 6 7 8 9 10   DOC/DOC 1 9 8 7 6 5 4 3 2 1 0

ISBN 978-0-07-171402-0
MHID 0-07-171402-2

McGraw-Hill books are available at special quantity discounts to use as premiums and sales promotions or for use in corporate training programs. To contact a representative, please e-mail us at bulksales@mcgraw-hill.com.

The views expressed herein are those of the individual authors in their personal capacity, and do not represent the views, positions or opinions of their respective employers, or any organizations with which the authors may be professionally affiliated.

To my late mother, Antoinette Verelst Gossieaux,
the first love of my life.

—Francois

To my smallest, but most favorite tribe:
Janet, Kelly, Eddie, Kate, and Grace.

—Ed

CONTENTS

foreword

Hyper-Social
Revolutions and Revelations

In the 1990s, with the advent of the Internet, there was a lot of buzz about how revolutionary the Internet was going to be. In my own field, marketing, everyone was thrilled about the possibility of selling things directly to consumers online, in a disintermediated fashion. E-commerce was the name of the game. And added to e-commerce were online advertising, Webvertising, and pay-for-content as the other big deals. Each was enthusiastically marketed as the Big Internet Revolution.

But time has proved these proclamations of business revolution to be wrong.

Although the ability of organizations to reach out to consumers in new ways has been extremely important, and has altered the way in which business has been done over the last decade, they really weren't all that revolutionary in their execution or implications.

Activated by the burgeoning Internet, however, there was another revolution brewing. Drawing upon the Situationist philosophers for inspiration, the great Sufi anarchist poet Hakim Bey wrote in 1994, "Meeting face-to-face is already the revolution."

Little did Bey seem to suspect that the Internet would bring some of the powerfully subversive social forces that arise when people gather away from their institutionalized circumstances into the homes of the mainstream. From where we stand today, it looks as if the bigger Internet revolution was not so much about organizations stretching out to reach consumers in new ways, but about consumers using the Internet to reach out and connect *with one another* in new, and endlessly increasing, ways.

Technologically facilitated social connection is the big revolution, the social movement, the transformation of our times. And yet, given that this is such an enormous change, we have a relative paucity of understanding of it.

That's where the book you are holding in your hands comes in. Revolutionary times call for revolutionary thinking. What Francois Gossieaux and Edward K. Moran have written in this book is nothing less than a guidebook to this new revolution, an initial charting of this new terrain. More than that, it is an action plan that not only enlightens managers and everyone else about *what* to do in these exciting, ridiculously scary new times of transition, but *why* to do it.

And that explanation makes a big difference.

I realize that there is no shortage of books about the Internet or about new technology and business. Over the last 20 years, I have read literally hundreds of them. I have stacks of what I tend to quickly dismiss as shallow pop business management books. You know the ones. Some of them are filled with examples, but there is no connection between the examples, and no principles that emerge from them. Some of them are loaded with how-tos and tactics. But although they tell us what to do, we never understand why we should do it, and with technology's rapid pace of change, those tidbits of knowledge spoil more quickly than an opened carton of yogurt. Then there are the big-picture pop business books that promise to deliver a whole new way of thinking. But that way of thinking often tends to be composed of just one idea. Usually, it's not even a great idea.

Academic books usually aren't much better. You know the ones I am talking about? Those thick, erudite academic volumes, usually written by B-school professors, that use complex and rigorous research and strong, original thinking, but that cloak them in inaccessible language and abstract sentences forms? Often when I finish reading one chapter of one of these books, I can barely remember what it was I was supposed to have learned. And because they are so abstract and high-level, they rarely engage us with examples or tell real, functioning managers what it is that we are supposed to do.

It is quite rare indeed to find to find a book about such an important topic that is accessible, well researched, and substantively deep. I am delighted to say that *The Hyper-Social Organization* is such a book.

Into a marketplace that is virtually starved for insight about social media, and filled with trivial how-to books or popular management approaches that treat only a small element of the vast social changes that are rippling through society, *The Hyper-Social Organization* is the real deal: an authentic, informed, and organized organizational eye-opener.

In recent years, talented scholar-authors like John Sherry, Doug Holt, Bernard Cova, and Grant McCracken have convinced a growing audience that adopting an anthropological approach can add enormous insight to the practice of brand and marketing management. How powerful is it to bring this same cultural approach to the understanding of social media?

Talented practitioner-thinkers like Don Tapscott, Marc Gobé, Alex Wipperfurth, and Sean Moffitt have demonstrated to wide general audiences how a focus on communities is changing the world of business. How useful and topical is it, then, not only to bring, but to explain and develop how these ideas about tribes and communities ripple throughout and completely transform the new, Hyper-Social organization?

How ironic is it that a book about the way technology changes our world would ultimately be about recognizing the most human elements of our social life, an idea that these authors summarize so nicely in their notion of Human 1.0?

To this list of outstanding recent thinkers, writers, and influencers, we must add Francois Gossieaux and Ed Moran, for with this wonderful exploration of the expanding universe of sociality, they share new and important insights for us all.

And it is ultimately not in its technical knowledge, nor even in its practical business acumen, that the biggest successes of this book lie. This book succeeds so well because it exemplifies and develops the still largely nascent ability of the Internet to humanize human pursuits, to connect the disaffected, to reorient, to deinstitutionalize at least as much as it disintermediates. It is a book about talent tribes, about social networks, about messiness, gift economies, consumer experiences, and the convergence of marketing management and general management.

But, much more than this, it is a book about our increasing humanity, the expansion of the frontiers of our sociality and connectedness. And I find this topic endlessly exciting.

So treat yourself to some brave new thoughts about one of the most, if not the single most, important revolutions of our time. Don't just buy this book. Read it. Absorb it. And use the ideas in *The Hyper-Social Organization* to humanize your organization and our world.

—Robert V. Kozinets
Professor of Marketing, York University, Toronto,
Marketing Researcher, and author of *Netnography:*
Doing Ethnographic Research Online

acknowledgments

The passionate, helpful interest the following people have taken in the development of this book are further proof of the power of Hyper-Sociality, and the strength of the Human 1.0 traits we discuss throughout the following chapters. These professors, researchers and businesspeople have generously shared what they've learned as organizations undergo the Hyper-Social shift, and have provided us with energetic and pointed feedback. We deeply appreciate the time these executives and managers have contributed, and how their involvement has kept the book firmly planted in practicality as opposed to solely theory.

We especially appreciate the input we received from Beth Comstock (CMO, GE), Marty St. George (CMO, JetBlue), Renee Hopkins (editor, Strategy & Innovation, lead editor for Innosight's InnoBlog), Robert Kozinets (Professor of Marketing, Chair Marketing Department, Schulich School of Business, York University), Utpal Dholokia (William S.Mackey, Jr. and Verne F. Simons

Distinguished Associate Professor of Management, Rice University), Caroline Wiertz (Faculty of Management, Cass Business School, London), Luis Suarez (IBM), Rawn Shah (IBM), John Hagel (The Deloitte Center for the Edge), Paul Levy (CEO, Beth Israel Deaconess Medical Center), Barry Judge (CMO, Best Buy), Mark Colombo (SVP Digital Access Marketing, FedEx), Janet Swaysland (SVP Social Media, Monster.com.), Mark Yolton (SVP Communities, SAP), Shel Holtz (author of multiple books, and principal at Holtz Communication + Technology) and David Rogers (Executive Director, Columbia Business School Center on Global Brand Leadership, and author of *The Network Is Your Customer*).

We are also grateful to all of the many CMO 2.0 conversation guests that have been interviewed over the past year and a half (http://www.cmotwo.com) and who spent hours answering our questions and sharing their experiences, including Mark Gambill (CMO, CDW), Porter Gale (CMO, Virgin America), Ram Menon (CMO, TIBCO), Susan Lavington (SVP Marketing, USA Today), Christa Carone (CMO, Xerox), Dan Ariely (author and professor at Duke), Don Peppers (author, and cofounder of Peppers & Rogers Group), Gail Galuppo (CMO, Western Union), Alan Webber (author, and cofounder of Fast Company), Ted Gilvar (CMO, Monster.com), Rob Spencer (Pfizer), Erin Nelson (CMO, Dell), Manish Mehta (VP of Social Media and Community at Dell), Pete Blackshaw (EVP, Nielsen Online), Will Prest (CMO, Transamerica Retirement Services), Jeff Hayzlett (CMO, Kodak), Jay Gillespie (CMO, Fiskars), and Larry Flanagan (CMO, MasterCard).

We also deeply appreciate the input of Valeria Maltoni (Conversation Agent), Rachel Happe (The Community Roundtable), Scott Wilder (Edelman), Rachel Makool, Geno Church (Word of

Mouth Inspiration Officer, Brains on Fire), Jon Husband (author), Richard Binhammer (Dell), John Puchalski (aka GRIZZ, Director of Ambassadors at Killington—for understanding and also for teaching me (Francois) a thing or two about large volunteer programs, Karim Lakhani (Harvard Business School), Kelly Morrissey (for keeping us on track and for reviewing early chapters), Chris Thoen (Head of Connect + Develop at P&G), Jen McClure (founder of the Society for New Communications Research), Robert Godes (University of Maryland), Nora Ganim Barnes, PhD. (University of Massachusetts Dartmouth), Dave Logan (author of *Tribal Leadership*), David Fugate, our literary agent who grasped the importance of Hyper-Sociality earlier than most people, Mary Glenn at McGraw-Hill, our colleagues, especially Phil Asmundson, Noel Spiegel, Jolyon Barker, Wally Gregory, Bill Ribaudo, Hylton Jolliffe, and Lois Kelly who supported our fascination with social media and online social activities, and who have generously contributed their knowledge and experiences.

This book could not have been written without the support of a number of tribes, including our families. As we gathered the Tribalization of Business data and as we analyzed it, passionate groups emerged that challenged us, educated us, and guided us. These groups include the many workshop and conference participants over the past two years who have listened to our evolving views on the Four Pillars of Hyper-Sociality and who have helped us make sense of the data we collected. We also owe a great debt to the hundreds of companies that participated in the Tribalization of Business Study, and the many companies who reviewed the data with us, and suggested insightful interpretations.

introduction

Your Customers and Employees Are Hyper-Social. Is Your Business?

In the beginning, business and commerce were social exchanges—if you sold poor products, people would bad-mouth you and shun your operation, forcing you out of business or pushing you to improve your offering. We have always bought things based on who else bought the same product. That is why the most popular songs are also the most successful. Perhaps more important, we buy things based on the opinions of others who observed the original buyers. But as commerce scaled (and by scaling, we mean growing exponentially), and firms and multinational organizations arose, the social infrastructure did not expand with them. You could still bad-mouth a bad product, but the impact of that social action remained very local and had little effect on the success of that product. Buying because of what others bought or because of what others thought of the buyers became a little easier, but it was still fairly local in nature as well. The social disappeared from business and commerce, allowing some companies to develop bad habits in how they sold their goods and how they treated their customers, prospects, and employees.

With the rise of social media, which provides a massive platform of participation and a social infrastructure that is finally catching up with the commerce infrastructure, the social element is reentering commerce and business with a vengeance. People can now claim a share of voice that is equal to or larger than that of companies, employees can now develop support networks that cross the traditional hierarchical organization charts, and people can once again behave the way they were hardwired to behave in business and commerce—tribally, humanly, and socially.

To understand the changes that are afoot in the world of business, you are better off understanding Human 1.0, which took tens of thousands of years to develop, rather than Web 2.0, which took merely a decade. Throughout human evolution, we developed characteristics and reflexes that allowed us to behave Hyper-Socially—to become the only Hyper-Social species that could work cooperatively with individuals who were not our brothers or sisters or otherwise related to us. There are other species that are Hyper-Social, such as bees and ants, but within their very large societies, they are all brothers and sisters. There are also species that can act socially across kinship lines, but they do so only in small groups. Humans can be social across kinship lines on a city, national, or even global scale, resulting in our being the only species that can act Hyper-Socially on a large scale, without everyone being related.

Humans are not a species that is characterized by individual action, nor has our species been so successful solely because of individuals. Humanity's development has been characterized more by our innate drive to live in groups, to work together for common goals, to compromise, to extend favors, to value fair treatment, to care what others think about us, and to bond with others more often around common beliefs or goals than around common genes. This Human Hyper-Sociality surpasses even the intensely cooperative behavior of other social species because we are not constrained by having to be related to other members of our pack or hive. We can belong to multiple packs or hives simultaneously (we call them tribes), and therefore we can communicate with, innovate with, and cooperate with far more individuals. Given the flexibility, scalability, and fluidity of that sort of Hyper-Social behavior, it is clear why humanity has managed to create what it has.

It is the growth of this Hyper-Sociality, enabled by social media and new communication platforms, to levels never seen before that is changing business as we know it. So, then, what should you and your organization do about it? After all, Hyper-Social human relations can be pretty messy and unpredictable, and companies like order and predictability.

Our research shows that those companies that embrace Hyper-Sociality and those executives who drive their organizations to become Hyper-Social will likely be best positioned to deal with volatility, marketing effectiveness, uncertainty, globalization, growth, innovation, and other issues that are currently top of mind with most CEOs. It will be Hyper-Social organizations that are poised to emerge from the current deep economic recession as the new titans.

This book is about doing business differently in a Hyper-Social world. We will define what a Hyper-Social organization looks like and how you can transform your organization to become fit for the future. Based on the extensive research data that we have collected as part of our annual Tribalization of Business Study (sponsored by our respective companies, Human 1.0 [formerly Beeline Labs] and Deloitte, as well as by the Society for New Communications Research), in which we surveyed and interviewed more than 500 companies to understand how they leverage communities as part of their business, we will review the benefits that major companies are deriving from leveraging tribes and communities and from becoming Hyper-Social.

While anthropologists talk about "tribes" and sociologists talk about "communities," we will use the terms interchangeably. We will use case profiles of well-known companies to highlight the perils of resisting these inevitable changes. After reading this book, you will better understand the impact of Hyper-Sociality on your human capital needs and your organization chart, and grasp the management skills that you will have to develop. We will also arm you with tools to benchmark your company's "Hyper-Social Index" against that of your competitors and your different business units.

This book also relies on the research, scholarship, and innovation of a number of scientists, thinkers, and academics. Taking our concept to heart, we knew that only by Hyper-Socializing the researching of this book would we be exposed to all of the implications and opportunities presented by Hyper-Sociality. So we have drawn widely from others' thinking on a number of topics, including behavioral economics, brain science, evolutionary sociology, and management theory, to build out our hypotheses. In addition, we have presented the ideas in this book at a number of conferences and to a number of business executives, and have used their insights to improve our theories. Many of these leaders in their respective arenas have graciously agreed to speak with us and to be interviewed, and you will see their thoughts appear often in the pages to come.

Finally, we agree with what Alan Webber, the cofounder of *Fast Company* and author of *Rules of Thumb*, told us when we spoke with him: "And one of the things that I've seen over and over again, is a change from leaders who have all the answers to leaders who know the best questions to ask." In the spirit of this, we will end most of the chapters with guiding questions instead of classic summaries. We don't profess to have all, or even most, of the questions when it comes to the Hyper-Social shift, but we hope that the ones we have will provoke discussion, collaboration, and further research. So whenever you find us starting to ask too many questions, bear with us. It's our Hyper-Sociality showing.

part one

RESIST THE HYPER-SOCIAL SHIFT AT YOUR PERIL

one

How Did We Get Here?

How Social Media Drives Hyper-Sociality and Why Businesses Must Change

Most companies that are thinking about leveraging social media as part of their business—whether in marketing, customer service, new product innovation, employee communications, or public relations—see it as a new way to reach people. They focus on the *media* in *social media*. Missing from this strategy is the idea that social media is not about media, nor is it about Web 2.0 tools or the new rules that govern them. Social media is all about our social nature growing to levels never seen in human history. Social media is about certain Human 1.0 behaviors finally taking hold in the business world, where they've been long absent.

Industry guru Tim O'Reilly calls social media a "platform of participation," and that is exactly what it is: a massive platform of participation. Social media allows us to behave in ways that we are hardwired for in the first place—as humans. We can get frank recommendations from other humans instead of from faceless companies. When things don't work out, we can get mad at people instead of organizations. Our reciprocity reflex,[1] which enables us to be the only Hyper-Social species without all being brothers and sisters, can once again take center stage. We can help others and be helped. We can form tribes again—except that this time, our tribes will not be bound by geography, and we can belong to multiple tribes at the same time.

Social media is what has enabled the hardwired Human 1.0 behaviors to scale to levels never seen before in business; we call it *Hyper-Sociality*. And while some people will argue that our social behavior changes when it becomes virtual and large-scale, as we are seeing now, early research on the topic has the social science community thinking that our social behaviors won't change.[2]

Human 1.0

We may be living in a Web 2.0 world, but the behaviors that this new environment triggers are solidly Human 1.0, and they can largely be explained by the evolution of humans to become the only Hyper-Social species without all members having to be related.

What we buy and how we buy have been studied extensively by evolutionary biologists and behavioral economists. For instance, the way people seem to want to help others and be helped is caused by a reflex called reciprocity; the fact that we like to mimic others is caused by what are called mirror neurons; the reason that we like to look cool, at least on a subconscious level, is that it may help us find a better mate; the reason we buy the same things over and over again, even if it makes no sense, is that we are herding animals and in some cases self-herding. What this means is that if we buy a jar of fruit preserve for no good reason, and we sort of like it, we will keep buying that brand forever. We are creatures of habit, perhaps because that consistency makes it easier for us to make decisions. All of these behaviors have been hardwired into us over thousands of years of evolution, and have permitted us to be as successful as we have been.

In contrast, the modern business organization is quite young. Throughout its short history, business structures required us to behave in ways that were unnatural. Think, for instance, about the specialization of skills, or about the unnatural interactions resulting from the information imbalance that exists between producers and consumers of goods, or between employers and their employees. That unnatural environment has also caused companies to develop many bad habits along the way—both with customers and with employees.

It wasn't until recently that customers were asked to provide input into the design of new products and services, and for a good portion of the history of the enterprise, people had very limited choices—you could buy a Ford as long as it was black. Fake-sounding commercials touting the virtues of goods and services became commonplace. These messages worked because they were the only source of information that consumers had, and because there were few other channels of communication that were vying for their attention. In typical business jargon, companies started using war metaphors to describe their competitors, suppliers, and customers—and in some cases they started behaving as though they really were at war. Marketers "mounted campaigns" to pitch new products, and "fought for marketshare," against "entrenched competitors," all the while fighting to "win" new customers and "raise barriers" to entry.

Internally, some companies came to treat their employees as commodities, or interchangeable cogs in a big machine. Transparency was something to be shied away from; instead, companies embraced secrecy and sometimes deception. The rumor mill at the company water cooler had very limited reach and little impact, and it could basically be controlled. Command-and-control methods of management took hold (and to a far greater extent than efficient organizational theory would call for), limiting communication within the company mainly to vertical silos and between small groups of people who had direct reporting relationships.

A by-product of all this command and control is that trust in business virtually disappeared. In fact, according to the 2009 Edelman Trust Barometer,[3] trust in business continues to decrease, with trust and credibility hitting an all-time low in Edelman's tenth annual study. When trust disappears from an environment, everything becomes more expensive for everyone. For producers of goods and services, it means that they need to spend significantly more on marketing and sales to achieve the same results with skeptical customers. For consumers of goods and services, it means that they must conduct a lot more due diligence before making their buying decisions. Fortunately, as we will see in later chapters, Hyper-Social organizations can leverage social media to bring trust back into the equation and reduce transaction costs for all parties involved.

What happens now with Hyper-Sociality is that we can behave like humans again—not like consumers or human resources. We can talk to one another and help one another. If we're not happy with the company or its products, we can not only talk back directly to the company, but also talk to thousands of the company's other customers if we choose. And if we're not satisfied with the response, we can bad-mouth the company or the employees that wronged us, organize grassroots boycotts, and have an actual and immediate impact.

In fact, this willingness to pay a personal price in order to punish a company or person that treated us unfairly is a Human 1.0 trait as well. In his "ultimate bargaining game,"[4] Vernon L. Smith, the winner of the 2003 Nobel Prize in economics, asked pairs of people to play a game that would test fairness. In the game, one of the two people receives a sum of money, say $50, and is responsible for deciding how to split it up with the other person. That second person can either refuse the offer, in which case neither person gets any money, or accept the offer, in which case both people can keep the money. If you were to put your economist hat on and consider humans as rational beings, you would predict that the second person would accept any amount of money being offered to him; after all, refusing an offer would leave him with less money, since the two people would have to return the money. Well, in playing the game all around the world, the researchers found that there is a trigger amount, which differs somewhat from culture to culture, but which is significantly different from $1, at which the second person will refuse the offer. So in effect, there is a point at which the second person considers an offer unfair and is willing to pay a personal price (giving up whatever amount of money is being offered to him) in order to punish the first person for being unfair. That is what you are witnessing when people go out of their way to bad-mouth your product or service: not only are they trying to warn others because of reciprocity, but they are willing to pay a personal price to punish you for behavior that they consider unfair.

It is also worth noting that people are more predisposed to punish other people than to punish the organization. It took us tens of thousands of years to develop this innate sense of fairness for other people. Since organizations in the modern sense have been around for only a few hundred years, we have not developed that same sense of fairness as it relates to them. When the financial meltdown happened in late 2008, people became truly outraged when a list of executives and their bonuses was published. Sure, people had been mad as hell before at what those companies had done, but the anger became visceral when they could take it out on people instead of organizations. The same happened in the summer of 2009, when British people became outraged at the parliamentary expense-account fiasco. If the scandal hadn't had the names of specific people associated with it, the outrage would have likely been much milder.

As a company, you can try to harness this powerful force to your advantage or see it used against you. But to understand how to harness the power of Hyper-Sociality, you need to understand Human 1.0 more than you do Web 2.0 or other social media technologies.

A good example of Human 1.0 in action is the SAP Developer Network, a community with more than 1.5 million developers. When SAP first started the community, it had an incentive system in place that gave individuals a reward for helping others and helping SAP. Here's how it worked: Every time you helped someone, that person could give you points for the help she received. Every time you were willing to help SAP by providing it with a quote in a press release or by acting as a spokesperson for it at a conference, you would get points. You could then turn those points into personal rewards. What happened next is that SAP started seeing some bullying behavior in the community. People became overly competitive with one another, exhibiting behaviors that could be characterized as aggressive. Eventually SAP decided to switch the reward system to one in which the total number of points doled out in the community would trigger donations to a children's cause at the United Nations. After SAP made that change, the bad behavior soon abated.

If you were tuned into Human 1.0 behavior, you could have avoided such objectionable results in the first place. Behavioral economists like Dan Ariely, the author of *Predictably Irrational*[5], or Ori Brafman and Rom Brafman, the authors of *Sway*[6], could have warned you about what would happen.

The Brafman brothers describe a research project at the National Institutes of Health (NIH) that predicts this behavior through neurophysiology. The NIH researchers placed participants in an MRI machine fitted with a monitor and a joystick to allow the subjects to play a game. At the beginning of each game, a circle, a square, or a triangle would appear on the screen. A circle meant that if you succeeded in completing the upcoming task—zapping a figure as it appeared on the screen—you would earn a monetary reward. Different circles meant different size rewards. A square meant that if you failed to zap the figure, you had a penalty of 20 cents, $1, or $5. A triangle meant that no money was on the line.

When the researchers monitored which part of the brain was active in the various stages of the game, they found that every time a circle or a square appeared (which meant that money was at stake), the pleasure center of the brain lit up—the same center that is associated with the "high" that results from drugs, sex, and gambling, and that can lead to addiction. When triggered, that part of the brain releases dopamine, which creates a feeling of contentment and pleasure—and as addicts will tell you, you need increasing doses of dopamine to achieve the same result over time.

In a separate study, subjects were asked to play the same game, but instead of making or losing money, the participants were told that the better their score, the more money would be donated to charity. Now the MRI revealed that the pleasure center was completely quiet, but instead the "altruism center" of the brain lit up. That is the part of the brain that is responsible for social interactions—how we perceive others, how we relate, and how we form bonds.

Understanding Human 1.0 is more important in predicting how Hyper-Sociality will affect your business than understanding the tools, the underlying technologies, and the new rules that govern them. And when we talk about Human 1.0, we don't mean only the individual characteristics that make us human and that have been tapped by advertisers for decades—we especially mean our *group behavior*, that which makes us social. That makes understanding the changes that are upon us and how to harness them simpler than in many of the previous waves of change.

This does not mean that the changes are any less profound—on the contrary. As we will see later in this chapter, they are truly game-changing. The good news for business is that the impending changes can be anticipated.

What Is Driving the Hyper-Social Shift?

A number of key technological shifts are enabling the Hyper-Social shift, and without the confluence of these major, long-term trends,

Hyper-Sociality would be an unrealized dream of our primate minds. Several of the more important drivers are the emergence of inexpensive social media applications, worldwide connectivity via the Internet, and the blurring of the line between expert and amateur.

Since humans are so fundamentally social, we have consistently developed tools and technologies through the ages that allowed us to share thoughts and information with others in some form. Cave drawings, art, the printing press, the telephone, television, the citizen's band ("CB") radio of the 1970s, and the bulletin boards of the early Internet days all point to the desire of humanity to increase one-to-one communication to one-to-many or many-to-many.

Combined with a number of factors like Moore's law (a doubling of computing performance every 18 months at a lower cost), the creation of common standards like TCP/IP (the technical protocols that underlie the Internet), and the ubiquity of wired and wireless connection to the Internet, the stage was set for the emergence of powerful platforms that would allow humans to act in the social mode in which they always existed. Indeed, with the scale and reach of the Internet and our natural instincts to behave as social beings, it's not surprising that tools like e-mail, wikis, blogs, and online social networks quickly emerged. It's also not surprising that people are spending so many millions of hours per month socializing online. When viewed in the larger context, the Hyper-Social shift is a natural result of the way we've always acted as humans. It's just that social applications and the social networking phenomenon have allowed that natural behavior to scale to a level never before imagined.

Companies have long controlled the tools of production and distribution, and have attempted to influence public opinion with their large corporate budgets and access to expensive and relatively scarce informational resources like newspapers, television, and radio. Now that the tools of production (print, video, and worldwide content distribution via sites like YouTube) have dropped in price and have been democratized, virtually anyone with an Internet connection has the ability to reach a global audience, and people can easily identify and collaborate with like-minded tribes of humans.

As a result, the dynamics of communication and relative power between amateur and expert and individual and company have changed forever. Even governments and police forces are not immune. Consider, for instance, how the story of a lost Sidekick mobile phone told by an outraged citizen blogger with spare time and a basic knowledge of HTML eventually located the phone and forced the New York City Police Department to arrest the teenager who found the Sidekick and refused to return it.[7]

As Clay Shirky describes in his book *Here Comes Everybody*, in May 2006, a New Yorker named Ivanna left her Sidekick mobile phone in a taxi. Since no one returned the lost phone to her, even though Ivanna's friend Evan sent an e-mail to the phone seeking its return, she purchased a replacement. When her phone company activated the new phone that Ivanna purchased, however, she was able to view her old phone's picture library, and she saw that a woman with the e-mail "Sashacristal8905" was now using the phone to take pictures. When Ivanna e-mailed the woman, the woman rudely refused to return the phone. Ivanna's friend Evan, indignant that someone would keep what she knew wasn't hers, posted a Web site called "StolenSidekick" that explained the situation and provided a picture of Sasha and her e-mail address.

Viewers of the Web site eventually identified the woman by her pictures and her e-mail address on a social network. Based on the evidence uncovered through subsequent online conversations, the New York City Police Department eventually escalated the dispute from a lost phone to a stolen phone, and arrested Sasha. Such a chain of events would not have been possible only a decade ago.

Social Media: A Massive Platform of Participation

As we've discussed, Web 2.0/social media is a massive platform of participation that allows the Hyper-Social wave to sweep across everyone—your employees, customers, prospects, and detractors—on a scale that is beyond anything that we've ever seen before. In effect, social media gives everyone a voice equal to that of your company. There are numerous examples of individuals who were able to stand up to the big companies and demand rectification of their problem or force lasting changes, the most famous external example of which is probably "Dell Hell," created by a well-known blogger, Jeff Jarvis.

Dell Hell started when Jeff Jarvis complained on his blog about a new Dell computer he had purchased. "I just got a new Dell laptop and paid a fortune for the four-year, in-home service. The machine is a lemon and the service is a lie. I'm having all kinds of trouble with the hardware: overheats, network doesn't work, maxes out on CPU usage. It's a lemon."

Dell had a policy of "look, don't touch" when it came to customer complaints voiced on bulletin boards and blogs, and so it did not respond to Jeff Jarvis's complaints. What happened next was that the *New York Times, BusinessWeek*, the *Houston Chronicle*, and other mainstream media outlets picked up the story—and that is when Dell Hell *really* happened for Dell. Jarvis had a platform that gave him a voice equal to Dell's, and his being social—in this case, criticizing a bad product to warn others not to make the same mistake, and punishing a company for what he considered unfair treatment—made a real difference. And by a real difference we don't just mean that Jarvis got his problem fixed, we mean that he was able to force Dell to become much more customer-centric, which made a difference for all future customers.

Thankfully in the case of Dell, this experience allowed them to transform themselves into a best practice example of how to leverage Hyper-Sociality as part of their business. When we spoke with Erin Nelson, Dell's CMO, he told us: "We launched into it in a fairly responsive manner. One of the things that [the Jeff Jarvis situation] forced us to do, is launch into this with full force. And it wasn't a question of the test, try, learn measure, it actually was a question almost of survival. So we actually turned what was a relatively negative situation for us into a phenomenal platform for learning, and for making sure that we really were exploring the vast opportunities these tools gave us." [8]

There are also plenty of internal examples, with the most publicized one probably being the Mini-Microsoft guy at Microsoft. In this case, a Microsoft employee decided to start an anonymous blog to shine a critical light on the inner workings of Microsoft, calling the company a "passionless, process-ridden, lumbering idiot." His blog, which started in 2004, quickly became a virtual central water cooler where other Microsofties could communicate with one another. Every time the Mini-Microsoft guy posts on his blog, hundreds and in some cases thousands of other employees comment on his posts—mostly venting their frustrations without fear of retribution. So what's going on here? Most of these people, including the Mini-Microsoft guy, are passionate about Microsoft, but disillusioned by the leadership and the official management channels of communication. So they do what comes naturally: They become social; they vent; they complain; they find support and strength in one another. They don't mean harm to Microsoft; they truly want it to become a better company.

Internally, this platform of participation is slowly changing the way companies work. No longer are communications limited to the channels of the traditional command-and-control hierarchy. People now find ways to communicate and help one another across conventional reporting structures.

Externally, the impact of this platform is not all that different from the internal impact. People can behave the way they were hardwired to behave in the first place—humanly and tribally. As we said before, the prevalence of those tools, both within and outside of your organization, is inevitable. Like many recent technology innovations and their subsequent adoption, this one is driven not by central IT departments, but by the individual users. Companies may attempt to control what technologies take hold in the enterprise and what sites people can access, but in reality they cannot—people will find a way to circumvent these controls. For instance, when a retailer's thousands of IT people could not access Twitter from work, many of them devised alternative ways of doing so, including using their personal iPhone to access Twitter and offer help across functional barriers.

Connectivity—Always On

At the simplest level, ubiquitous connectivity to others (usually via some sort of wireless connection) creates far more opportunity for your customers, your potential customers, and your detractors to move from *thinking* about your company to *saying* or *doing* something about your company. Such connectivity also permits tsunamis of sudden sentiment about your company to rise incredibly fast, fueled by the many people who are on the network and hear the chatter. An example is the uncomfortable position that Domino's Pizza recently found itself in when a video of employees performing distasteful acts with the food they were preparing for customers appeared online. The company did not learn of the video until it was tipped off by a blogger, and by the time Domino's posted an apology, about 48 hours after the video was posted, the video had been viewed *almost 1 million times*. It's a safe bet that the company, and those other companies that were watching from the sidelines, has developed new policies for scanning the horizon and learning of events of this sort much sooner.

Another subtle impact of this ubiquitous connection with a possibly global community is the disappearing transition between stimulus and response; indeed, as we experience and think, we are able for the first time to reach hundreds or thousands of humans with our immediate, unfiltered sense of what's taking place. With mobile technologies and real-time social applications, there will no longer be the buffer period between when we think something and when we communicate it. This transition is likely to be disconcerting and ultimately embarrassing for some, but for other companies, it will present a rush of incoming data that need to be parsed, understood, and acted on in short order.

This immediacy and real-time nature of communication will also create greater expectations of immediate response and redefinitions of what "responsiveness" looks like. It is hard enough now, at this early point in the process, for us to respond to all of the communications we receive, but when the Hyper-Social shift is well underway, we may find ourselves feeling inundated by our tribes' real-time narrative of what they're thinking and what they would like us to do.

Summary: The Hyper-Social Organization—an Anti-Fad

As we have seen in this chapter, the main driver for much of what is happening in business today is not technology, nor is it a fundamental change in media. What is really happening is that social media, connectivity, and always-on technology have allowed the Hyper-Social Human 1.0 to expand to levels never seen before and reenter business with a vengeance. That makes Hyper-Sociality the *reverse* of a fad in some ways. It's not something new, as humans have always behaved socially.

Hyper-social organizations will not use social media as a new channel to reach and interact with customers; instead, they will realize that social media fundamentally changes the way you identify, develop, educate, and support those customers. Not realizing that distinction will result in companies not being able to achieve their business objectives. And those objectives have not changed; they were best described by the late Peter Drucker when he said: "Because the purpose of business is to create a customer, the business enterprise has two—and only two—basic functions:

marketing and innovation. Marketing and innovation produce results; all the rest are costs. Marketing is the distinguishing, unique function of the business."

Your end goal has not changed; it is still to create a customer. It is everything in between to get to that goal that has changed!

In the next couple of chapters, we will take a closer look at what has actually changed and how those changes are not only inevitable, but truly game-changing.

two

The Human 1.0 in a Web 2.0 World

While early research shows that fundamental social behavior does not change as Hyper-Sociality scales, there are fundamental differences between our Human 1.0 ancestors, who roamed the earth for tens of thousands of years, and our Human 1.0 contemporaries, who inhabit our Web 2.0 world. For one thing, our ancient tribes were limited by geography, and we usually belonged to only one tribe. Now we can belong to tribes that span the globe, and we typically belong to multiple tribes at the same time.

As Rob Kozinets, marketing professor at York University and one of the editors of *Consumer Tribes*,[1] said in a recent interview we conducted with him: "Today's tribes have looser affiliations and are more hedonistic in nature than ancient tribes. They are nomadic by interest, rather than geography, and centered around expertise and commercial culture."[2]

Let's take a closer look at some of the differences between the Human 1.0 in today's world and in the ancient world, and what that means for Hyper-Social organizations.

How Tribes Form

Humans form tribes because they have evolved to gain advantages as tribes, not just as individuals. We developed a symbiotic relationship between individual biological evolution and culture as a way to bypass what would have taken us too long to achieve through natural evolution. This whole yin and yang relationship between individual natural evolution and culture is best described by evolutionary biologists Robert Boyd and Peter J. Richerson, who write:

> Culture is information that people acquire from others by teaching, imitation and other forms of social learning. On a scale unknown in any other species, people acquire skills, beliefs, and values from the people around them, and these strongly affect behavior. People are heirs to a pool of socially transmitted information that affects how they make a living, how they communicate, and what they think is right and wrong. The information thus stored and transmitted varies from individual to individual and is a property of the population only in a statistical sense.[3]

In a Web 2.0 world, social media allows modern tribes to form in an instant, and because we are driven to be tribal and to learn from our tribes, tribes appear around almost any topic your imagination can conjure up—Belgian American fly-fishing enthusiasts who love beer and work for Cisco, passionate scrapbookers who use Fiskars tools, or passionate private BitTorrent communities interested in Asian action flicks and Manga. Combine that with the fact that we don't seem to trust what organizations are telling us,[4] and you have a new world order in business—one in which the most important conversations are no longer the ones that organizations have with their customers, prospects, and detractors, but the ones that happen among tribal members.

So how do business tribes form and coalesce, and how do you know that they have the right attributes and forces to support your efforts?

If you want to become a Hyper-Social organization and leverage the power of modern tribes as part of your business, you need to be able to identify the types of tribes that are most likely to benefit your organization. Failing to understand who your tribes are, where they hang out, and who their leaders are will result in misguided efforts that will have no measurable impact on your business—or worse, misguided efforts that will anger your potential tribes and their constituents.

Modern tribes almost never form around products, services, or companies; they form around shared passions (e.g., fan clubs), shared pains (e.g., cancer survivors), a shared sense of duty (e.g., police officers), or categories based on common traits (e.g., poor frugal moms). So the Harley community is not a vibrant community centered around a brand, as some would lead you to believe, but rather a community based on a common sense of belonging to a shared lifestyle—riding. Tribes are also different from market segments, which are centered around categories based on individual traits, mostly geographic, demographic, or psychographic (e.g., moms), rather than categories based on behavioral traits (e.g., frugal moms who love the art of the deal). We'll touch more on segmentation vs. tribes in Chapter 6.

Another important distinction between communities and tribes can be found in how they deal with diversity. Understanding this distinction is key to determining the value that a community or tribe can bring to your business.

Defenders of Belief and Seekers of Truth

On the one hand, some communities and tribes are made up of people who share a common belief and simply prefer to hang out with other people who share that belief. We call these folks *defenders of belief*. They frown upon diversity and operate in an insular fashion. Business communities and consumer tribes that fall into that category can be found everywhere—think of the Apple zealots, who would not want to be caught anywhere near a PC owner; or the Ducati motorcycle riders, who certainly don't want to be confused with Harley riders.

On the other hand, you have communities and tribes that embrace diversity—within certain limits. We call them *seekers of the truth*. They realize that the best ideas and solutions come from diverse groups of individuals, not from groups with a common sense of belief, since the latter often perpetuate an echo-chamber effect, or groupthink. Commercial communities and tribes in the seekers of the truth category include cross-industry professional affinity groups, like IBM's global CIO community, and software developers, like the SAP community that we discussed in Chapter 1, where people are willing to help one another and share even with competitors in order to find the best solution in a timely manner.

Why is it so important that you understand this distinction? For starters, if you are looking for input into your product innovation process, a community full of defenders of belief would yield pretty poor results. If your goal is to involve customer tribes as part of designing new products, you need a community of people who are seekers of the truth, embrace diversity, and enjoy a good difference of opinion. The more diverse your community is, the better the products they will codesign with you. Some companies, like Intuit, will go so far as to embrace what many would consider extreme diversity, inviting not just their customers and prospects but also their detractors as part of the process.

Cisco's 2008 I-Prize was a good example of the power that a diverse community can bring to new product development. Cisco likely did not even know that it would end up with a community. It launched the I-Prize looking for the next billion-dollar product line—sourced from the outside. People and teams would submit their ideas and business plans online, where they could vote and comment on one another's plans—even though those comments and votes did not count toward moving a business plan to the next stage. That task was reserved for a review board made up of Cisco employees. To Cisco's surprise, a true community started forming online. People would team up, and some would form posses to "out" other groups suspected of unfair voting practices (even though those votes did not count). By the time the business plans moved to the quarter-finals, half of the business teams had formed online. The jury is still out on whether the winner, a "smart power grid" solution, will indeed result in a new billion-dollar business for Cisco, but what is for sure is that if the pool of participants had been mostly defenders of belief, Cisco would not have received more than 1,000 new business ideas from 104 countries.

Note that diversity is not a steady state. People mostly prefer to associate with others who are like them. The scientific term for this phenomenon is *homophily*.[5] Research has proven the existence of homophily in all kinds of environments, which leads to a natural tendency for groups to be homogeneous rather than diverse. Even if you work really hard to hire diverse individuals, you cannot avoid the outcome that people in groups will influence one another over time. It is a well-known phenomenon that a conservative justice on a three-judge panel where the other two are liberal will start voting more liberal, and vice versa. So unless you shake it up every now and again, what starts as a diverse group may easily end up as a pretty homogeneous group. Take in-house product development teams, which are still the largest source of new products. They suffer from groupthink big time! How do we know? Because many product development teams have a homogeneous makeup, and here are the results: 80 percent of new products fail.[6] In Japan, that number is actually 97 percent.

If, on the other hand, your goal is to increase word of mouth through communities and tribes or to leverage the power of the crowd to help you with customer service, then having communities full of defenders of belief can work even better than those made up of seekers of the truth. Note how many such communities are using goods with powerful symbolic values—e.g., BMW owners, who consider themselves drivers of the ultimate driving machine. This brings us to the next topic, the role of symbols, signs, rules, and culture in making communities and tribes scale beyond the smaller groups that we used to associate with in ancient times.

Symbols, Signs, Rules, and Culture

As we saw in Chapter 1, reciprocity is one of the key factors that allow communities to work—you scratch my back, I'll scratch yours. In small tribes and groups, reciprocity is often based on face-to-face interaction—helping someone move his stuff, and expecting him to return the favor later on. In modern tribes and communities, reciprocity can work on a much larger scale—think of people supporting the green movement in Iran by traveling to New York and demonstrating in front of the UN. Think about how, after 9/11, empathy from around the world was so strong that even the French all felt like Americans.

What is going on here, and how does reciprocity scale beyond face-to-face interaction?

In his book *Us and Them: Understanding Your Tribal Mind*, David Berreby[7] says: "My fellow feeling for the people of New York does not depend on everyone of us taking turns doing each other's dishes. . . . For a city or nation to exist, its members must be good at satisfying their need for reciprocity with symbols, not actions."

Bingo!

Symbols, signals, and rules are the key to scaling reciprocity and, by proxy, one of the keys to making large communities and tribes work. If I read advice coming from a community of firefighters, I may well trust that advice, even if I do not know anyone in that community, because in my mind I equate being a firefighter, and all the symbols that go with it, with a strong sense of duty and trust.

There are symbols and rules that are very strong; race, religion, and language come to mind. But there are others that are much more artificial—think of people who have a shared experience based on attending one of the Burning Man events, people who enjoy the riding lifestyle by riding a Harley, or the importance of uniforms in conveying a common belief or shared sense of duty.

Scaling reciprocity, however, is not enough to explain the existence of the large-scale communities that we find in modern business. In order to understand the other side of the equation, we need to take a walk through Robin Dunbar's neighborhood.

Dunbar, a British anthropologist, first suggested that people can maintain a stable social relationship with only about 150 people.[8] That number is related to our ability to remember people and their relationships with one another, so that, among other things, we can keep track of those who are truly reciprocal and those who are free-loaders. While inferring this number from data on other primates, Dunbar did verify that 150 is in fact the number of people you would find in ancient farming villages, ancient tribes, and Roman army units. Modern tribes and communities scale beyond that magical number of 150 not only because people use symbols, signs, and rules as proxies to scale their capability for reciprocity, but also because we have developed strong social and cultural norms for right and wrong. So the key to scaling communities is symbols, signs, rules, and culture.

If you are building business communities, not only do you need to make sure that those communities are based on a shared passion or pain among their members, but you also need to think about symbols, signs, or rules that you can leverage to make the bonds deeper—and you need to constantly monitor the community culture to ensure that it is one that fosters trust and cooperation.

And when you do leverage symbols and rules, make sure that they have a shared meaning and are top of mind among the people you want to engage with. Sometimes there are multiple symbols associated with the same category, as in New York firefighters—are they firefighters first, or are they New Yorkers first? Sometimes symbols have multiple meanings; for example, Harley may be associated with the love of a riding lifestyle for most owners, but may also be associated with a gang lifestyle for others. If some people feel that they are New Yorkers first and firefighters second, then you have to have a separate area for New York firefighters in your firefighter community. If a majority of people associated Harley with a gang lifestyle, then hosting a community centered around Harley would not be in the company's best interest.

How Affinity Expands through Technology

Because of their strong shared sense of duty, firefighters and police officers have always liked to hang out with one another. It was not until the advent of the Internet and social media that they could do that on a large scale. Today, PoliceLink (http://policelink. monster.com), an affinity-based community hosted by Affinity Labs, a division of Monster.com, has more than 1 million members. FireLink (http://firelink.monster.com), run by the same company, has an estimated 250,000 firefighters as of this writing. Of course, affinity groups would not grow to this level without technology, but they also would not be able to do so with technology only—they need symbols, signs, rules, and culture in order to scale. In both the PoliceLink and the FireLink communities, the symbology of the uniform is very strong.

Technology allows affinity groups to scale, and the larger an affinity group becomes, the more powerful it is. If there are only 20 members getting together to talk about a shared passion, they have a group. In fact, that was the original definition of affinity groups: small groups of activists (usually between 3 and 20) who worked together on a direct action.[9] Groups can be powerful, of course, especially when they federate with other similar groups, but they have limited reach. When you get tens or hundreds of thousands of members that rally around the same affinity, however, you get a movement. And as most people will agree, it is hard to stop movements.

Why People No Longer Listen to Companies

As we saw in Chapter 1, in the beginning, *all* commerce was social. As organizations grew, however, the social aspect slowly disappeared from the scene, and some companies developed terrible habits. One example is the way companies started abusing communications, which led to the current communications breakdown between organizations and their customers and prospects.

To understand what went wrong, we need to turn to the reciprocity reflex once again, as communications is in fact a reciprocal process. Thomas Gilovich, in his book[10] *How We Know What Isn't So*, best describes it when he says:

> Because communication or conversation is a reciprocal process, it is not surprising that many of the needs and goals of the speaker and listener are complementary. This is well illustrated by one of the most basic goals of communication, to ensure that the act of communication is "justified." For the speaker, this means, among other things, that his or her message should be worthy of the listener's attention; for the listener, it means that the interaction must in some way be worthwhile. To satisfy this basic goal, it is necessary

that certain preconditions be met. The message should be understandable (i.e., not assume too much knowledge on the part of the listener), and yet not be laden with too many needless details (i.e., not assume too little knowledge on the part of the listener).

Of course, that is what most companies do not seem to understand. For communications to truly work, they need to be reciprocal—there has to be value in them somewhere. Value in communication can come in the form of warnings (e.g., don't use that product; it doesn't really work), useful information (which in most cases is different from product specs), and, of course, entertainment (nothing beats a good story or a funny one). Throughout most of the twentieth century, however, this process was not always reciprocal, because companies did not need it to be that way. The only information you could get from some companies about their products and services came directly from them, and the only thing they wanted from you was your money. They did not care whether the communication was truly based on a "you scratch my back, I'll scratch yours" relationship—because they did not have to care.

So now that we have companies with really bad habits and a platform of participation called social media that allows people to engage with other people in conversations that are truly reciprocal, it is no wonder that two-thirds[11] of all buying decisions are made based on information that does not come from the company selling the product or service. When people have a choice between a reciprocal conversation and a nonreciprocal one, they will tune out the one that is not. For instance, consider your level of interest in someone who babbles about himself at a cocktail reception.

Summary: The Human 1.0 in a Web 2.0 World

As we saw in Chapter 1 and expanded on in this chapter, the Human 1.0 in the Web 2.0 world clearly has a lot in common with the Human 1.0 who roamed the earth thousands of years ago.

What that means for the world of business is that we have to understand the role of reciprocity in everything we do—from internal/external communications to new product development and customer support. Teaching leaders and workers by using the philosophy from *The Godfather* (you scratch my back, and I'll scratch yours) may be a better solution than using Dale Carnegie or other classic business training courses.

Business executives need to stop thinking in terms of abstract business concepts and constantly evaluate what they do in the context of what makes people tick (in groups, not as individuals). They need to start asking some of these questions: Can I create a retellable story around what we do? Can I create symbols, rituals, or culture around our offerings? Can I create and mobilize tribes to help our cause? Can I leverage the power of every individual within my company to humanize our brand and create more passion around what we do?

In the next chapter, we will look at how the Human 1.0, along with Web 2.0 and new business practices, is affecting all areas of Hyper-Social organizations, and how the changes that are afoot are truly game-changing.

three

The Impact of Hyper-Sociality on Your Business

Whether you embrace the Hyper-Social shift or not, it will ultimately have an impact on all aspects of your business. Since people are social by nature, and since social media is giving them the ability to behave Hyper-Socially again in business, it is likely that some parts of your business have already gone social—think of the customer's buying process as an example. If you want to be proactive, you need to evaluate which parts of your business would benefit the most from becoming Hyper-Social. In doing this exercise, you will quickly realize that you can reduce transaction costs and improve efficiency by making *most* business processes Hyper-Social.

Scary? Yes. Inevitable? You bet!

How the Hyper-Social Shift Affects Various Parts of Your Business

While we will be reviewing the impact of Hyper-Sociality on the various parts of your business in detail in later chapters, it is important to highlight the scope of this impact in an overview. We should stress again that our research indicates that Hyper-Sociality is not a fad that will pass, as so many other fads have done. Indeed, Hyper-Sociality is the *reverse* of a fad in some ways. It's not something new, as humans have always behaved socially, but their ability to behave socially in the business world has long been suppressed by distance and lack of communication tools. Now that social media and the Internet have arrived, we are returning to the preindustrial social status quo, albeit on a much larger scale.

Companies that proactively tap into the Hyper-Social shift will find themselves conducting business with people whose job it is not to work on the things they work on—customers helping them design better products, nonmarketing employees helping them amplify launch activities, or noncustomer service employees and other customers helping resolve customer issues. They will be able to scale those business processes to levels not possible with traditional management techniques and budgets. Like Christa Carone, the CMO at Xerox, they will find that tapping into the social contract that people have with your company, as employees as well as customers, can be much more powerful than tapping into the market contract that they have with you. When we spoke with her, she described how Xerox was able to unleash virality never seen before during a recent product launch—simply by tapping into existing social media enthusiasts across the company. "So as a result we were seeing posts from employees who would typically blog about a hobby that they have—about antique cars or something—who said, 'Hey. I rarely talk about what I do at work, but I am really proud of what the company launched today,' and then shared information about the product. So we had this very unique viral effect of our employees feeling empowered to communicate on behalf of the company... it's amazing what you can do when you empower people with information..."[1]

Sales and Marketing

Deloitte's 2009 *State of the Media Democracy Survey* indicates that 63 percent of American consumers learned of a new product for the first time online, and 51 percent say that they purchased a product because of an online review.[2] A study from McKinsey[3] found similar results: more than 50 percent of U.S. electronics consumers now rely on Web-based research to narrow the choice of brands rather than following advice from sales staff when choosing among products in stores. In a Hyper-Social world, the most important conversations are no longer the ones that you have with your customers, prospects, and detractors—the critical conversations are the ones that are taking place *among* your customers. Now, if people are increasingly making buying decisions based on information that comes not from you, but from other people within their tribes, you will have to change the way you create and distribute branded content. You will also need to change the way you get people's attention and the way you sell to them. Out are "interruption marketing," corporate-speak-laden sales materials, and "the hard sell," to name just a few now-antiquated tactics. While those strategies are out, what is "in" is reciprocity-based actions, helping people, affiliating with others, and delivering true value to

Table 3-1 Examples of Hyper-Sociality in Various Corporate Functions

Process	Before Social	After Social	Benefits	Case Studies
Sales	One-to-one	Many-to-many	Sales is social networking	TIBCO, Zappos
Market Research	Based on small groups and financial incentives	Based on tribes and social contract	Much more accurate market data and increased success	Eli Lilly, Pfizer, IBM, Fiskars
Lead Generation	Interrupt-driven	Become findable, be generally helpful in public conversation	Leads that actually want to buy something	EMC, Dell
Customer Communications	Mostly between companies and customers	Primarily among customers, detractors, and prospects	Reduced cost and increased effectiveness	Best Buy, Dassault Systemes, Fiskars
PR and Thought Leadership	Rolodex-based and focused on traditional media	Community/tribe-based and focused on social media	Much more amplification of the messages	Microsoft, Intuit
Product Innovation	Constraint to a department	Includes all employees, customers, prospects, and detractors	Reduce product failure rates (now at 80%)	Cisco, Netflix
Talent Acquisition and Development	Board, interrupt-driven and based on weak ties WOM	Endorsed by the tribes people belong to	Social context provides better matches	Monster.com
Employee Communications	Mostly within silos	Cross enterprise	Increased serendipity, increased support	IBM, FedEx, Cisco
Customer Service	Conducted by employees	Conducted by employees and other customers	Customer service as a revenue source instead of cost center	SAP, Zappos
Knowledge Management	Top-down process	Federated and user-driven process	KM that works, changes in work habits	IBM

everyone—friend or foe. In other words, Hyper-Sociality can completely transform your sales and marketing approaches, including lead generation, PR, communications, and product positioning. We will go into the details of how Hyper-Sociality is poised to fundamentally transform all those practices in later chapters.

Product Innovation and Development

Next, let's consider Hyper-Sociality's impact on product innovation and product development. Although these departments are the heartbeat of most companies, they consistently suffer from an 80 percent failure rate. The companies that leverage Hyper-Sociality as part of their new product development are highly likely to experience higher product success ratios—and that is money that goes straight down to the bottom line that their competitors will not have. As part of our yearly Tribalization of Business Study, we have seen the early signs of tribe-based product development and the impact they have on overall business success.

The bottom line is that if someone in your industry starts leveraging tribe-informed product development, you have no choice but to follow suit, or be ready for severe margin pressure and market share loss. Getting customers involved in the creation of new offerings not only will result in better offerings, but will result in higher levels of customer engagement. Innovation cycle times may also be reduced, as outside experts can be used to accelerate problem solving.

Given the networked nature of Hyper-Social product developers, many organizations will also develop new ideas of when a product is finished or complete. We have heard companies refer to the concept of "constant beta" when describing their product development processes: Since creation is so collaborative with customers, it is an ongoing process that does not seem to have a middle or an end. And the phenomenon of Hyper-Socialized innovation is not limited to a few business sectors. Companies that have turned product innovation into a social process can be found in every industry—Pfizer, Fiskars, Intuit, Procter & Gamble (P&G), and Dell, for example.

Customer Service

Customer service may be the part of your business that is first and most dramatically affected by the Hyper-Social shift. Customer service is a perfect place for companies to use social media and to leverage Hyper-Sociality—people love helping others. In fact, you won't be able to stop it—the drive for people to help one another is just too powerful a social force to stop. Not only that, but customer service and support conversations may be the last market conversations in which people want companies to engage, calling for a much tighter integration between marketing and customer service. And again, the benefits of leveraging Hyper-Sociality in customer service will change the competitive dynamics within your industry, with those that do it right not only reducing their costs, but also increasing their customer loyalty and market share at the expense of those that don't.

Interestingly enough, an informal poll that we conducted among 50 companies revealed that almost none of them were making social media investments in customer service. For most companies, customer service remains a cost center, not the potentially rewarding and profitable customer interface point that companies like Zappos and TiVo have been able to tap.

Talent Acquisition and Development

Recruiting won't escape the Hyper-Social shift either. As tribes begin to alter company products and marketing, Hyper-Social companies will need to adapt in order to better interact with their customers, employees, and business partners. Organizations will suddenly find themselves ill equipped on the talent front, lacking individuals who can manage frequent, multichannel discussions in real time with important constituents. Former star employees will find themselves in unfamiliar territory and possibly in need of retraining, and management will need new employees who can operate in a messy Hyper-Social environment.

Management will also have to become comfortable with employees crossing over former organizational boundaries in search of information, and being privy to information and knowledge flows that formerly were off-limits. Initially, recruiters are likely to wrestle with job descriptions, pay scales, and career paths for these new Hyper-Social-savvy workers, as the organization has never had to identify or recruit these people previously.

Organizations will need to rethink how to train and reward these new employees, as their ability to create a more Hyper-Social organization will at first seem difficult to quantify or to assign monetary value to. For instance, today, customer service reps may be rewarded for resolving a customer question in the shortest possible time; a Hyper-Social company may well be more concerned with gleaning meaningful product development or marketing information during a customer service interaction.

Another change driven by the Hyper-Social shift is the increased opportunity for companies to work with volunteers in a fashion that is almost identical to actually employing them. Although this might not be recruiting in the classical sense, it presents a new opportunity for organizations to attract and profit from passionate volunteers who wish to help, but not necessarily to become employees.

Employee Communications

Companies such as IBM are already using social media to permit their employees to communicate better within the company and to locate needed expertise. Other companies are enabling employees to reach outside of the organization, and to communicate with non-employees who can add value. Yet other organizations are providing employees with social tools that allow them to find mentors and career advice among colleagues. Vast improvements over the corporate newsletter or lunchroom memo board, these systems facilitate the flow of information up, down, and across organizations.

Knowledge Management

Increasing Hyper-Sociality will have a profound impact on how organizations capture and communicate knowledge. As with the other corporate functions we've just considered, Hyper-Socializing knowledge management within companies will greatly improve the generation, sharing, and locating of knowledge. Capturing knowledge and then sharing it effectively has typically been a tough process for organizations to optimize because of a number of obstacles. For instance, knowledge management systems typically are created without consulting users, and do not provide demonstrable value to contributors. Progressive and visionary knowledge managers are developing tools and systems that tap into Human 1.0 behaviors such as reciprocity and status seeking among peers, so that people are given incentives to create and share more information.

And as we discuss later, knowledge may well start flowing from the organization to the customer, providing a significant new value.

The Hyper-Social Shift Is Inevitable

While we have pointed to the inevitability of the Hyper-Social shift in Chapter 1 and in parts of this chapter, it is critically important that you understand what that means for your business. In order to continue keeping Hyper-Sociality out of your business, you would need to turn your company into a North Korea–like fortress— not exactly a wise move in this hypercompetitive age. In a recent interview that we conducted with leading business thinker John Hagel,[4] he talked about the intensification of competition and how this has led the mean length of company survival to come down to 10 years, compared to 75 years in the 1930s. One of the best ways to cope with this situation, according to Hagel, is to shift from a *knowledge stock* mentality, where you aggressively hoard proprietary knowledge and extract value from it for as long as possible, to a *knowledge flow* mentality, where you refresh your current knowledge stocks, which have rapidly diminishing value, by participating in knowledge flows. Of course, one of the big challenges for companies is that, unlike information or data, knowledge does not flow easily, as it relies on long-term trust-based relationships. Indeed, data and information are facts that describe a situation and can be generated by machines, whereas knowledge consists of truths, beliefs, methods, solutions, ideas, and other elements that are created by humans and shared among people who trust one another. So one of the keys to success in this new economic reality is to move from a transactional world to a long-term trust-based world. Examples of taking on a knowledge flow approach include letting your key customers participate in product innovation and turning them into affiliates to allow them to help one another. In other words, the best way to prepare your company for the intensification of competition is by embracing Hyper-Sociality instead of keeping it at bay!

And even if you think that you can keep Hyper-Sociality at bay, those competitors who do embrace it will gain benefits that are game-changing and that will cost you significant market share and lead to profitability pressure.

In reality, however, you won't be able to stop the Hyper-Social shift from taking hold in your environment. You can try to block your employees from accessing Twitter, Facebook, MySpace, and other social networks from work, but they will bring their own tools to gain access. In addition, they can and will access these services from home, whether you like it or not. You can set up Soviet-era-style policies to block people from engaging in social media, but unless you are willing to burden yourself with the repercussions of having a Soviet-era-style policing department, that too won't work. And even if you could stop all your employees from being social, your customers, prospects, and detractors will behave Hyper-Socially and dislike the fact that you are dealing with them as a corporate entity instead of as a set of human voices. Besides the increased competitive pressure, you could also face a severe brain drain once the economy picks up and your top talent flocks to other companies.

The Hyper-Social Shift Is a Game Changer

As we saw earlier in the book, many companies are merely looking at leveraging social media as part of their business, with a heavy emphasis on the *media* part of social media. They set up corporate Twitter accounts to disseminate their press announcements, they set up Facebook fan pages that offer coupons, or they set up corporate blogs full of anonymous company and product blurbs. Clearly, that is the wrong way of looking at this latest wave of change.

Unlike e-mail, social media is not simply a new channel of communication with customers. Social media, and the Hyper-Social shift that it has helped usher in, is completely transforming the rules of business—from marketing to customer service to product innovation to internal collaboration. By providing a platform for participation to your employees, customers, and prospects, social media has changed the fundamental pillars of the business game. Not only have the rules of the game changed, but so have the players, the scope, the tactics, and what's at stake.

Let's take a quick look at the different elements of the business game and how they have changed.

The New Rules

- People do not want to hear from companies anymore.
- People want to hear from other people.

Some people will argue that it has always been like this, and they are right. The problem is that prior to social media becoming commonplace, you could not hear from other people in a scalable way, and so you had to listen to what companies were telling you.

The New Players

- Customers

- Employees
- Prospects

Except for competitors not being on the list, it sounds like the old players, doesn't it?

The difference is what Clay Shirky calls "here comes everybody" in his latest book,[5] which explains many of the changes that are afoot. It is not just the employees that are in your direct line of command who are playing key roles in your decision-making processes; it is all your employees. And it is not just your largest customers, or those whom you pay to advise you, who will participate in your decisions—it is all of them, including people who have not yet bought from you.

The New Scope

The scope of business for many old-school executives was primarily focused on presales activities and new product innovation. The new scope of business is across the complete customer life cycle and involves understanding the holistic context in which humans make decisions.

The New Tactics

- Tapping into business communities
- Harnessing social media and social networks
- Using people-speak and authenticity
- Faster speed of response

Those are big changes in how companies will have to think and work in order to create new customers. No more corporate-speak, no more interruption-based marketing programs, and no more targeting. It is now all about attracting humans, building relationships and trust by helping them and letting them help one another, and leveraging the tribal nature of people.

Is this how business tactics should have been all along? Absolutely! But how many companies were doing that when they did not have to? Almost none. Now they will have no choice if they are to survive.

What's Now at Stake

- People's attention
- People's trust
- Talent in employees and customer champions
- Externalized business processes that include employees, customers, and prospects
- Retellable stories to market *with* your customers instead of *at* them

So as you can see, gone are the switching costs, the better mousetraps, the big advertising budgets, market share, and other added values that determined your competitive value in the marketplace before social media shifted the power away from companies and into individuals' hands.

The business of identifying, developing, educating, and supporting customers has become a new game *because* of social media. Social media is not just a new channel for reaching and interacting with customers. Failing to realize that distinction will result in companies not being able to achieve their business objectives.

And as we have seen earlier, your end goal has not changed—it is still to create a customer. It is everything in between to get to that goal that has changed! The only way you will get there is if you understand the new rules, the new players, and all the other elements of the marketing game.

Examples of How the Game Has Changed

Still not convinced? Fiskars, a $1 billion North European scissors and garden tool manufacturer, was able to create a passionate community of 5,000 scrapbookers, who call themselves "Fiskateers." It's a real movement that the company probably could not shut down if it wanted to. But why would it want to? The Fiskateers increased the company's online chatter by 600 percent and its scissors sales by 300 percent, and it now derives most of its new product innovations from the community.

Another well-documented case study is eBay. When it created customer support forums for its buyers and sellers, where they can exchange tips and tricks on how to buy and sell with other people, eBay discovered that those who were active in the customer support forums were bringing in 50 percent more revenue and profits to the company.

Surely those are not level-setting figures. They are, by any definition, game-changing.

Of course, when a tidal wave of this magnitude hits your business, it will inevitably transform all aspects of that business. In Part Two of this book, we will take you through the various changes that you can expect and how you can prepare for them. We will review how Hyper-Sociality will affect your human capital needs; how it will force you to think differently about organization charts, management skills, and the informal networks through which information really flows; and how you may actually have to change or adjust your values in order to capitalize on the power of the emerging social behavior.

Summary

By now we hope you realize that Hyper-Sociality will affect all parts of your business. You can get ahead of it and make a proactive strategy for how Hyper-Sociality will change your business, you can let it happen to you, or you can resist it (not recommended).

While we will go into much more detail about how to leverage Hyper-Sociality as part of all of your business processes in Part Four of this book, at this stage there are some questions that you should already start asking yourself and your teams.

How good are you at engaging your employees and your customers as part of your most critical business processes, like product innovation or customer support? How good are you at engaging your detractors? How much of a "perpetual beta" culture do you have in your company? Do you consider your customer service department a cost center, or something more? Have you seen signs of leaders within your company who resist Hyper-Sociality or feel threatened by it? Are there signs that your competitors are embracing it at a faster pace than you are?

four

The True Drivers of a Successful Community

M ost Hyper-Social organizations leverage the power of human Hyper-Sociality through online communities. They integrate these communities as part of customer support, product innovation, thought leadership, and public relations, and to increase word of mouth—all with various levels of success. Research in the field of virtual communities shows that most business thinkers agree on the fact that there are four fundamental elements of successful communities:

- Members
- Content
- Member profiles
- Transactions

When managed properly, these four elements lead to economics of increasing returns that characterize the most successful communities—those that seem to take off like virtual whirlwinds.

The Four Drivers of All Successful Communities

Let's discuss these drivers one at a time. Understanding the workings and seeing the benefits of the dynamics of each of these drivers is easy. Many of those dynamics, as they relate to the increasing returns that characterize successful communities, were first described (more than a decade ago) by business thinker and management consultant John Hagel in *Net Gain*.[1]

Even as an executive, you need to understand those pillars of community building, as they are not only the potential drivers of increasing return in your business, but also the main culprits for community failures.

The Importance of Members in Communities

The more members you have, the more they will tell other potential members, and thus the bigger the growth in your community membership. You may realize that you cannot have a successful community without the "right" members, but what does that mean? It means that you cannot select your members from generic market segments, which are based on the individual characteristics of the people in those segments. Instead, you need to think of them as tribes, groups of people whose desire to hang out with one another is rooted in shared passions (e.g., knitters), shared pains (e.g., parents who have children with disabilities), a shared sense of duty (e.g., military personnel), or categories based on common traits (e.g., women-owned small businesses). In order to succeed, you also need to make your community member-centric, which means that the members and whatever ties them together are at the center of the effort, not your company or your products and services.

A large office supply company set up a community that ran afoul of both of those tenets—and is no longer around to tell the story. First, the company decided to build a community for small businesses—a hugely profitable market segment for it, but clearly not a well enough defined tribe. Small businesses include mom-and-pop stores, restaurants, and automobile dealers, but they also include technology and biotech start-ups. Add to that the fact that these companies are populated with employees who have vastly different job responsibilities, and it becomes clear why there is very little commonality among the individuals within this market segment that could draw and keep them together in an online community. The company also decided to put products (shredders, staplers, paper, and so on) at the center of the community rather than the members, with their issues, pains, and joys as owners of small businesses. So even if the company had been able to tap into a small business tribe, say women-owned small business owners, it would still have had an uphill battle to make that community successful.

Besides having the ability to attract the right tribes to your community, you also need to identify the leaders of those tribes and find a way to engage them as part of your efforts. We call these ambassador programs, programs in which you recognize the leaders by giving them some special status or assigning them a specific role. Our tribalization research shows that only 20 percent of companies that have online communities have a formal ambassador program—a surprisingly low number considering that most documented successful communities have such programs. Think of the Microsoft product support communities and their widely replicated MVP (Most Valuable Professional) program, a distinction that gets bestowed on members for outstanding past performance, without any expectations of future performance. The Fiskateers would not be what they are without the original three lead Fiskateers, and the SAP developer community would certainly be a whole lot less effective without its 70 mentors, who are nominated by the community but selected by SAP. Note that it isn't the quantity of leaders that makes these communities successful; it is usually the strength of the social contract that the leaders have with you and with the community that determines success.

When you engage people in conversations, be it in communities or in other social media–based environments, remember that you are dealing with humans, and that they will expect you to reciprocate by fully participating in those conversations. Communication, as we have seen before, is a reciprocal process. Unlike with other, more traditional marketing programs, you are asking people to invest their social capital with you. Being human, they will expect something in return—solutions to their problems, good advice, new people with whom to network, or simply entertainment value.

Our 2009 Tribalization of Business Study shows that more than 50 percent of companies that have communities have one or fewer employees (by "or fewer" we mean part-timers) dedicated to the community effort. What are they thinking?

That is, of course, what led to a somewhat comical scenario that one of us ran into less than a year ago. A part-time community manager of a sizable loyalty program in the hospitality industry called us in a panic, saying, "People in our community are outraged by recent changes we made to the loyalty program, and since there is nobody here who has the time to engage with them, some have started trashing the place and put profanities on our corporate blog—can you please help?" What? The company expected its most loyal customers to engage with it in its community, but no one at the company had the time to engage back with them? Come on—just as communications cannot function without being a reciprocal process, communities won't work unless they too are based on reciprocity. It's just another example of the legacy left over from years of not being Hyper-Social, and developing bad corporate habits.

The Importance of Content in Successful Communities

Now let's turn to the role of content in communities—one of the most important and yet underutilized sources of value in communities. The more "quality" content you have in your community, the more value you are delivering to your members and the more they will proselytize the virtues of your community to other members, which will increase your membership. Content can come in a variety of ways, but for this exercise, let's divide content into professionally created content and user-generated content. Both are critically important in order for communities to work, yet most community organizers don't think about professional content at all. Note that professionally created content is not the same as your traditional marketing materials. Professionally created content for your community has to be developed with the goals of your community members in mind, rather than your company's products or services.

If yours is like most companies, it does not have the critical mass of potential community members that would allow it to rely on the likely meager content coming from those members to provide enough value for the rest of the community. Companies like Microsoft, Intuit, and Apple may have enough potential customers to start vibrant customer communities based primarily on user-generated content, but if yours is not like those, you will have to hire content developers to kick-start the process. In fact, even companies with very large numbers of potential community members are far better off hiring outside content developers to kick-start their community. The reason for this is best explained by Clay Shirky, the author of *Here Comes Everybody*,[2] when he says: "The number of people who are willing to start something is smaller, much smaller, than the number of people who are willing to contribute once someone else starts something."

American Express understands this. While it clearly has a large enough number of small business customers, it hired a small army of outside content providers when it launched Open Forum, its small business community.[3] When you first reach Open Forum, you immediately get the sense that there is a lot of valuable content there—developed just for you. A large office supply company, on the other hand, launched its small business community, without any external, professionally created content. As we mentioned earlier, that community ceased to exist in less than a year. In fact, the company missed all of the key success factors that we describe in this chapter, including not integrating the community with its online transaction infrastructure (which we will get to in a bit), not putting the small community member at the center of the community effort, not leveraging member profiles, and launching a community with only product-related content.

A large retailer, parent of two clothing chains, had a number of communities that violated this rule of community building as well—and those communities are no longer around to tell their story, either. It invited customers to sign up for its "What's In" community, where they could get alerts from other members about new arrivals at their local clothing stores—except that there were no alerts to speak of, and no other valuable content that would have made a person to want to come back. You could tell when the company blasted mass e-mails to invite its customers to the community by browsing the member list and seeing wave after wave of new members who set up a profile once—never to come back again.

Content created for your community has to have value for its members. It also has to be findable and retellable as part of the reciprocal communications that members will have with one another. As Ted Gilvar, the CMO at Monster.com, told us recently: "People vote on the quality of your content with their time and attention, and that is why you need to produce content worthy of consumption." We think that professional content is best developed by outsiders and managed in an editorially independent fashion. Not only will this add more credence to the claim that the community is designed around its membership and not the company sponsoring the community, but it also avoids the natural tendency of corporate marketers to talk in the dreaded "corporate-speak" about themselves. Unfortunately, our research shows that most companies would disagree with us on this point—only 35 percent of them use external professionals for their community content development.

While advertising can work in communities, advertising and other marketing materials are not typically the content that provides the core value to your community. There are some exceptions here, like the use of job listings in professional affinity communities. Job listings in professional communities such as PoliceLink, which we discussed earlier, are advertising, but in an affinity-based professional community, they are valuable content as well.

User-generated content is a bit more tricky, especially for companies that have a command-and-control marketing mentality. For user-generated content to work, companies need to embrace some of the messiness that comes with the Hyper-Social shift. Sure, you need to monitor your user-generated content constantly to ensure that it is free of spam and that it does not contain libelous or nefarious content, but that does not equate to "controlling" what appears on your site. You can set up guidelines for what content (comments, posts, discussion threads, reviews, and so on) you will accept on your site, but once those guidelines are published, you need to live by them. Assuming that your guidelines don't contain language saying that you will reject reviews that are critical of your company or its products (which those of some well-known companies actually do), you have to allow negative as well as positive reviews. If you fail to allow both positive and negative comments, your community will be perceived as another nontransparent corporate mouthpiece of the sort that people have come to mistrust.

Content alone will not make for a vibrant community. There are plenty of communities out there that have high-quality professional content but do not enjoy the forces of increasing returns that characterize successful communities. Like the IBM-sponsored Internet Evolution community (http://www.internetevolution.com), they are nothing more than online publications, with the same economic characteristics as those of traditional online media outlets. Content needs to be married with the other three forces of increasing return in order for your community to take off.

The Importance of Member Profiles in Communities

If you capture information about your members and use that information to make it easier for them to find relevant new connections or knowledge in your community, you will increase the value of being a community member to the members, which again will cause more members to join. It is amazing how much people will tell you about themselves if they see the benefits of doing so. Not only will they disclose a lot of information about themselves as part of their static profile, but through their actions and behaviors within the community, they will tell you things about themselves that are more valuable than any data about them that you could uncover through classic market research. What you can get from community interaction is not just information about your community members; it is deep knowledge steeped in social context.

As with anything else in social environments, you need to give your members something in return for all this rich knowledge. That something is useful recommendations for new connections with content and with other members. Think about it: The reason that most of us are willing to share as much information about ourselves as we do with Amazon is that Amazon recommends new books to us (and for some of us, it does an amazing job at increasing our dollars spent not only with Amazon, but also on books as a relative share of our overall budget).

Unfortunately, most communities do not use the information that we give them, or the knowledge that they can gain through our ongoing behavior within that community, to improve our experience within that community. Although this is frustrating for the members who knowingly provide that knowledge about themselves, smaller, tight-knit communities may survive the fact that community organizers do not leverage that knowledge. In larger communities, where it becomes harder to find relevant content, and where we can no longer keep track of who is who by name, it can actually become a deterrent to success if the system doesn't help us find the right connections.

In order to make it easier for members to populate their profiles, some communities, like *Bloomberg Businessweek*'s Business Exchange (http://bx.businessweek.com), are connecting to other services, like LinkedIn or Google, to allow the automatic population of member information. As the world of business communities continues to fragment, such federated community management solutions will become more of a necessity.

The automatic population of member profiles with information that you have about them based on other relationships is something that needs to be member-driven. We have seen too many internal communities fail because the profiles were automatically populated with information coming from the company's human resources database. People take offense at some of their personal information being made public without their consent—e.g., the number of years they have been with the company (which may make them look old if they have been there for a very long time).

The Importance of Facilitating Transactions in Communities

The easier you make it for community members to engage in a transaction (find support, buy something, or discover relevant information), the higher the value they will derive from it and the more they will tell other members, which will increase your membership once again. Whatever the purpose of your community, make sure that people can get to what they came for in the first place as quickly as possible and with the least amount of distraction. If they came to get support, give it to them fast; if they came to buy something, make the experience as smooth as possible; and if they are there to help you design new products, don't exhaust and confuse them with unnecessary steps. Research has shown that people who participate in online product design communities have a higher willingness to pay more for the products that they cocreated, so these are community members who you do not want to turn off from participating.[4]

If you already have a transaction-based relationship with your customers, think seriously about connecting that transaction-based infrastructure with your communities. Coming back to the office supply company, when it launched its community, it was impossible for people who already had an account with the company to connect their buyer profile with their community profile or to go from a product recommendation by another member in the community to actually ordering that product within their account.

Monster.com, on the other hand, is a company that got it right. After it purchased Affinity Labs, a collection of affinity-based professional communities, it realized the benefits of connecting the communities with the Monster.com job board, a transaction-based job search and recruiting platform. Not only are the combined profiles much richer for recruiters looking for talent (they now include social context), but they changed the nature of the relationship that the company has with talent from an episodic, transactional relationship to an ongoing relationship in the context of rich tribal behaviors. The company also created the potential for community members to become part of the talent acquisition and development process, thus turning the whole process more social, with community amplification and higher levels of trust.

Other Important Factors to Consider When Building Communities

There are other elements that drive and define communities, such as the social infrastructure and the technology foundation of communities, or the integration with the business processes that they support. None of those characteristics has the same power as the four forces of increasing return that characterize successful communities.

The social infrastructure of communities, however, deserves some special attention, as it is frequently the cause of community failures.

Social Infrastructure

Too many companies with communities think that they need some sort of monetary contract with their community members, or at the very least with the leaders of their tribes. Much of that thinking goes back to the tradition of focus groups, where we pay people to come and fool us (and themselves) about what they intend to buy or how they perceive our products or brands. Humans are Hyper-Social, and within well-oiled communities, the strongest contract you can have with them is a social contract based on reciprocity. People will help you design better products knowing that they will be able to buy better products down the line, or just knowing that it will make them look cool or intelligent within their tribe. People will help you support your products because they are hardwired to help other members of the tribe, and trust that they will get help in return when they need it. In his latest book, *Predictably Irrational*, behavioral economist Dan Ariely argued that we live in two different worlds: one in which social norms prevail, and one in which market norms prevail.[5]

The social norms include friendly requests that people make—for example, when a neighbor or friend asks you to move a couch. You do not expect to get anything in return right away, and the feelings associated with helping the person are usually warm and fuzzy (for both parties). Market norms, on the other hand, are cold and calculated, with exchanges being sharp-edged: wages, prices, rent, and so on.

One of the experiments that Ariely recounted involved three groups of people who were asked to do a repeated task for five minutes—combining circles and squares on a computer screen. The first group was given $5 for the task, the second was given $0.50, and the third was asked to do it as a favor. The group that was paid $5 worked harder than the group that was paid $0.50 by about 50 percent. The group that was not paid, and that evaluated the request in the social framework instead of the market framework, beat both other groups. Ariely then repeated the test, but instead of giving money, he gave the members of the first group a gift of chocolates worth about $5, but without telling them that; the second group got a Snickers bar; and the third group was again asked to do the task as a favor. This time all three groups achieved the same positive results.

Another point that Ariely makes, supported by more experiments, is that once a person evaluates something within a market framework, he will continue to do so even after payments are no longer given. Therefore, it is a very bad idea to create situations in which the two frameworks are mixed.

Pfizer is one of the companies we interviewed that understands this. When we spoke with Rob Spencer, the so-called chief idea management officer (not an official title),[6] he explained to us that the company never uses rewards in its collaborative problem-solving or social innovation exercises—it relies exclusively on recognition instead of rewards. For Rob, it's extremely important not to monetize what are essentially social contracts.

There is not much to say about the role of the technology infrastructure in community management, other than to note that, unfortunately, many community initiatives start off as a technology platform exercise rather than a social one. That is the wrong way to look at setting up communities—and, our research has found, a large cause for failure. As Intuit's vice president of communities, Scott Wilder, would say: "If your community cannot survive in a bulletin board, it will not survive anywhere." We could not agree more.

Summary

What we've covered in this chapter is not exactly new ground. Much of the basic information was available at the end of the last century. Nevertheless, most Hyper-Social program failures today can still be attributed to what we covered in the chapter. So when people come to you with plans and programs that touch on Hyper-Sociality, make sure that you are armed with questions to challenge their assumptions.

Why did we come up with this technology plan—would a bulletin board not have sufficed? Where is the content going to come from that will provide value when members first check in (and when they come back)? Why are we not tying the community efforts to our e-commerce site? Are we allowing people to bring in their profiles from other sites?

part two

THE FOUR PILLARS OF HYPER-SOCIALITY

five

Forget Market Segments and Consumers—Think Tribes and Humans

"Argh, please stop calling us consumers (or worse, users)—you'll miss the boat on what we are all about if you insist on doing that."
—**People**

The next four chapters will discuss the Four Pillars of Hyper-Sociality:

- Tribe vs. market segment

- Human-centricity vs. company-centricity

- Network vs. channel

- Social messiness vs. process and hierarchy

Let's start off by looking at the way companies think about the people whom they depend on to stay in business. If they keep thinking of these people as consumers, companies will develop such a narrow view—one limited to people's context only as it relates to brand equity—that they will miss the opportunity to increase the public's love for their company and its products. If, on the other hand, companies could expand their view and think of people as humans—social beings with needs and wants that go beyond what any company has to offer—they could get a much larger share of most people's wallets (for a very long time).

Who is going to be the more loyal customer: the apartment-renting "consumer" to whom you've just recommended a 1,000-square-foot apartment with two bedrooms and two baths based on his requirements or the "human," with his rich ethnic background, family configuration, and love of dogs, to whom you've recommended a duplex in a neighborhood of pet lovers and with the right school system? We are all humans, and we are influenced by our social context when we make decisions. By calling people consumers, you are stripping away that rich context and missing the true reasons why we buy things.

If companies can think of their patrons as human and consider the rich social context of those patrons, they may be in for some surprises. A good example of such a surprise is that people are not just a herding species; we are, as Dan Ariely puts it, a self-herding species, one that keeps buying the same brands, even if there was no good reason for buying those brands in the first place—that is, until a company screws it up.[1] Some companies have known this for years, even though they may not have been able to pinpoint the reason why. A senior executive from the HP Inkjet Printer division told one of us many years ago that his company (and other vendors in the space) was enjoying almost perfect customer loyalty, with people continuing to upgrade to the same brand of printer, until one of the manufacturers screwed it up—e.g., by

being late to market with a new release when com
had theirs available.

OK, so now that we've passed that hurdle, let's dwell on this issue some more. Seriously, language is a very important factor in how we evaluate things and how we make decisions. Using the wrong language can limit our thinking. Using the right language can expand our horizons tremendously. And language happens to be something that, as humans, we have not had enough time to adapt to. As Gary Marcus, the author of *Kludge: The Haphazard Construction of the Human Mind*, concludes,[2]

> The linguistic world is much less trustworthy than the visual world. If something looks like a duck and quacks like a duck, we are licensed to think it's a duck. But if some guy in a trenchcoat tells us he wants to sell us a duck, that's a different story. Especially in this era of blogs, focus groups, and spin doctors, language is not always a reliable source of truth.

Are we getting too academic here? Does anyone really care about all this stuff?

You should. If your team is thinking about building a new product to meet people's needs, and it thinks of the problem it is addressing as a "calendaring issue" instead of a "meeting facilitation issue," your team will build a different product. You should care about language in everything you do. Another confusing term that gets bandied around the corporate world is *markets*. By definition, a market is a place where the sellers of goods or services can meet with the buyers, and where there is a potential for a transaction to take place. The sellers must have something that buyers want in order for there to be a transaction. So by thinking about markets, we are automatically focusing on the transactions and losing sight of the human behaviors that cause people to buy products and services in the first place.

Tribes have their own language and their own terms, and it's important to understand and speak their language and meet them on their own terms. If you want to succeed in engaging tribes, you will need to listen for how they talk, and adjust everything that you do with them accordingly. Companies need to stop thinking about consumers, stop thinking about markets and market segments, and instead start thinking about humans and their tribes. Tribes are based on group behavioral characteristics, while market segments are based on individual "consumer" traits. People in market segments do not necessarily want to hang out together, but those in tribes do, and if you want to leverage the Hyper-Social shift in your business, that is how you will have to look at your markets from this point forward.

Most businesspeople have been trained to use market segmentation as the basis for their strategy development. Unfortunately, in this Hyper-Social era, markets and market segments are no longer where buying decisions get made. In a Hyper-Social environment, you need to reach the tribes whose members influence one another—not the market segments that can be targeted with direct mail and ad campaigns.

In this chapter, we will also tackle some of the business world's sacred cows. Some might be instinctively inclined to disagree with us, but we are confident that when you see the business world through the Hyper-Social lens, you will also see the limitations of certain business fads. They are the one-to-one marketing and product customization wave that never was, the end of market research (aka "market deception") as we know it, and the long tail niche strategy, which never became profitable for anyone.

Stop Thinking Market Segments— Think Tribes Instead

Classic market segmentation is based on people's individual characteristics, not their social behavioral characteristics. Unfortunately, these individual characteristics about people do not tell companies much about whom people like to hang out with and what they are likely to buy.

Knowing that a person owns a small business may be an indicator that she will subscribe to a small business magazine or belong to the local chamber of commerce, but it will tell you little about the tribes that influence her buying decisions or with whom she discusses her frustrations, which could lead to the design of better products and services. When we spoke with Mark Colombo, senior vice president of digital access marketing at FedEx,[3] he described how his department uncovered two tribes within the small business market segment: women and people who live near the Canadian border. First, the department found that two-thirds of its small business clients are owned by women. Now, don't you think that the conversations in a community of women-owned small businesses will be much more vibrant than those in a generic small business community? For instance, women who own small businesses likely share a common set of issues and pains and may experience a strong sense of duty to help other women, which you would not find in a more broad-based small business community.

FedEx also found that most of its small business customers have shipping areas that look like circles around their physical location—for some, the circle is 50 miles; for others, 400. When it started looking at companies that are right by the Canadian border, however, it found that most of those companies had half-circles, with the shipping circles cut off right at the border. The reason? Not enough understanding of the export regulations. If you could create a community for the half-circle tribe that is sharing a common pain point, that too would lead to more vibrant exchanges and value creation than you could create in a generic small business community.

Let's take Jeep owners as another example.[4] The company could have used classic market segmentation methods to find the right target market segments to advertise its Wrangler or its Cherokee— much the same way that Nissan and Honda did. Nissan marketed its Nextera to single, 32-year-old, outdoorsy males who enjoy mountain climbing, biking, and surfing. After the launch, the company found that more than half of the buyers were women. The same thing happened to the Honda Element; the firm targeted it at active, suburban twentysomethings,[5] only to find out that most buyers turned out to be baby boomers. Instead, Jeep found a tribe—a tribe with a shared passion for adventure, which tribal members express by "off-roading" their vehicles. The tribe has young people and old people; mechanics, teachers, lawyers, and doctors; women, men, couples, and whole families—all sharing that same passion. The people who participate in Camp Jeep, Jeep Jamboree, and Jeep 101 events form a tribe, and it would have never surfaced in classic market segmentation research. Not only did Jeep uncover a real tribe, but it had the foresight to create an environment, in the form of company-sponsored events, in which the tribe could operate as a Hyper-Social group.

There are other such examples, including the Harley-Davidson riders and their HOGs (Harley Owner's Group), the MINI Cooper owners, and the Fiskateers, to name just a few. While many people would call these "brand communities," we will refrain; in fact, we believe that using that term is very misleading for marketers, as it leads them to think that they can build brand communities, whereas in fact they cannot. Brand communities imply that the brand is at the center of the activity—which it is not. In order for communities to work, the members need to be at the center of the community, and so the motivations have to be different from the pure hedonistic pleasure of owning a brand or product. The Fiskateers may be the people who come up with most of the new Fiskars product ideas, and they may be the firm's staunchest defenders when the brand comes under attack. But the reason they form a tight-knit community, one that some members say has changed their lives,[6] is that they share a passion for scrapbooking. The reason that Harley owners get together is that they share a common passion for a riding lifestyle. Jeep owners have a shared aspiration for adventure by off-roading their cars. What about MINI Cooper owners, though? The reason they form a community is that they share a sense of humor and have an intense desire to express their creativity, not for the car, since according to ethnographic research,[7] even people who no longer own a MINI Cooper stay with the community.

As we saw in Chapter 2, people use the Jeep, the MINI, the Fiskars scissors, or the Harley as symbols to associate with others who share their passion. In some cases, they take that a step further and create rituals around those brands, which make the brands even stickier. But at the end of the day, these are not brand communities; they are passionate rider communities, scrapbooker communities, and adventure seeker communities. Professor Bernard Cova, who is also the coauthor of *Consumer Tribes*,[8] says it best: "We can hypothesize that consumers value the goods and services which, through their linking value, permit and support social interaction of the tribal part, products or services that support AB and not the fact of being A or B."[9]

So why Jeep, why Fiskars, why MINI, why Harley? Because in each of those cases, the company has provided an environment in which the member community can operate and thrive. Jeep marketers are providing training camps for off-roading and are organizing barbecues at which members can share their passion. Fiskars provides an online environment in which its members can thrive and connect, and it provides offline events as well. In all cases, the brand marketers act as enablers of a shared passion that exists within a tribe or community. And while these are not brand communities, when they are done right, they obviously affect the brand in more ways than one—such as increasing sales by 300 percent for Fiskars.

Analyzing people based on their individual characteristics is not a good predictor of what they will buy. So market segmentation will be of limited use in helping you market, sell, and develop new products. Buying is an inherently social process, and that is true not just in the Business-to-Consumer world, but also in the Business-to-Business world and the Consumer-to-Consumer world. As Dan Ariely found, "The decisions and judgments of individuals in a group are dependent upon the decisions and judgments of other group members such that choice or opinion shifts are induced."[10]

People tend to herd, and that affects their buying behavior—they buy the music that gets the most downloads, see the most popular movies playing, and vie for reservations at the restaurant with the longest wait time.

Engaging with Tribes

Depending on the tribes that you want to interact with, you will need to define an appropriate engagement model, including where and how to engage with them. Some tribes will prefer to contact one another primarily online, while others might want to add a hyperlocal, face-to-face component to their community. For example, if there is such a tribe as frugal moms who love the art of the deal and cannot stop talking about it when they find one, they may best be served by a Twitter-like environment with an SMS component to send one another alerts about those good deals.

In some cases, you will be able to engage tribes on your own platform (your own e-commerce site or your hosted community), and in other cases, you won't. That is what happened to TiVo, where a strong independent community of TiVo enthusiasts had already formed by the time TiVo decided to leverage communities. Instead of trying to lure those people to its own platform, TiVo wisely decided to engage them where they already were—an online forum set up by passionate users that attracted thousands of enthusiasts. That probably meant forgoing the detailed monthly reports with all the stats about the community and other goodies that corporate executives are used to. But at the end of the day, it's the best place to get support and one of the best sources of new ideas for the TiVo new product development team. In most cases, companies will have to embrace a federated model of tribal engagement, as people wander around cyberspace and have discussions about the things that you care about in multiple places.

All tribes have their leaders. Once you find the tribes that will help you with your business, you will also have to find their leaders and decide how to engage them. Leaders can be fans, employees, associates, contributors, customers, bloggers, or other independent content providers. They can be detractors or the real captains of their industry. But they are out there, and unless you know how to find them and to tap into their power, you will have limited success with your Hyper-Social efforts. That is why it's surprising that barely 20 percent of all the companies that participated in our 2009 Tribalization of Business Study have tapped into the leaders of their tribes. For each of the tribes you engage with, you will need to develop a leader strategy that includes where and how to recruit them, if and how to compensate them, whether or not to have a tiered leadership model, expectations (e.g., for content) for the various leader models, and whether leaders from one tribe can be used for other programs. In some cases you can start communities and wait until the leaders emerge, but in most cases it is well worth the effort to identify and engage them before you launch your Hyper-Social tribal initiatives.

Last, you will need to tie the various tribal engagement models to your strategic objectives—e.g., amplifying word of mouth, gaining product insights, improving customer service, and so on. Doing so includes setting expectations for which part of the company can expect to benefit from these initiatives, and how the company should measure progress and success.

So stop thinking markets and consumers, and instead focus on humans and their tribes—they are the ones who will help you market, sell, and design better products.

The Limitations of Business Fads

Now on to debunking some of the sacred cows that are out there — we hope you will still be with us at the end of this chapter.

One-to-One Marketing and the Product Customization Wave

One-to-one marketing was supposed to be the holy grail of customer relationship management. Companies would no longer have to isolate us from the rest of the world as a group to sell to us; they could actually do it on an individual basis. The problem is that we are Hyper-Social beings who prefer to operate within our tribes. We do not want to be isolated from our group so that salespeople who know more about us than we feel comfortable with can give us the hard sell. We want the buying process to be a social process. We don't trust companies to be on our side, and so we prefer looking to our peers for the information that will let us make sound buying decisions. The good news is that those Hyper-Social tribal peers cannot wait to help us and warn us about bad products and services.

As a team, we may want to customize our group workspace, the tools we use, or the T-shirts we wear, but we don't want one-on-one product customization. In fact, we do not like having too many choices. Research has shown that an overabundance of options significantly reduces our willingness to actually buy something[11] — it's as if mass customization leads to mass confusion.[12] Now, wait — don't throw that customer relationship management system out just yet. While people may not like to have companies try to sell to them on a one-on-one basis based on all that rich marketing data they've accumulated, people love actually being ready to buy a product, and people love it when a call center recognizes them and treats them as if they were a long-lost relative. Think of the CIO who made his buying decision based on his peers' recommendations, and is now ready to buy that solution from your company. How do you think he would feel if, during the ordering process, someone from your company decided to warn him that what he wants to buy is actually incompatible with some other applications that his organization relies on, rather than just push the sale? He would stay with you forever, or at least until you had a major screwup—and even then, he would probably be more forgiving.

People also like it when "the system" (an e-commerce site or an online community) recommends other content that is highly valuable because it's based on what is known about them—much like Amazon recommending books or the Apple Genius recommending music. If companies leverage communities or social networks, they can make a big impact without one-to-one marketing. People love it when the software they are using enables them to help others; it makes them look great, and they also feel warm and fuzzy inside for having helped someone. Think of it as the next generation "refer a friend" program, one for the Hyper-Social times. The old "refer a friend" programs were very lopsided in terms of who was getting the most value from them. Almost all the value went to the company. A "refer a friend to valuable information to help her make a good decision" program (granted, we need a pithier title) is much more reciprocal in nature, and has a much higher likelihood of becoming viral among your customer tribes.

Remember this: When people are ready to buy or when they have a problem with a product or service, they want to be treated as individuals. When people are in the process of making a buying decision, they want to be treated as a member of their tribe. And yes, the logical extension of that thinking is that a company's behavioral and contextual targeting campaigns may in fact be a colossal waste of time and money now that we are undergoing the Hyper-Social shift. During the sales cycle, it's important to target tribes!

The End of Market Research (aka "Market Deception") as We Know It

We have already seen that market segmentation research is not a good predictor of what Hyper-Social beings will buy, because it does not tell you anything about the group behavioral characteristics that make people want to hang with one another. On top of that, there is also evidence that the data that companies are collecting as part of that process may actually be flawed. According to a major neuro-marketing research project led by Martin Lindstrom,[13] we humans tend to lie to market researchers. It's not a conscious decision to lie; it's just that our unconscious minds are better at interpreting our behavior (including why we buy) than our conscious minds. Dan Ariely adds that he is "very suspicious of focus groups because of the research on irrationality and because people have very bad intuitions about their own behaviors."[14] Taken together, we would say that these findings spell new challenges for the market research industry, on which companies spent $12 billion in 2007 in the United States alone.

One of the biggest problems with classic market research is that it assumes that people make buying decisions on their own and does not compensate for the fact that most such decisions are in fact influenced by groups or tribes. Another problem with traditional market research and focus groups is that they do not account for the fact that most of the time people deceive themselves by making up a socially acceptable story for the reasons they bought the product or service *after* the purchasing decision. And that story can be vastly different from the real reason they bought that product. Another problem, this one more specific to focus groups, is that people are often paid to participate in those efforts. The result is that they will evaluate everything they do during that session in their market framework instead of their social framework, meaning that they will evaluate the value of what they give you in monetary terms rather than in social terms, as we saw in Chapter 1. That could lead them to focus on quantity of feedback rather than quality, or to tell you what they think you might want to hear just because you pay them.

With this much uncertainty around market segmentation research, it's no wonder that CMOs like Simon Clift from Unilever profess that they just don't believe in predictive research and don't use it.[15]

Again, don't close down your market research department just yet. There are things that market research, especially ethnographically based research, can help you uncover, including information about tribal behavior. Let's take the example of a global clothing manufacturer. When the company decided to relaunch a women-based brand of jeans, it decided to center the launch around a worldwide tribe—a community to which they expected to attract 3 million young women. The theory was that they needed to find one commonality among all young women worldwide to attract them to the community in the first place, and then allow sub-tribes to form in order to keep the members of the community engaged. It turned to ethnographic-based market research to find that one common trait and discovered one that is very counter-intuitive, especially for classic market researchers. The emerging common trait among all young women worldwide is the process of *individuating*—getting out from under the influence of parents and masculine dominance. The counterintuitive part is that even though the thing that binds these women together is their becoming individuals, they experience this process as part of a *tribe*.

Other useful things that can be gleaned from classic market research are trends involving pricing or usage, and even root cause analysis of why certain things turned out the way they did. But these are mostly trailing indicators and should not be used to predict the future—especially as it relates to buying decisions!

Why the Long Tail Never Materialized

Interestingly, many of the markets that were predicted to be "long-tail" opportunities (think media and entertainment content, for instance) turned out to be much more hit-driven than logic might have led us to believe. The long tail, a principle articulated by Chris Anderson of *Wired*, suggests that deep catalogs of songs, movies, and the like will be highly valuable in a world of cheap digital storage and search engines because consumers can browse and purchase entertainment that is precisely interesting to them (rather than settling for mainstream fare). Curiously, people seem to be intensely interested in "hits," however, there are very few songs or movies that enjoy broad success. One key reason for this is that humans enjoy consuming and talking about the content that others are consuming and talking about. The majority are not consuming large amounts of obscure music, films, or novels; rather, they rush in droves to see the movie that opened that weekend or the television show that everyone is talking about, and they tend to spend their valuable time consuming hits as opposed to more unpopular long-tail content. Google's CEO, Eric Schmidt, nicely sums up the business import of this fact when he observes,

While the tail is very interesting, the vast majority of revenue remains in the head. And this is a lesson that businesses have to learn. While you can have a long tail strategy, you better have a head, because that's where all the revenue is.

And, in fact, it's probable that the Internet will lead to larger blockbusters and more concentration of brands. Which, again, doesn't make sense to most people, because it's a larger distribution medium. But when you get everybody together they still like to have one superstar. It's no longer a US superstar, it's a global superstar. So that means global brands, global businesses, global sports figures, global celebrities, global scandals, global politicians.[16]

Summary

Forgetting market segments and embracing tribes instead is a big cultural shift. As you guide your team through the changes, keep asking yourself and your team the hard questions. Why would the members of our target audience want to hang out together? Is there any way that we can play a role in increasing their Hyper-Sociality? Are we relying on faulty market research in making our business decisions? If we could rethink our go-to-market strategy, would we go after our customers? Do we have a tribal mindset? Have we identified the leaders of our tribes? Have we found ways to engage them? Have we looked at what platforms we will need to engage our tribes on? Are we trying to chase the one-to-one marketing myth? Do we make proper use of our CRM system? Are we chasing the long tail for no good reason? Should we instead be focusing on the head of the curve instead of the tail, and do we know which members of our tribes consistently can identify the head?

six

Forget Company-Centricity— Think Human-Centricity

Peter Drucker once said that the single most important thing to remember about any enterprise is that there are no results inside its walls—the result of a business is a satisfied customer. We businesspeople get so absorbed in our own world that we start thinking of our products, services, and companies as the center of the universe (and in fact, they are often the center of *our* universe). As we talk about the space we live in day in and day out, we start suffering from the curse of insular knowledge, with the result that few people outside of the company, other than a few industry insiders, have a clue of what we're talking about.

In addition, companies often develop jargon, specifications, and categories of products largely from their own perspective, not from the vantage point of potential customers. Consider, for instance, how a multidivisional technology company may market printers, computers, and monitors as separate products on separate Web sites, although the customer may consider the products to be so linked that they are one integrated purchase. Products are often designed, named, and priced not as a result of external input, but rather as an outcome of what the company has done before or what influential internal groups have required. It seems as though even in our personal lives, the company comes first. Indeed, history shows us that game-changing, disruptive products are suppressed not because they are not what the customers want, but rather because they *are* exactly what customers want, and so they threaten existing corporate power structures.

Once upon a time, there were no corporations—the legal profession and the business community had to create the "legal fiction" concept of a corporation to make it sufficiently analogous to a human, i.e., an entity that is able to sue and be sued. Once created, corporations became almost super-beings, with the potential to outlive their creators and their critics alike. Management structures became aristocracies of sorts, where power was handed down from one generation to another, and the supremacy of the company over the individuals who managed it was rarely questioned. "Company men," as loyal workers are still known, were expected to subjugate themselves to the interests of the company, and willingly did so. Indeed, legal principles were developed that created a "fiduciary relationship" between many managers and the abstract companies they work for; in plain terms, these executives are legally required to act with the best interests of the corporation (and not their own) in mind. They have become servants of the corporation.

Considering this long history and acculturation, it is no wonder that most companies' management and owners believe that in all interactions with others (be they customers, employees, or business partners), the same rule should apply—the company comes first. Indeed, we should clarify that this book is not about helping companies leverage the new tools of human Hyper-Sociality to gain some sort of advantage over their customers or employees. Our message is starkly different: you must understand and leverage Hyper-Sociality if you are to properly connect with, and delight, your customers and your employees, which should be your goal.

Simply put, by becoming Hyper-Social, you will benefit the humans with whom you interact, and in doing so, your company will gain much. As a result of conducting the Tribalization of Business Study and studying scores of companies' attempts to navigate the Hyper-Social shift, we believe that the failure to be human-centric is the most commonly breached of the Four Pillars of Hyper-Sociality, as we will discuss in Chapter 9, and one of the greatest challenges that organizations face.

Human-Centricity

First let us consider what "human-centricity" means. In essence, it is seeking, first and foremost, to direct all company activities and decisions toward providing value to the humans who are the company's customers, employees, or business partners. For instance, when someone attempts to order a book that she has previously purchased from Amazon, the order system will remind her that she already purchased that book. From a traditional sales perspective, that is probably a terrible policy: if the person wants to give your company more money, why would you create any impediment to that transaction? From a Hyper-Social perspective, though, reminding someone that she might have forgotten that she'd already ordered that book is *exactly* what people expect from a member of their tribe. If there's going to be someone who is given the benefit of the doubt or cut a break, a human-centric company will extend that break first to the customer, not the company. It also means that the qualities that matter most to humans and that make them feel best, such as fairness, transparency, respect, openness, and the opportunity to help and be helped, will be practiced throughout the organization.

Given that human-centricity, not company-centricity, is one of the Four Pillars of Hyper-Sociality, the typical manager's inability to embrace the concept has the potential to materially suspend the move toward Hyper-Sociality. Unfortunately, too many executives put company-centric philosophies at the center of their corporate social environments (such as their communities). Of the Four Pillars, human-centricity vs. company-centricity is the one where corporate culture is most clearly implicated. Accordingly, it's no surprise that trying to move the organization ahead on this thinking often pits change agents against the inertia of corporate culture. But on the other hand, if and when human-centricity becomes embedded in your corporate culture, it will become an enduring strength, passed from employee to employee, that competitors will find difficult to duplicate.

Let's consider again the myopia that many of us suffer when we work for company-centric organizations. As a result of our working in these companies, we often think that our brand is more important than it probably is, and that consumers view our company through a brand or product lens. Consider this: Human prospects rarely think of products as the center of their universe, and while some companies babble about their products using all the fashionable industry buzzwords, their customers use much simpler terms to talk about the same products. And when people are talking about a company's products, they're much more likely to be speaking with others with whom they've developed some sort of affinity (i.e., members of the same tribe) than with someone *from* the company. In a Hyper-Social world, it is not about the company or its products; it is about how the company should subordinate itself to what the tribes around it use the company for. Sometimes it is a product that solves a problem or fills a need. Other times, it's a product that lets the tribe discuss related issues and ideas that interest it. But it's very unlikely to be the hallowed product itself.

Factors That Stand in the Way of Human-Centricity

The historical bias toward company-centricity and away from human-centricity is perpetuated by a number of factors. One key factor is that the most influential functions within organizations are inherently company-centric. For instance, legal departments are typically oriented in a fiduciary relationship with the company, and they seek to resolve every contingency and unintended consequence that may arise in favor of the organization, not the human employees or customers. Indeed, legal representatives have little discretion in this regard; they are sworn guardians of their clients' interests, and in the perceived zero-sum world of competing interests, if I let the customer "win," I have caused my client to lose.

Company-drafted "terms of use" that control participation in most online communities, for instance, often provide clear illustrations of the legal department's bias against acting Hyper-Socially. Indeed, there is little customer voice expressed in the terms of use—if you examine the terms, you'll see that there is little evidence of a customer advocate's voice. In addition, the public relations function typically is not a key advocate of human-centricity. "Spinning" communications to persuade, as opposed to reaching a better understanding with, external human stake-holders is often demonstrative of poor Hyper-Sociality. This con-trasts dramatically with the viewpoint of the CEO of Mozilla, a company that clearly has shifted closer to human-centricity:

> So when some significant part of the community gets upset, we pay a lot of attention. Sometimes our responses are defensive at first, but I think we're pretty good at opening up. It's pretty interesting to look at what somebody is complaining about and find the truth behind that. We also try to be very low spin. In fact, sometimes we joke that we're negative spin. We don't need the press or anybody else to do that; we'll do it ourselves.[1]

This inquisitiveness about customer complaints, a genuine desire to understand what it is that has upset the customer, is a human-centric trait that a number of Hyper-Social companies demonstrate. They are not challenged by an upset stakeholder, or repelled by antiproduct or anticompany sentiment. On the contrary, Hyper-Social organizations seem to be driven to understand why there has been a disconnect between the value that the organization thought it should be delivering to the customer, and what the customer felt was actually delivered. Hyper-Social organizations view these exceptions as key learning experiences, as opposed to regrettable but explainable outliers among their typically very sat-isfied customer base.

Other factors that stand in the way of human-centricity include efficiency-centricity and the simple fact that the customer has often had no forum where his voice could be clearly heard. Historically, efficient corporate operations have often required bureaucracy and strict policies that concomitantly placed the interests of the corporation above those of the humans it transacted business with. Customers had to accept delivery, payment, or return policies so that the company could manage complex systems in the most efficient (and cost-effective) manner. Because of the limitations imposed by communications infrastructure, distance, and lack of feedback systems, large organizations frequently had a limited ability to understand their customers' desires and needs, and to place these in the center of their business operations. For instance, unless there was a massive boycott, the distant corporate executives might have no idea how displeased some customers had become. Diminishing market share or revenues might be the first nonspecific notification of dissatisfied customers that the managers received, and they probably got it months after the fact.

Acting in that same traditional company-centric fashion in today's new Hyper-Social world, however, is a strategy that is fraught with disaster. The evidence lies in a virtual landscape littered with dead online communities whose companies did not put humans and their tribes at the center of their efforts. These unsuccessful attempts at interacting with Hyper-Social communities serve as petri dishes of a sort, where customer colonies failed to thrive despite significant amounts of corporate investment and attention. As we have argued throughout this book, in order to become Hyper-Social, organizations need to put humans and their tribes at the center of every business process, decision, and policy.

And organizations need to always remember that sometimes the human is a customer or prospect, and at other times the human might be an employee.

As a result, if your organization's communities and other social media are about you and your products, people will not drop by in the first place, or they may come once and never come back. In fact, the Tribalization of Business Study indicates that the "company" aspects of online communities are far less important to humans than being able to connect with like-minded people, to discuss hot topics, or to be able to help and be helped. The context of the conversation has to be about the humans, what makes them tick, and what makes them want to hang out with one another.

A popular online parenting community found out what happens when corporate goals trump the wishes of the actual members of the community.[2] In order to make room for advertising, the sponsoring organization reformatted the site and altered the arrangement of blog posts in a way that greatly upset community members. Despite a groundswell of demand for a return to the old format, the sponsoring organization did not heed the tribe's requests. Within a week, disgruntled tribe members created a replica of the beloved legacy community, and the new community soon enjoyed a multiple of the traffic that the original site was experiencing.

Our research has also uncovered a potential pitfall worth noting in shifting companies toward greater human-centricity. Many companies are applying return on investment (ROI) metrics to social media in a way that has them thinking in terms of, "What is this investment doing for me?" as opposed to, "How can I improve the value for the customer? What can I do now for my customer that I couldn't do in the past? How can I use the participatory nature of Web 2.0 tools to improve the customer experience?" Would online retailers, applying that logic, ever have permitted candid, uncensored online reviews of products that they sell, knowing that they might lose some sales as customers discussed product benefits and shortcomings? To these retailers' credit, they eventually did adopt this measure of customer-centricity, but only after the ROI of *not* doing so became very hard to articulate.

Steps to Becoming More Human-Centric

Fortunately, the successes of some pioneering Hyper-Social companies indicate the steps that companies can take to become more human-centric. Key actions include being responsive to customers' suggestions, criticisms, and questions and having strong moderators managing the communications between tribe and organization. Permitting detractors within the tribe to speak their mind and providing access to competitors' information or products that might be valuable to the tribe are common steps that organizations take to shift the bias from company-centricity to human-centricity. Permitting the members of the tribe to boost their reputations or status in the context of the tribe, perhaps by recognizing particularly helpful or competent members, is another common feature organizations add that help to position the humans as preeminent.

Now granted, there are some cases in which you will be able to get away with a little more company-centricity. If your goal is to gain market insights into your new product innovation process, then you probably can get by with a smaller community of people who are primarily focused on your products—something that they care about. If your goal is to both gain market insight and leverage Hyper-Sociality as part of your word-of-mouth efforts, however, it is unlikely that you will be able to achieve that with a focus-group-like community centered on your products.

Truly Hyper-Social companies put customer-centricity into much more than their social initiatives. They extend customer-centricity to their

- *Value proposition.* Instead of being product-centric, a value proposition needs to become consumer-centric. Look to position your offering as a customer-centric solution, not as a set of features, functions, and benefits. Tribes often use products or services for reasons other than the simple features or benefits of those products or services. They will use products, for instance, that they believe raise their status in the community. People who drive hybrid-technology cars are probably interested in saving money on gas, but they also happily pay a "hybrid premium" on the purchase of the car. This contradiction indicates that there is probably another motive in their purchase: broadcasting their concern about the environment, and their willingness to invest in improving the environment, to the people around them.

- *Brands.* Most brands are product- or company-centric. They need to become customer-centric. Do companies really think that most customers are highly concerned with how accurate their luxury watch is, especially when they can buy a perfect timekeeper dirt cheap? The real question is, how do people feel about themselves in the context of your brand? Do they look cool, smart, or informed? That is what really counts, and it is what they are probably interested in doing as they interact on luxury watch online forums.[3]

- *Focus groups.* Focus groups are usually "focused" on the product itself or the company. They need to become customer-centric and understand why that tribe finds your products so engaging. Ideally, a company will derive insights from ongoing customer communities instead of having focus groups, and won't run those communities as focus groups.

- *Product platforms.* These are important, but in addition to them, companies now need to look for customer platforms. Customer platforms focus multibusiness, diverse companies not on a particular product, channel, or internally generated view of the market, but rather on customers and their tribes. Goods and services are then delivered to those customers on their terms, rather than in the ways that corporate legacy platforms formerly dictated. When a company as diverse as GE can find consumer platforms in addition to product platforms, which is what Beth Comstock, GE's global CMO, told us in a recent interview, that means that most other companies can find them too.

Again, if a company wants to become Hyper-Social, it needs to put the Hyper-Social engine—humans and their tribes—at the center of everything it does. But this begs the question, what's in human-centricity for the company? As we discuss at various points throughout the book, the benefits of becoming Hyper-Social accrue in many places across your company. First, moving to human-centricity begins to shift the corporate culture to one that's truly customer-centric. In addition, the shift in attention to the human elements of your business can help to improve product development, marketing, sales, talent management, knowledge management, and customer service (as we will discuss in upcoming chapters).

Becoming human-centric also creates new knowledge flows for the company that may not have existed in the past. For instance, if everyone at your company began receiving daily reports on the top social media opinions expressed about your company, its brands, and its executives, instead of just monthly market share or sales data, wouldn't this transparency profoundly affect decision making across various groups? Wouldn't it provide customer support with insights into how that function could be improved? Wouldn't such knowledge improve the planning, pricing, and promotion of your next product? Wouldn't it give your salespeople new ideas on new segments (think tribes) that they should be targeting?

And these are just a few of the potential benefits to the organization from putting human-centricity above company-centricity. Since you are appealing to Human 1.0 sociality by putting humans at the center of your corporate efforts, word of mouth about your company and its products may well increase. This is especially valuable, since it has been shown that word-of-mouth marketing is typically much more effective than conventional marketing.[4] Moreover, your company's voice within the tribe may well enjoy greater authenticity and credibility as your human-centric organization proves to be clearly committed to providing value equal to or greater than the value that people are seeking in return.

Given that this human-centricity is nothing more than what most companies already pay lip service to (putting the consumer at the middle of everything they do), you should explore how existing programs can be used to move your company in the direction of human-centricity. You may also consider doing what some companies have done: create the role of "chief commercial officer" or "chief customer officer." This is a senior role where a respected manager is given the task of serving as a customer advocate of sorts. Upon reflection, it is curious that, given the importance of the customer, no leader has yet been appointed in the C-suite to look out for this critical stakeholder.

Another step in the right direction of putting customers at the center of its corporate activities has been the creation of the "chief culture officer." Grant McCracken, author of *Chief Culture Officer* and researcher at MIT, notes that corporations need to extract value from the zeitgeist, from the outside world, and deliver that to customers. In McCracken's view, this newly identified executive needs to "know culture, both its fads and fashions, and its deep enduring structures" both to serve the customer, as well as to protect the corporation from unanticipated cultural shifts. Without a chief culture officer, McCracken observes that the corporation "lives in a perpetual state of surprise, waiting for the next big storm to hit."[5] Given the new social media tools available to the corporation, and its ability to better understand the external culture through many new touchpoints, the time indeed appears right for the rise of the chief culture officer to use this newfound understanding of the culture to help company and customer alike.

Summary

In this chapter, we show how the Hyper-Social organization is customer-centric, not self-centric. While most organizations espouse the importance of the customer (and the employee), and many probably truly believe that they need to be human-centric and not company-centric, few organizations have taken sufficient steps in that direction. There are a number of reasons for this inertia, but careful self-examination quickly shows organizations how they can improve their human-centricity. For instance, are there customer advocates in the organization who are fighting to break company-centric mindsets? Does the organization willingly share information and value with its customers, or does it attempt to use information asymmetry against its customers? Is the relationship with customers and employees viewed in a zero-sum way, where value derived by customers or employees necessarily diminishes the organization's gains?

seven

Forget Information Channels— Think Knowledge Networks

M arketing executives have traditionally been weaned on the use of information channels to reach customers and prospects. First we had print advertising, then radio, then TV, then e-mail and the Web, and now social media. It's important to make a distinction here, though. At the risk of sounding repetitive, let us again reiterate: social media is not a channel, it's the platform that allows the Human 1.0 social instinct to scale.

Unfortunately, some marketers are in fact using social media as a channel—rehashing old press releases to tweet or to send to bloggers, and putting old customer testimonials or, worse, speeches by their own company executives on YouTube. Why is this happening? The answer: panic and a rush to fix what's broken. Have you been hanging around a direct marketing department, an ad department, or a PR department lately? If you have, you may have noticed the severe mood swings that have been hitting those groups in the past few years. What they used to do is no longer working.

What we're witnessing today is nothing less than a tectonic shift that is making the use of channels—any channels—to interrupt and intercept customers and prospects obsolete. Let's go now to a couple of parties so that we can make this point clear.

In the old channel days, you used to go to parties where nobody knew one another. When nobody knows one another, it's easy to start a conversation or interrupt an existing one to start a new one. OK, so now flash forward a few decades. The parties that you go to now have strong social cliques. When there are strong social cliques, you can stand in the presence of a group that is having a conversation for minutes (or hours in some cities) without being noticed or having anyone acknowledge your existence. That is exactly what Hyper-Sociality has done to the ability to have conversations with your target audiences. In the past, your customers and prospects had no way of communicating (in a scalable way) with one another, or to form tribes. Thus, it was easy for you to use channels of communication to interrupt people and bombard them with information and messages. Now they have found one another, and they are socializing around powerful networks and tribes. Combine that with the fact that most people no longer trust information that comes from the company, and you can stand there at the party all day, waving your arms, only to find out that not one person will acknowledge your existence.

In this chapter, we'll take a closer look at the fundamental differences between channels and networks and how they require different approaches. We'll also look at the differences between data and information, which typically flow through channels, and knowledge, which can flow only through trusted networks, and what that means for your corporate content strategy and your knowledge management strategy. Finally, we'll explain, with some compelling case studies, how you can find and engage the networks that matter to your business. Sound like a good program? Let's get started.

Understanding the Way Channels Used to Function

Channels are typically separate (and sometimes competing) ways of reaching customers or business partners with products, information, or messages. In the old days, information about the product traveled along with the product itself. When mass communication channels came into being, we could separate the two, and information about products and services started to travel alone. Increasingly, decisions to buy products and services were no longer made based on those products and services, but rather on the information about them. That was the beginning of advertising, direct marketing, and public relations.

With the number of channels proliferating—not only more TV channels and more print outlets, but also new channels such as e-mail, the Web, and more recently the mobile platform—it became easier to target specific people with messages, but at the same time it became much harder to get their attention. Take this passage from Martin Lindstrom's book *Buyology*,[1] which, we believe, illustrates that point beautifully:

> By the time we reach the age of sixty-six, most of us will have seen approximately two million television commercials. Time-wise, that's

the equivalent of watching eight hours of ads seven days a week for six years straight. In 1965 a typical consumer had a 34 percent recall of those ads. In 1990, that figure had fallen to 8 percent. A 2007 ACNielsen phone survey of one thousand consumers found that the average person could name a mere 2.21 commercials of those they had ever seen, ever, period. Today, if I ask most people what companies sponsored their favorite TV shows—say, *Lost* or *House* or *The Office*—their faces go blank. They can't remember a single one. I don't blame them. Goldfish, I read once, have a working memory of approximately seven seconds—so every seven seconds, they start their lives all over again. Reminds me of the way I feel when I watch TV commercials.

Scary, isn't it? The typical response of marketing executives to this conundrum is indicative of the push that many felt to come up with the next breakthrough in spreading awareness as the statistics turned unfavorable. Some went looking for new channels to continue to interrupt people—for example, by placing promotional messages on the interactive voice response systems that sometimes prohibit you from talking with a human being when you make a call. Others thought of putting promotional messages on conveyor belts at supermarket checkout counters.[2] Still others, like Procter & Gamble (P&G), are trying to turn everyday social relationships into a channel by commercializing them. Through Vocalpoint, P&G mobilized an army of 600,000 moms to chat up its products and distribute coupons for them.[3] The company makes sure that it recruits well-connected mothers, those who generally speak to 25 or 30 other moms during the day, instead of typical moms, who speak to an average of only 5 other moms a day. Prior to Vocalpoint, it set up Tremor, a similar program for teens to chat up teen products. In the case of Tremor, it recruited 225,000 teens who had social networks of 150 friends in their instant message buddy list, compared to a teen average of 25.[4]

One of the biggest issues with programs like these is that not all sponsors require "buzz agents" to disclose that they are being compensated for buzzing about the products. As a result, some people fear (and probably rightfully so) that such practices could result in "the commercialization of human relations" and the erosion of social trust.

There are myriad examples of companies that have tried to turn social media into traditional marketing communication channels. Think of those that are setting up company or product profiles on Facebook and measuring their success by the number of "friends" they have. Is that really success? In most cases, the only reason that people "befriend" brand fan pages is the couponing that takes place on these sites. So these companies are failing to leverage the Hyper-Social potential of social networks—they are merely using the age-old monetary bribes known as discounts. Doing so continues to destroy the market for the rest of us. Companies like Xerox, on the other hand, which uses its Facebook fan page to engage with alumni, are leveraging the Hyper-Social potential of social networks to their advantage.

The Importance of Networks in Hyper-Social Environments

Channels stop working when the customer is collaboratively involved in the delivery of the message. With the customer's involvement, the message (and sometimes the very definition of the product and its value) changes as it is propagated through the network. Moreover, some customers will be more "important" than others because of their status or their location in the network, which could be more central, and thus better connected.

The message may also change in response to what the network feels the message is or should be, or simply because of the typical sharpening (emphasis)[5] and leveling (deemphasis) that happens to messages when they travel through networks made up of Humans 1.0. (Think of the kids' game Telephone.) Accordingly, the company might have to clarify the message, or the actual propagation might force a review of what the desired message was or should be. What's the upshot of all of this uncertainty? One clear answer is that discrete business "channels" are an endangered species.

In a networked world, where your customers, potential customers, and detractors are all nodes that are equally visible to every other node, there is no opportunity for the company to control "the channel" as it might have done in the past. In a Hyper-Social environment, where you don't know who will be participating in the conversation until the conversation actually begins, it is impossible to create separate pathways over which you can send a message to a retailer, a customer, or a business partner.

That being said, you need to be aware of the topology of the networks that exist within your tribes, as differences among them call for different approaches. In some cases, you will have very tightly connected members at the core of your network, with others at the fringes who are less connected; in other cases, you may have more evenly distributed networks; or you may even have networks that have ring networks inside of them. The characteristics of the tribal network will determine where you might want to position yourself within the network (if the tribe allows you to become part of it) and how to have your content travel through the network most effectively. In some cases you will want to target the members who are the most connected at the center of your network, and in other cases you will be better off if you target those who are loosely connected to them.

You should also understand the nature of the social bonds and leadership structures that exist within your Hyper-Social networks. If the leadership does not rotate on a periodic basis, or doesn't allow newcomers to achieve status within a reasonable amount of time, that is a problem. The type of bonds that people have with one another is also an important characteristic. In certain environments, such as sites with product reviews, connectedness is not all that important, but status might be. In other environments, such as those where people are helping one another in the context of complex problem solving, connection is an important factor that will determine how knowledge flows within those communities. In all cases, you will need to gather network characteristics for active lurkers—the largest and potentially most influential participation group within your community. They are those who participate and share information with others, but do so using channels (phone, face-to-face, or e-mail) other than the public community forums.

Another fundamental difference between channels and networks lies in what flows through them. Data and information flow through channels, whereas networks allow knowledge to flow. As John Hagel said when we talked with him,[6] "Unlike information or data flows, knowledge does not flow easily—as it relies on long-term trust-based relationships."

Buyers and companies both have reasons why it is important to make this distinction.

Besides the fact that as potential buyers, most people don't trust the nonreciprocal communications that companies want to have with them through fixed interruption-based channels, they also turn to their trusted networks because there they can gain actual knowledge about products and services—a commodity that is much more valuable than plain old data or information about them.

As for companies, they need to increase their external knowledge flows if they are to survive. When we spoke with John Hagel, he explained that he believes that in this era of intensifying competition, we need to shift from a knowledge stock mentality, where you aggressively protect and hoard proprietary knowledge, build scalable offerings around it, and then extract value from it for the longest possible time, to a knowledge flow mentality, where you realize that what you know today has rapidly diminishing value and where you refresh your knowledge stocks by participating in knowledge flows. So the key to success in this new economic reality is to move from a transactional world to a long-term trust-based world. Examples of taking on a knowledge flow approach include letting your key customers participate in product innovation and turning them into affiliates to allow them to help one another, as many tech companies do with their developer communities.

The complexity of many-to-many networked communication requires different management activities and an ability to cede some formerly corporate functions to the other people in the conversation. Corporate marketing, sales, public relations, and communications professionals have grown up in a world in which the channel was clearly defined, the product was immutable, and the flow of the channel was basically one-to-one or one-to-known. Developing a culture, management processes, and tools that permit the company to leverage these knowledge-based neo-networks instead of well-understood information-based channels is proving to be a formidable challenge for companies as they make the Hyper-Social shift.

But when companies do successfully leverage networks of users, potential users, and even detractors, wonderful things can happen. As SAP demonstrated with its Developer Network, a network of humans can often leapfrog over what would have been obstacles to more conventional, rigid "channels." By simultaneously leveraging a network of developers, potential users, and consultants (all of whom would have been engaged only individually via different, discrete, and more expensive "channels" in the past), SAP was able to inexpensively and expertly kick-start the adoption of its new software.

How to Find and Engage with the Networks That Matter

Chances are that your company has already started putting the infrastructure in place that will allow you to find the networks that matter. "Emerging Best Practices: Social Media Monitoring, Engagement & Measurement," a Beeline Labs research project[7] sponsored by FedEx, found that many companies have started monitoring social media conversations on blogs, forums, social networks, and microblogging platforms. They do this mostly as extensions of existing functions, not as part of new functions, which presents a potential danger if you count on this form of monitoring to switch your corporate mindset from a channel mentality to a network mentality. The function that is most likely to initiate a social media monitoring and engagement program is corporate communications. Not only is this the most channel-centric group within your organization, but its communications are often tightly controlled by the legal department, which makes it less likely to become part of network conversations that lead to buying decisions.

In order to find the networks that matter to your business, you will first need to map the ecosystem of the network conversations that relate to your company. While you will typically find the strongest networks in communities or tribes, you may also find them within the audiences of influential bloggers, microbloggers, or social network connectors. As we saw in Chapter 5, you may even discover networks with no home and decide to host them yourself, the way Jeep, Fiskars, and Monster.com were able to build vibrant communities. Most social media monitoring tools will allow you to start the process of identifying where your networks of influence are. Some even come with powerful "netnographic" tools, which are especially useful for mostly text-based online environments.

Once you understand where your networks are, you need to develop knowledge about the people in those networks—who they are, what makes them tick, who their leaders are, how they would like (or dislike) to have you engage with them, and so on. At this stage, it may be useful to develop some personas (fictional characters that represent groups of customers)—not based on individual demographic traits, as they are often developed for Web usability or store user experience projects, but based on their tribal traits. Personas will also help you down the line when you need to involve others within the company as part of your content and knowledge management strategy as well as your network engagement strategy.

At the end of the day, you want to have a deep understanding of the networks that matter so that you can participate in them and benefit from all the knowledge flows that happen within those networks. To the extent possible, you will want to participate in those knowledge flows—you want knowledge from the external networks to flow back into your product innovation processes, and you want knowledge from your internal networks to be used when people make their buying decisions or when they need help.

In order for this knowledge flow to happen, you will need to humanize your company. While the term is often misused, what we mean is this: People want to interact with other people and not with organizations, so you have to have "actual humans" participate in those knowledge flows, not "company spokespeople." For some companies, especially tech companies, that may come more naturally. Companies like IBM, Microsoft, Cisco, and EMC will allow most of their employees to engage in social media circles, with few dos and don'ts in their corporate policies regarding social media. The biggest "don't" is usually "don't embarrass us." In general, they trust their human employees to do what's right for the customer, and also for the company.

Many companies outside of the tech sector have very different policies. They may not have as many tech-savvy employees who feel comfortable tweeting, blogging, and Facebooking, and they may also have much stricter legal departments that want much more control over what employees are saying in the marketplace. If that is your case, then you will have to select a group of internal ambassadors and train them on the use of the tools, and also on legal compliance. We have seen very traditional companies become highly successful in doing that.

In almost every case, you will also need to train your people on how to develop content that will travel in those networks. As we saw earlier, McKinsey estimates that two-thirds of all buying decision–focused conversations do not involve anyone from the company. In a separate study, IDC estimated that only 20 percent of all content developed by the typical marketing department is actually being used by the typical sales organization. What we can extrapolate from this information is that the content developed by most marketing departments is used in less than 7 percent of all buying decisions. Surely, if more than $100 billion is collectively being spent on sales enablement tools, and if people are going to increasingly turn to their trusted networks of peers to gain knowledge from which to make buying decisions, some CMOs must be lying awake at night thinking about how to reinvent marketing content. To make one's marketing content become part of the knowledge flows, it needs to become more findable, more retellable, more to the point, and clearly more mashable. Out are the corporate-laden white papers and press releases, and in are the short YouTube customer testimonials and the customer reviews.

When you are defining your engagement strategy, it is important that you not become just a sophisticated corporate response system for things that are being said about the company in social media. If you want true knowledge flows to happen among your internal and external networks, everything you do has to be based on reciprocity. That means that in some cases, you simply need to have some of your people be helpful to outsiders, even when being helpful does not involve recommending one of your products or white papers. If you base everything you do on reciprocity, which is what makes us human, value will flow back to your company in the form of ideas and profits. Dell, Best Buy, and EMC are examples of companies that have been successful in their efforts. They don't just respond; they are generally helpful to others within their community.

How *USA Today* Tapped into Knowledge Networks

Let's close this chapter by looking at a company that truly made the transformation from a channel-based mentality to a network mentality—*USA Today*. Now, this is not just any company; this is a player from the publishing industry, the ultimate channel-centric industry. It made the transition successfully by embracing a community- or tribal-based approach to its Web site instead of a more channel-centric portal approach, which many other publishers used. When we spoke with Susan Lavington, the senior vice president of marketing at *USA Today*, she told us how the company's mission, "Capture the National Conversation," may have helped it to have the right mindset to make the transition from a news delivery site to a relationship-based environment—its subsequent ability to offer advertisers not just target audiences, but participation in network conversations that matter. [8]

The way the organization started was by having online sections on topics for which it knew there was an audience, but for which it could not have dedicated sections of the paper. One of the first online sections was a travel section on cruises. *USA Today* posted articles and allowed people to comment on them. Quickly it found out that people were leaving really thoughtful comments, and so it decided to turn this into a full-fledged community. As Susan said, "It's been hugely successful not only with our readers, but with our advertisers. And we found we have this group of people that are cruise enthusiasts that really rely on USA *Today* to be their guide about all things cruising."

USA *Today* constantly keeps looking for conversations that its marketing partners might have an interest in and for which it already has the tribes, and when it finds one, it creates a community around it. In some cases it has even found unexpected tribes, like video gamers who are into mixed martial arts.

Another area where USA *Today* is having success is to humanize its brand by putting the user at the center of all its efforts, rather than simply making the user the target of its content. As we saw in Chapter 6, doing so is one of the key ingredients in making communities work. It also realizes the value of reciprocity in communities by being generally helpful to its readers, even when that means pointing them to valuable but competing sources of information. Susan gave this example:

> Gene Sloan, who's the moderator of our cruise community, frequently points back out to what may be considered his competitors who are also covering the cruise industry. And, as a result, we've just found that the more you link out, the more you get back in and we've embraced that. Another great example is our pop culture community writer, Whitney Matheson. Again, she links out all the time to what other people are saying, what other people are covering and brings it into the conversation for her community and the more she does it, the more she grows.

In the end, *USA Today* doesn't just deliver an audience to its advertisers, as many other publications do; it allows the audience to participate in those tribal network conversations that matter.

Summary

We hope that by now, you are thinking tribe and not market segment. As we saw in this chapter, not all tribes are created equal — it's important to understand the networks that exist within those tribes. The way they look and operate will affect your strategy. Making the shift to a network view of the world is a hard one for most executives. In order to lead your team in the right direction, you will once again need to ask the right questions.

Is our Web site connected to the networks that matter? Would you send the content that comes out of your marketing departments to your own friends? Have you identified the types of networks that exist within your tribes? Do you understand how people achieve status in the networks, or how they become leaders? What sort of bonds exist in our tribal networks? Can we position ourselves within the networks? Do we understand why we are trying to influence which people? Are we trying to commercialize social ties? Are we thinking of social media as a channel? Do we participate in the external knowledge flows that are happening? Do we even understand what those knowledge flows are? Do we understand our internal networks and knowledge flows? Have we consciously tried to humanize our company so that we can become members in the networks and participate in their knowledge flows?

eight

Forget Hierarchies—Embrace Social Messiness at the SEAMS

E mbracing Hyper-Sociality as part of your business strategy can be scary. After all, social environments aren't limited to nice people who are motivated by reciprocity; they also have freeloaders, bullies, sociopaths, and even nasty people. Those social detractors can do a lot of damage to your organization. Unfortunately, those people are already in the mix. They may be employees of your company or employees of your customers. And if they haven't already started to hurt you, they will do so soon—whether you embrace Hyper-Sociality or not. The difference is that if you do embrace it, chances are that the Hyper-Social champions among your employees, customers, and prospects, motivated by their Human 1.0 characteristics, including altruistic reciprocity and a deep sense of fairness, will keep those social deviants in check, or at least help you do so.

It's not just socially awkward people who will try to hurt you with an online smear campaign. Sometimes angry customers and employees will use their newfound Hyper-Sociality to punish you if you screw up. As we saw in Chapter 1, humans are hardwired to punish and take revenge against people who (they feel) have treated them unfairly. In fact, they will be willing to pay a personal price to punish you. That means that if your customer service department wrongs a person, chances are that he will join a community like Planet Feedback (http://www.planetfeedback.com), or Who Sucks (http://www.hoosucks.com), where he can go out of his way to bad-mouth you. Worse still, he might use his own megaphone, as Jeff Jarvis did when he created Dell Hell, or set up a site and create a vibrant community at "yourbrand"sucks.com.

Just like everything involving social environments, the Hyper-Social shift includes some messiness. You can choose to embrace it or fight it—but as you may have guessed, we strongly encourage you to take the first option. In order to embrace it and fully capitalize on the Hyper-Social shift, you will have to let go of some hierarchical command-and-control structures and top-down processes.

Companies and markets are not just made up of individuals; they are also made up of tight-knit communities and tribes that have come together because of a shared passion or pain, a shared sense of belonging, or in some cases a common enemy. Their contract with one another is not a monetary-based contract—it's a social contract. And yes, even within your employee base, you have tribes that are bound together by social contracts (hopefully not because of shared animosity toward management), and the bonds that result from those social contracts are much tighter than the bonds that these employees have with the company itself based on their legal contract. So if you want to innovate or solve problems within your company, you are far better off tapping into those tribes and their social framework than focusing on their sense of responsibility as employees or customers based on their actual contract with your company.

Fixed hierarchies and processes tend to clash with Hyper-Sociality and the messiness that comes with it. As Professor Patrick Cohendet, Professor of Economics at the University of Strasbourg, France, said,[1]

> A too strict control of hierarchy enforcing members to follow the rules decreed by the "visible structures" would prevent the firm being able to benefit and derive value from the knowledge accumulated by the "invisible communities." Such decisions certainly would not eliminate the functioning of community (people would continue to talk and exchange ideas), but the useful knowledge accumulated at that level would presumably be hampered from flowing to the rest of the organization. The hierarchy cannot influence the internal functioning of communities, but it can and should find ways to let the knowledge accumulated by communities flow and bring value to the firm.

So how do you embrace social messiness? How do you let go of hierarchical structures and processes enough to enable the Hyper-Social shift and to stimulate innovation without having to kill the corporate culture that took decades to establish itself? And what can you expect from fully embracing it? What might happen if you resist it? These are some of the topics we will tackle in this chapter, showing you real examples to help you figure out how much you should embrace social messiness and how to do it in the first place.

Embracing Social Messiness
Should Not Hurt Your Company

Some great companies have been able to embrace messiness without too much pain. One such company is JetBlue. When we spoke with Marty St. George, its CMO, he told us about the values-based culture that drives everything at JetBlue. The company's original mission was to bring humanity back to the airline industry. So how can you humanize a brand when there are so many employee touch points that can make or break that brand promise? It turns out that for JetBlue, the most important ingredient for success is having a values-based culture—one in which every single employee bases her actions on those values. Not surprisingly, the values that drive the JetBlue culture are fairly straightforward and easy to live by: safety (the most important, of course), caring, integrity, fun, and passion.

All employees are screened for those values during the hiring process, go through extensive training on them after being hired, and are constantly reminded of them for as long as they are with JetBlue. The end result is that everyone at JetBlue feels part of a big tribe, single-mindedly focused on improving the customer experience and by proxy JetBlue's business. Front-line crew members are empowered to make independent and human decisions based on those values.

JetBlue did not develop a traditional rule book, a huge manual full of rules and legally reviewed processes to prepare employees for every possible scenario that they may encounter as they interact with their tribes. Instead, it developed five core values that form the social contract among its employee tribe and then let those employees be humans in dealing with all customer situations. The power of this approach is obvious, as Marty told us: "I think 95 times out of 100 we can predict what a crew member's going to say in a situation because obviously the values are very important, but also because there are certain pieces of our contract of character with our customers that we know are going to be interpreted the same way pretty much every time."

Do you suppose JetBlue could have developed that high a predictability of response with a rule book? Of course not. This values-based approach, which is actually built on Hyper-Sociality and shows the power of letting go of fixed processes, also ensures a self-enforcing culture with built-in organizational learning. Marty further talked about the importance of transparency in forming a cohesive workforce, one that focuses on them (the customers) and not on us (the employees). For JetBlue executives, briefing employees on how the business is doing and addressing their concerns in a timely manner is just as high a priority as briefing and informing investors.

Contrast this approach with that of another airline company whose CEO recently was recognized as one of the worst CEOs, partly for not treating employees respectfully. When executives manage their employees without respect, their tribes start operating at what Dave Logan categorizes as level 2 in his book *Tribal Leadership*[2]—driven by the motto "My Life Sucks" and resulting in very *Dilbert*-like behavior. People take long breaks, there's no innovation, there's no collaboration, and they do the minimum required not to get fired. Does this sound like the experience you've had with businesses you've used recently? According to Logan, 25 percent of all companies operate that way.

JetBlue is a relatively new company, so you could argue that it had the opportunity to design its processes from scratch and that it would be much harder for existing organizations with deeply entrenched cultures of command and control to achieve the same results. Think again.

The poster child of process-driven organizations and the beacon for Six Sigma quality control programs, GE, was able to embrace it. When we spoke with GE's global CMO, Beth Comstock,[3] she told us how the firm was able to embrace social messiness on multiple levels. On the innovation side, it created an online employee-based imagination network to complement its formal innovation processes. To stimulate innovation in marketing, it set up a team of "rogue marketers" whose job it is to come up with rogue marketing techniques—and in the process also serve as catalysts to make marketing people think differently about how to market.

NASA Langley is a 92-year-old government agency. It is probably the last organization you would expect to embrace messiness. Think again! Under the leadership of its chief technologist, Richard Antcliff,[4] the Strategic Relationships Office did just that. Not only did it embrace Hyper-Social messiness, but it ditched its hierarchy and its formal processes altogether. Imagine trying that in a 92-year-old government agency. Based on the lattice management structure popularized by W. L. Gore, of Gore-Tex, it created an environment based on "cloud leadership," with no titles, no formal job descriptions, no bosses, and no rules, and where people can work on whatever they want. The work gets done by enlisting people from throughout the organization who share a passion. Even contractors can spend 20 percent of the time they were hired for to work on whatever they want. The results: unbelievably high morale among the employees, who can now work on whatever they are passionate about instead of specifically what they were hired for.

Embracing customer and prospect Hyper-Sociality should not hurt, either. Let's take the example of Fiskars and the Fiskateers one more time. The folks at Fiskars and Brains on Fire (the agency that helped them build the Fiskateer community) focused on a lot of things right in building this community—they found an area of passion (scrapbooking), and they put the customers and prospects at the center of their community, not the company or its products. A community centered around scissors probably would not work as well, but that is exactly the kind of community that most companies are trying to build.

In a nutshell, the Fiskateer community is a community of passionate scrapbookers who are helping one another in every aspect of the hobby, from providing social interaction guidelines for the community to finding the right tools for the job. A handful of community leaders are paid by Fiskars; all others are volunteers. What started as a modest PR project, with a goal of recruiting 250 community members within 6 months, ended up with a movement of 5,000 passionate Fiskateers in 18 months. In fact, the community achieved its original goal of 250 members in less than 48 hours. Another goal was to increase chatter by 10 percent; it increased by 600 percent. The company also blew past its original goal of increasing store sales by 10 percent and instead increased store sales by 300 percent. What's even better is that the program, which was originally funded by Fiskars to the tune of $1 million per year, is now fully paid for by the big box art stores.

As we found through our own Tribalization of Business Study, there were also unexpected benefits from the community. Many new product ideas have originated within the community, the community helps Fiskars cocreate its advertising, the community members took over the primary role of customer support within the arts market, and the community rallied to help Fiskars when it came under attack for supposedly shipping products using cancer-causing materials.

"The key to success," said Fiskars's CMO, Jay Gillespie, "is to keep yourself accountable to the fans—not the company." And if you have doubts about the commitment and passion that Fiskateers have toward one another, check what Debby Lewis had to say after we interviewed Jay Gillespie:

> Being a Fiskateer has changed my life. The social networking that takes place on the message board—sharing about our family and friends through the gallery and meeting other Fiskateers—makes an impact. I have very close friends now in IL, FL, SC, CT, PA, and the list goes on. Fiskars as a brand has been supportive of the community members and of all the Certified Fiskars Demonstrators. The blog, to me, is the lifeline of the Fiskateers with our Five Leads. Fiskars products are innovative, designed with the consumer in mind. It's not about the product, it's about the people who will own the product to enhance their stories.

That, ladies and gentlemen, is game-changing!

A Framework for Embracing Hyper-Social Messiness

Many people, especially people from traditional advisory service providers, will recommend that you get started by doing what you're already doing, except with a social media twist. Ad agencies will recommend that you focus on engagement through multiple media, or start a Facebook fan page that is powered by couponing instead of by Hyper-Sociality; new media consulting firms will recommend that you start communities, but will build nothing but fancy Web sites with lots of bells and whistles; and some PR agencies will push you to approach social media the same way you approach traditional media. All of these are bolt-on strategies for existing programs and processes, some which have been characterized by decreasing returns for the past few years, if not for decades. On the other end of the spectrum, you will get the self-anointed social media gurus, who will gladly sell you Twitter feeds, blogging programs, or grand social media strategies that have no connection to any of your business processes.

What you need is a process that is grounded in the traditions of business change management, one that has a high likelihood of success and little chance of causing you or your organization unnecessary losses. Fallout associated with change, after all, is one of the top reasons that change management programs fail. We refer to this process as "embracing social messiness at the SEAMS." If you think that innovation happens at the edges, think about what is on the other side of those edges, and you will have to agree that what is really happening is innovation at the SEAMS. OK, so we are marketers and love acronyms, and like all Human 1.0–wired marketers, we fall in love with our own inventions. Make fun of it if you will, but what you won't do is forget it!

SEAMS

When you are embracing social messiness by the SEAMS, you are implementing the following steps: sensing, engaging, activating, measuring, and storytelling. But before you can start with SEAMS, you need a tribal ecosystem map, showing both internal and external tribes. You need to figure out where those tribes hang out, what motivates them, who their leaders are, and what stage they are at. As we have seen before, finding out some of that information will require both ethnographic and netnographic research.

The SEAMS process starts with *sensing*—sensing what is going on in your various environments. Sensing needs to go beyond merely listening for what is being said about the things you care about. It's about understanding what is being meant and mapping that knowledge to the relevant business processes within your company, e.g., product innovation, customer support, knowledge management, human resources, marketing, and sales.

The next logical step is *engaging*—going beyond sensing and starting to engage your various tribal constituencies (e.g., customers, prospects, promoters, detractors, employees, partners, and so on) on their own turf. This step is not about engaging them through your advertising, corporate communications program, and other marketing campaigns; this is about good, old-fashioned engagement. That means talking *with* instead of *at* them. If they do not have a vibrant existing place to hang out, there may be an opportunity for you to host a virtual watering hole for them (as we discussed in Chapter 5). Based on the sensing and engaging stages, you should be able to identify those tribes that are the most ready to help you. So, for example, you may have vibrant tribes externally that hang out with one another, tinkering and inventing new uses for your product and helping newbies use the product properly. Internally, you may find advanced tribal stages in product development, but have a really rotten culture in customer support (we know, it happens). This knowledge will help you move to the next stage.

Next up is *activating*. Once you get a better handle on the new dynamics of the social situation out there, you need to devise a plan to activate some business processes with these newfound capabilities. Product innovation, customer support, PR, lead generation, talent acquisition, and knowledge management can all be transformed into social processes. Once these processes are activated, these social tribes will get involved through their social contract with one another rather than any contract they might have with your company. Based on which tribes are the most ready, you will be able to set priorities on which process will go Hyper-Social first.

Of course, you will have to justify all these new programs to your management team, so after activating, you must *measure* them. It is more critical than ever to understand what to measure and what goals to set. Unlike more traditional business change management programs, in which measurements do not interact with the actual programs, launching Hyper-Social programs with misaligned measurement goals can maim or even kill the program in the long run. We will discuss how to measure the impact of Hyper-Social programs and what to measure in Chapter 11.

This being a Hyper-Social environment, you cannot, of course, forget the *storytelling*. Regardless of what you officially call it, storytelling is important in all aspects of the SEAMS methodology. However you decide to engage with your tribes or get them involved as part of activating various business processes, you need stories that will be compelling and can easily be retold. Stories are how humans have passed on culture from generation to generation, and while your company has product and service stories that you want to see travel in the tribal networks that matter, you also want others to know, write, and care about stories about your Hyper-Sociality. You need to shape and share those stories and find a voice and an angle that differentiates your efforts and gives customers, employees, partners, and media an avenue into what makes your Hyper-Social projects tick. Even when you are measuring the effectiveness of your programs, you should always be on the lookout for interesting anecdotal stories—they will gain a life of their own and sometimes do more than stats in conveying the importance and success of your efforts.

Getting the Legal Department on Board

We can hear the nagging question in the back of your head right now: "How the heck am I going to get the people in my legal department to agree with all this soft Hyper-Social uncontrollable messiness?"

For some people, the answer might seem obvious: don't tell them about it.

But seriously, now, we know that your legal department is out to protect the company's and its shareholders' interests; we also know that sometimes it is doing that through too much process and cocooning of the company—protecting the interests of the company, but stifling the Hyper-Sociality and all the innovation that can come with it. There are some serious legal issues involved when you are trying to leverage Hyper-Sociality as part of business, including privacy matters, copyright issues, sexual harassment complaints, equal employment opportunity issues, and, of course, labor laws that were conceived in the early stages of the Industrial Revolution and have no bearing on social tribes.

One way to begin introducing Hyper-Sociality to the legal team is by putting everything that is new in the context of what you used to do in the past, and explaining how Human 1.0 behavior hasn't changed. Sure, your employees can now connect more widely with other employees using online environments, but how is that different from their connecting in smaller groups around the watercooler or at your annual sales kickoff? Your existing employee policies and procedures may be providing employees with useful guidance about behavior in online environments, as this forum is not all that different from face-to-face situations, or when people use e-mail and telephone to connect with one another.

When it comes to customers and prospects, what's so different about having more employees interact with them in online communities and other social environments compared with having your salespeople and customer service reps interact with them over the phone and through e-mail? Again, your existing policies and guidelines may provide you with a solid platform from which to expand your new ones—if you even need new ones. The other good news is that if you feel that you need new and expanded policies and guidelines, there are many companies that have developed them before you and made theirs available for others to study. By bringing your legal team to the Hyper-Social discussion earlier as opposed to later, you stand a much better chance of rapidly developing necessary new policies, guidelines, and training that will permit your organization to act more Hyper-Socially.

The issues related to labor laws can be a bit trickier. While some companies, like Best Buy, can serve as best practices examples (it has hourly wage workers who participate in its Blue Shirt Nation employee community), some legal departments won't allow you to move forward until controlling legal principles are well settled. As a last resort, and if your company culture lends itself to these sorts of arguments, you could suggest quantifying the risk and the cost of doing nothing, or of having your closest competitor acting before you. If you do that, again make sure to involve your legal department in the exercise, as some of the data needed to make your case may be protected by privacy laws and policies, and you will need your legal team to help accurately determine the risks.

Summary

We have covered quite a bit of ground in this chapter, and as usual, doing so triggers a lot of questions that you should be asking yourself and your team as you embark on developing your Hyper-Social programs.

Does your organization have the right balance between fixed hierarchies and processes and self-organized activities and processes? Do you know where your internal tribes are and what social contract binds them? Do you have a true values-based culture that people buy into? Is your organization getting the right advice in terms of how to move forward? Is your legal department being open-minded and collaborative? Do you know what part of the SEAMS process your organization excels at, and what part needs improvement? Do you have great stories to tell?

part three

PRACTICALLY SPEAKING: YOUR BUSINESS THROUGH THE HYPER-SOCIAL LENS

nine

How Hyper-Social
Is Your Company?

Measuring the Hyper-Sociality Index

B ased on what it takes to become a more Hyper-Social organization, as described in the earlier chapters of this book, you can now begin to measure how Hyper-Social your company really is. In fact, the concepts introduced in the earlier chapters enable you to benchmark your Hyper-Sociality against that of your competitors, or that of one part of your organization against that of another part.

This benchmark, which we call the Hyper-Sociality Index (HSI), is a framework that companies can use to evaluate how well positioned they are to take advantage of the Hyper-Social shift, and where they lie on the migration curve. After calculating their HSI, organizations will better appreciate their Hyper-Social weak points, be better positioned to compare themselves to the competition, and be able to better define those steps that will move them toward Hyper-Sociality.

The Hyper-Sociality Index

The HSI is built around the Four Pillars of Hyper-Sociality:

- Tribe vs. market segment
- Human-centricity vs. company-centricity
- Network vs. channel
- Social messiness vs. process and hierarchy

As we consider the Four Pillars of Hyper-Sociality, you will see that we have included in the framework specific questions that suggest or highlight practices that we have seen successfully employed by companies that participated in the Tribalization of Business Study. These questions have been carefully selected to raise the relevant issues for each pillar that will help you to "grade" a company on that specific pillar.

As part of the Tribalization of Business Study, we have surveyed more than 500 companies, and interviewed many of them, to begin ranking them relative to their peers. By assigning simple relative scores (−2 for significantly behind its peers, −1 for slightly behind its peers, 0 for on a par with its peers, +1 for slightly ahead of its peers, and +2 for significantly ahead of its peers' progress), company management can generate an accurate and consistent assessment of a company's location on the Hyper-Social shift.

First, a word on measuring your HSI score against those of your competitors effectively. Looking at the organizations that your constituents (employees, members, customers, or business partners) would consider to be your competitors, compare your *outward behavior*, as seen by the market, with your competitors' *outward actions and expressed attitudes*. For instance, although it is encouraging that your organization may have recently realized that it needs to pay greater attention to its tribes, without overt actions in the furtherance of this pillar, you shouldn't give your organization credit for only this newfound *awareness* in calculating its HSI. Hyper-Social behavior requires overt actions that are visible to the people that matter (customers, members, employees, and business partners), not just corporate resolutions or internal memos avowing greater human-centricity. Talk is cheap, and talk alone shouldn't be allowed to influence an HSI score.

Figure 9-1 is an actual HSI that was calculated for a large retailer. The company has stood well above its peers in the recent past in identifying and interacting with its tribes (notably, women looking for bargains because their families are on tight budgets). As the company learned by listening to this tribe, these women don't want to brag about buying luxury products cheaply—that is a different tribe. These women are much more interested in sharing

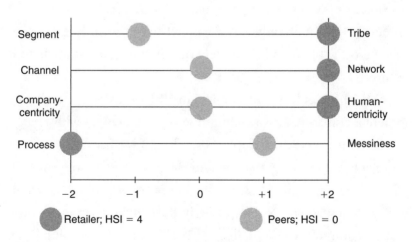

Figure 9-1 Example: HSI of Retailer

tips with their tribe on how to stretch a budget and how to prepare nutritious, but economical meals.

After discerning what the passion of the tribe revolved around (helping one another to find bargains and to make ends meet), the company did a great job of speaking to the tribe as a tribe, not as single individuals. The company took a minor role in the community (as it should) and allowed a network of people to educate it and one another on how and why they bought what they did. It was not primarily a disguised marketing campaign or just another channel for distribution of press releases.

Could the company's performance in helping this community find value around its passion be improved? Absolutely—look at the weakness around process. If the company eased up a little on how it managed the somewhat rigid application process, and used different sorts of incentives to keep people engaged, it might develop an even more powerful and sustainable discussion forum, with even more people participating for longer periods. In other words, if the company made this even less of a marketing program than it already is, we suspect that it would become an even more vibrant and ultimately sustainable community than it is now.

At the highest level, developing an HSI allows one to easily see where a company risks running into trouble dealing with Hyper-Social consumers and employees. Think of a package shipping company, for instance, that focused 100 percent on a conventional market segment, small businesses, and missed the important tribes within that segment. Not surprisingly, the company's product innovation community effort failed. Thankfully, it was a small failure, and many lessons were learned. Here, the company clearly failed to satisfy the pillar that requires organizing to interact with tribes, instead of with more standard market segments.

Or think of a mobile handset company that acquired a gaming community to better codevelop and comarket the company's mobile gaming platforms. The new product development process in the larger mobile handset company was so rigid and lengthy that people in the community felt that they were not being heard and started to desert the community, forcing the company to redesign a new product development platform centered around the community. Here again, the company had to try twice before it embraced the reality that Hyper-Sociality can be a messy business that is not easily shoehorned into a legacy corporate process.

Now, not all cases are as black and white as the ones we just described (where the companies would likely have scored a –2 in the categories of tribe vs. segment and messiness vs. process, respectively), and we need to add some measure of degree to the various pillars that we use to determine the HSI. An effective way of doing this is to develop a series of questions that, when answered honestly, help you to assign scores to the various pillars as they are practiced at your company and at your competitors' organizations.

And in addition to honesty, we find that having a broad functional perspective improves the process as well. For that reason, we encourage you to include people from across the company when you are assessing your HSI. It is tempting for the sponsoring group or business function (often marketing) to have all of the members of the HSI-measuring group be from that function. As we will see from the analysis involved, however, you will be better served if you include representatives from marketing, product development, talent, knowledge management, sales, and any other function that

shows interest and insight. You should also include a representative from the legal department so that you can understand the
reasons why some practices and attitudes may exist, and the steps
you would have to undertake to reform or change those processes
that appear to be having a negative impact on your HSI.

So as you embark on the HSI journey, consider which specific
aspects of the company's Hyper-Sociality you will initially focus
on, and who your target stakeholder will be. Perhaps you will
examine how the company interacts with customers, or perhaps
with business partners or with employees. Since at this point, you
may well have different organizational levels of Hyper-Sociality for
dealing with these different stakeholders, consider which would
profit most from the Hyper-Social shift, and focus on that group
as your target stakeholder. As Hyper-Sociality is adopted across the
company, you will, of course, be aiming for a consistently Hyper-
Social relationship with all of your stakeholders.

Let's jump into it. Let's look at how we would approach
developing an HSI in the following example. The company being
measured, whose target stakeholder is the consumer, should ask
questions like these when assessing its score along the Four Pillars
of Hyper-Sociality.

Tribe vs. Market Segment

- Have you identified tribes that are consumers of your products,
  but that differ from your legacy segmentation understanding
  of your customers?

- What is your relative rank as against your competitors? (Give
  yourself the following points: –2 for significantly behind your
  competitors, –1 for slightly behind your competitors, 0 for

on a par with your competitors, +1 for slightly ahead of your competitors, and +2 for significantly ahead of your competitors' progress.)

- Have you discovered the existence of tribes on social networks or online communities that you have identified as viable target customers?

- Have you increased your understanding of the collective passion that causes these people to participate in these online communities?

- Have you developed a "win story" that you've circulated within your organization about interacting with a previously identified or unidentified tribe in the past six months?

- Have you implemented features that permit members of your target tribe to help one another and enhance their status with one another?

- Do members of your tribe seem to trust your authenticity?

- Have you added offline or real-world activities that allow the members of your tribes to interact with one another (e.g., conferences, Webcasts, and conference calls)?

Human-Centricity vs. Company-Centricity

- Can the tribes discuss discomforting things, such as what they like about the competition or what prices they are paying to whom?

- Are the people who communicate with your tribes on the front line chosen for their special skills, their level of interest, or their rapport with the community, or are they given that job as a part-time role, or because they are not fully utilized elsewhere?

- Are competitors and detractors allowed to join the conversation?

- Are there social media tools that are not being used, compared to what other active Hyper-Social companies are using?

- Were customers and employees included in the drafting of the terms of service?

- Have you deployed a social Q&A system that permits users to ask one another questions and to draw upon your knowledge databases?

Network vs. Channel

- Do you listen to all of the methods that your tribes use to communicate and to receive information? (Receive higher scores for the degree to which the answer is yes, and negative scores for failing to listen to the tribes through disparate channels such as Twitter, blogs, phone, e-mail, and text messages.)

- Do you use technologies to listen in real time to the conversations about your company, your brands, your products, your executives, and your employees that are taking place in the social media?

- Do you share information gleaned from conversations with your tribes between internal functions such as sales, customer support, marketing, and product development in a nearly real-time fashion?

- Have you implemented a customer experience system that tracks all customer touch points (both direct and indirect) with your company?

Social Messiness vs. Process and Hierarchy

- Is the bias toward responding to tribe communications, or toward thinking about and analyzing how to respond?

- Is there a formal workflow or process that requires more than one person to approve responding to an inbound communication?

- Do you have a process in place that ensures that all incoming communications from the tribes, as well as references to your companies, brands, and executives, are responded to immediately?

- Are there processes in place for determining whether a communication should be engaged with?

- Do you respond to both explicit communications and informal "chatter" from your tribes?

- Have you given your people who communicate with the tribes explicit abilities to move that information around your company and to seek assistance from places outside of their function within the company?

- Have you included representatives from all divisions of your company in the group that hears what the tribes are saying? Is this cross-pollination effective and casual, or is it involved and lengthy?

- Have you ever been surprised by information being communicated to you about your tribes that didn't come from your tribes directly? For instance, did you hear about what your tribes were saying as a result of a news story, not from the tribes themselves?

- Are registrations required for users to join the conversations with the tribe?

- Are negative tribe comments broadcast as widely to management as the positive comments are?

- Are employees across the company able to see what's being said by the tribes?

- Does content have to be approved before it is posted where the tribe can see it?

- Can the tribes link to information on their own and post their own comments (without censorship for impermissible hate speech, and so on)?

- Has a Google Labs–like beta feature been created that permits users to vote on new products and innovations that they like?

- Are small innovation experiments that are expected to fail and that are expected to only create learning or customer satisfaction encouraged?

- Do you permit negative reviews of your products or positive reviews of your competitors' products?

- Will you go to where your tribes are already assembling, or do you try to bring them to your online properties?

This is by no means an exhaustive list of the questions that companies should develop to assess their location on the continuum that exists for each of the four pillars, but it does identify the sort of thinking that will assist you in scoring yourself on the four pillars, and that will lead to accurate determination of your company's HSI. Indeed, there is no end to the questions that you should and will develop as you begin to think within the Four Pillars of Hyper-Sociality, and as your company becomes increasingly Hyper-Social. As you become more familiar with the four pillars, you will soon identify specific issues that you are struggling with as a company—for instance, should we allow our competitors' thought leadership materials to be posted on our site? This is a significant human-centricity vs. company-centricity question, and it would be a terrific issue to track over time, and to see how your organizational resistance or acceptance changes over time.

Ensuring that employees from different functions are involved in the process, and different generations of employees as well, will yield better and richer questions. As a result, you will be able to engage in a robust, eye-opening discussion as your organization tallies up its scores. We say scores because you are likely to develop several HSIs as part of the process: one number that is your overall calculation of your HSI, others comparing you with each of your competitors, and perhaps others for specific business functions within your company. As you consider the questions given previously, you will undoubtedly realize that you probably cannot answer some of the questions for your competitors or your peers, as the information that the answer requires is not the sort of information that is broadcast externally or shared widely. It is fine to exclude those questions from your calculations of your HSI for purposes of comparison.

This should be a flexible tool that you can adjust for the idiosyncrasies of your industry—both the companies and the consumers.

The compass to follow as you go through the analysis is to keep returning to the Four Pillars of Hyper-Sociality; any question posed that gets you closer to advancement on those four fronts will be useful and should be considered.

We should also stress that since expectations and social media advance so quickly, it is advisable that you benchmark yourself every six months to ensure that you are not losing ground to rivals and that different business functions within your organization are not falling behind relative to one another. As we've shown, humans will flow to the companies that interact with them Hyper-Socially; you cannot rest on your laurels, as other companies will be moving forward on their Hyper-Social shifts. You can be sure that the interested tribes will broadcast any changes that they perceive as being important to their interests. Indeed, tribes will often follow online community terms of use closely, and carefully scrutinize any changes; if your organization begins to depart from what the community expects in terms of Hyper-Sociality, you are likely to hear about it promptly. The same is true if you fail to adopt a technology platform that the tribe has adopted for communication.

Also, we must note that severe underperformance on any one pillar can have a disproportionately higher impact on your progress along other pillars. For instance, failing to be human-centric can outweigh a terrific understanding of who your tribes are and how well you manage the social messiness. The tribes will eventually see through the veiled attempt to extract undue benefit from them, and will go to another organization that they trust to provide them with greater value and to respect their interests.

In addition to comparing yourself to your peers and tracking your migration to Hyper-Sociality, the HSI may provide other valuable insights. For instance, select a key operating metric, and determine which identifiable factors affect it. If it is customer churn, for instance, identify the best thinking on what is likely to be causing the churn. If you suspect that it is poor customer service, try Hyper-Socializing customer support, and then carefully track both the change in HSI in that area and the change in churn (if any). Such an experiment not only helps you improve your measurement and management of the HSI of the customer support function, but also provides you with a possible validation of your Hyper-Sociality efforts.

We also encourage you to compare the data you use to compose your HSI with the Tribalization of Business Study findings that we regularly update and publish at www.hypersocialorg.com. These results provide updated cross-industry data on how companies are performing across the four pillars, and provide trend information to show where the changes have been greatest. It is a terrific way to determine where you stand in relation to the larger population of Hyper-Social companies, and where you might improve.

The HSI can also be used to identify and develop business functions or areas that need to be improved, to set a goal to strive for, to identify possible reasons that competitors are moving ahead or falling behind, and to detect that if a competitor has increased its HSI, it may be targeting Hyper-Sociality. Since it is our observation that an HSI score rarely rises on its own without management support and direction, a rising HSI score at a competitor indicates that that competitor may be actively trying to raise its HSI. Not only does this have strategic implications, but it also provides a learning opportunity for your organization. Indeed, whenever you identify a competitor that has increased its overall HSI or its HSI in a particular function, track performance in that area. You can learn much about your weak spots that way.

Summary

To improve an organization's Hyper-Sociality effectively, managers must be able to measure their organization's Hyper-Sociality accurately. The Hyper-Social Index is a straightforward way of measuring an organization's performance across the Four Pillars of Hyper-Sociality, one that yields a numerical rating that can be used to gauge progress and to compare one organization's Hyper-Sociality with others'. By answering a series of questions, managers can identify areas of strength and areas that require improvement.

ten

Old Management Thinking Won't Work in the Hyper-Social Organization

The Tribalization of Business Study and other outside research indicate that some of the key impediments to organizations moving toward Hyper-Sociality are rooted in management thinking that is dramatically out of sync with the expectations and traits of the humans who are a firm's customers and employees. Indeed, the Tribalization of Business Study shows that current management practices are failing to adequately develop, interact with, and support the tribes that are important to their businesses. Organizations' efforts to interact with their tribes are frequently characterized by underinvestment, poor management, and flawed implementation. Other commentators have noted a striking general lack of innovation in management over the past years.[1]

Although we believe that many formerly viable management practices, strategies, and tactics may well be past their prime, we want to clarify here that the need in a Hyper-Social marketplace is not for less management; in fact, there is likely to be a need for *more* management. We perceive a sentiment among some that in a Hyper-Social world, more and more organizational functions will be assumed by the tribe, and that over time, the organization will shrink to a small nucleus. We are not convinced that this is the case, however, and we believe that even if companies do shrink in size, their need for expert management will either remain at current levels or increase.

Let's take a look at classical business management thinking first. In contemporary business, much of what constitutes "management" is the process of maintaining the status quo while growing by an annually reevaluated amount above that point. A critical aspect of this function is allocating limited resources (marketing spending, human capital, expenditures, and so on) in furtherance of executing on short- and long-term tactics designed to take advantage of (or cause) certain anticipated outcomes. A couple of key assumptions here are that many resources are scarce, and that the future can be predicted with some sort of certainty.

Going forward, however, we believe that some of these assumptions need to be reevaluated. In an increasingly digital world, scarcity needs to be reconsidered, as many of the constraints that we formerly faced have been erased by Moore's Law, the Internet, and technological advances. Also, in a Hyper-Social company or marketplace, what was formerly scarce needs to be reevaluated (for example, marketing spending is no longer a scarce resource — your ability to get your tribe's attention and its desire to retell your messages is now the scarce, sought-after commodity). Similarly, in an increasingly complex marketplace in which new entrants, new products, and new information are being created faster than ever, how will the ability to predict future events change?

Also implicit in all this is the assumption that people on the "inside" of a company control how that company interacts with (and influences) the external environment and, through careful control and action, can maneuver the company toward success. Consider for a moment the principle of market share as it is classically understood and viewed: It is a share of market that results from the actions or inactions and choices of the company and its competitors. By changing price, advertising, or product, or through the missteps of a competitor, a company can act in a way that is reasonably expected to affect consumers, and therefore the company's share of their wallets, in a relatively short time frame.

Given the Hyper-Social shift, however, it's clear that while management may be able to do a lot of things as part of its job, "controlling" what it formerly sought to control is increasingly unlikely. For instance, no matter how large a company's marketing budget is, or how talented its marketing professionals may be, it is difficult today to control a righteously unsatisfied customer who starts a "YourCompanyStinks.com" Web site or blogs about your company's shortfalls. Likewise, as we've stated already, the data indicate that customers are becoming less influenced by and receptive to advertising and marketing. Instead, significant numbers of people are purchasing products based on the online reviews of strangers.[2] Given these facts, which levers should management now pull to reach the same level of influence that it formerly enjoyed?

Similarly, no matter how much corporate resources are directed at product development, the mathematical reality is that there's a far greater chance that the next great product idea will come from outside, not inside, the company. And now, because of globalization, there are many more companies from many more regions developing their own competitive products.

And given the dynamics of communities, we see that the levers that we thought were effective may no longer be. For instance, even if you have robust fan communities discussing your products and creating disdain for competitors' products, research indicates that these same fans can become very vocal and persuasive traitors if they discover that the competition has introduced desired features that their (formerly) preferred company hasn't.[3]

Management should spend less time trying to exert control by pulling conventional levers, and put more resources toward *sensing, understanding, acting upon, and then immediately assessing feedback* based upon the new voices and Hyper-Social abilities that your customers, your members, your business partners, and your employees have. The importance of the feedback element here cannot be overemphasized; human interaction is a constant action/feedback/action process. And this needs to be operationalized in the organization. As Porter Gale, CMO of Virgin Airlines, told us:

> We kind of close the loop with the employees too. So, we give them feedback. We let them know that we're getting e-mails from guests and that this behavior is, you know, very positive.
>
> We also talk to people about even basic things about keeping the planes clean and how that creates a better experience and how people's actions on the frontline are going to affect the longevity of the company.
>
> So, our employees are very well informed and they recognize their part in the process.[4]

Managers should strive to understand the subtleties of the new communities, explore the nature of those "lurkers" who hang around but don't actively comment or register, determine why tribes of people are investing their valuable attention in the firm's product, and understand how companies can delight a customer before the competition learns what they know about the humans who engage with their company. Similarly, managers need to consider how each stakeholder group has grown or changed as a result of Hyper-Sociality. Stakeholders have grown and changed, and they have a new level of control and expectations. Customers, for instance, know how your products performed for others, they know how much others paid for your products, they know who your fittest competitors are, and they are inclined to share their opinions with your existing and potential customers. How will you manage that to your benefit?

The Changing Organization Chart

If an organization's "org chart" is dictated by its strategy, then how will shifting toward becoming more Hyper-Social affect the way the company is organized?

As we noted earlier, the typical business spends much of its time allocating scarce resources (human, production, information, and others) to develop goods and services that it then pushes out to meet projected demand. The firm collects information, spends appreciable amounts of time parsing that quickly aging information, and then passes that information across structural features (divisions, silos, and reporting structures) that developed largely because of historical forces. Moreover, generally speaking, unless there have been deep changes in its markets or recent high-level management turnover, a company's organizational structure probably bears a striking resemblance to its structure of five or ten years ago. And experience shows that in the majority of cases, the specific arrangement of the organization chart was driven primarily by the interests of past corporate executives or past business strategies, not the interests of emerging strategies, present employees, current business partners, or potential Hyper-Social customers. Organization design is often company-centric, not human-centric.

Accordingly, we expect to see widespread reformation of organization charts as companies become increasingly Hyper-Social, realign corporate functions around tribes and new knowledge flows, and start interacting with customers more effectively. Responsiveness to both customers' very visible feedback and competitors' accelerating moves will become increasingly important, as will decision makers' awareness of what is being said about the company and its wares. Will traditional hierarchical organizations, with multiple levels of management between the tribes and the corporate decision makers, enjoy any sort of advantage in a Hyper-Social future? It seems unlikely. Similarly, will decisions to create geographic or specific product divisions be critical in the future, as technologically enabled means of coupling with customers and partners in various regions lessen the need for dedicated geography-based divisions, and the definitions of products may change overnight in response to changing preferences?

Ominously, we have seen the early cases in which people in middle management roles have scuttled new social software and systems that encourage greater interaction and communication up and across the organization chart. Acting as a conduit between the executives and the rank and file has long been the province of middle management, and many people in this middle band may well be challenged by Hyper-Sociality between those colleagues who are above and below them.

As Hyper-Social companies find themselves increasingly sharing information with partners, collaborating with customers on product development, and reaching outside of their enterprise to find expertise within tribes or other companies, we believe that the *porosity* of corporate boundaries will increase. For instance, it will become more difficult to define where corporate marketing ends and the tribe's marketing begins. Similarly, the boundary between customer support provided by the company and that provided by volunteers or other customers will blur as people share common help documents and share expertise with one another. This may lead to management's reexamining exactly what it is that the company should be selling and what business it is really in (or should be in). As the communities better define what it is that they want and what they would rather do themselves, it is foreseeable that companies will unbundle irrelevant functions and abilities, and seek to acquire others where they can either enjoy a competitive advantage or differentiate themselves.

Immediate Steps That Management Can Take toward the Hyper-Social Shift

Our research indicates that by taking immediate steps, companies can deploy new ways of managerial thinking that will accelerate their shift toward more Hyper-Social organizations.

Partnering with Organizations

One such step is realizing that the Hyper-Social future will require greater partnering between organizations, and then implementing this practice. There are several reasons for this increase in partnering, driven largely by the reality that your target tribes are probably already members of existing tribes, and that rather than trying to win their attention away, you should partner with the existing sponsors of those tribes and bring the humans better value through this partnering. The Tribalization of Business Study shows that although a majority of managers considered partnering when setting up their online communities, only a minority actually included it. This tendency is a clear indication that there's a feeling that this can all be done in-house. This possibility is bolstered by the fact that the majority of the firms studied also declined to hire outside experts for creating content and declined to use external ambassadors.

Allocate Human Resources

Another key step that managers can take to accelerate the Hyper-Social shift in their organizations is to better allocate corporate resources against their tribes. One common misallocation that we see frequently in our interaction with these companies is the over-weighting of investment in social media tools and technology infrastructure, and the underweighing of organizational investment in the human resources who will interact with the tribes and who will move tribe-generated knowledge throughout the organization. It is curious how so many companies, as they attempt to exploit social media, view the technology as the key input, and the people who will manage the new information flows and the new interactions with customers as being of secondary or tertiary importance. Indeed, the majority of companies polled in the Tribalization of Business Study report that one or fewer full-time employees are responsible for managing their corporate communities! This stark underinvestment in the human talent involved in managing corporate communities is especially troubling when respondents cite community "facilitation and moderation" as being among the top four most effective community features.

Forget about "Monetizing" Social Media

An additional area in which management will need to think and act differently is in its attempt to "monetize" social media and tribes as if they were discrete product lines. In our research, we see this discussion distract and undermine Hyper-Social shift activities repeatedly. The debate goes something like this: "We will begin using social media at our company when we have determined how to monetize it. We don't want to start a customer community or use Twitter until we've figured out the proper economic model. Right now, no one is making money with social media, and we don't intend to jump in just because everyone else is. This is not a wise use of our funds."

We urge executives to stop thinking about social media and its use as a Hyper-Socializing toolkit in such a way. Just as the telephone and e-mail were not technologies that most companies ever went on to monetize in the conventional sense, this is also the case with Web 2.0 tools and social media. The desired outcome of adopting and using these elements is the increased participation of customers, business partners, and employees in the organization's key activities, not charging the customers for them.

A Questioning Approach to the Hyper-Social Shift

We also see this approach to the Hyper-Social shift as being productive: asking, "What are the big, thorny problems that your company needs to solve? Do they include creating better products? Differentiating itself from the competition in a decisive and sustainable way? Attracting the best talent and keeping it for life? Creating an organization that learns more effectively than its competition?" As we will discuss in the coming chapters, becoming Hyper-Social works well on problems like these, and enables the socializing of key business functions.

If your business model is failing, you will need to develop a range of options that will provide you with strategic flexibility and a path to success. Can Hyper-Socializing the ideation process improve this situation? Venture capitalists understand that only a small fraction of ideas will end up being successful. Why, then, do management teams try to rely on a small group of leaders and consultants to generate enough ideas to give birth to that one idea that will actually help? By opening up key value-creation processes and making them Hyper-Social, organizations tend to generate more and better ideas, and to improve their ability to learn.

Although this is difficult for product-centric companies to acknowledge, carefully cloaked business processes can be much more important to a company's success than products. Several commentators have noted that visible portions of business models and processes will eventually be copied. Those companies that can create subtle linkages between visible processes can create sustainable advantages because the linkages can't be copied. Inventing an innovative process may someday eclipse product development or making large capital investments in these same companies' agendas. By leveraging Human 1.0 tendencies to cooperate, share, and collaborate, management should invest more effort in innovating these imperceptible business processes and improving linkages between processes. These management-driven innovations, properly done, will be difficult for competitors to emulate, and will provide more value to the human customers and employees. Unfortunately, most managers today have excelled by delivering on the old strategies with ever-increasing efficiency.[5] Managers in the Hyper-Social future will need to innovate new managerial models tailored for a Hyper-Social marketplace.

As we discuss in later chapters, business processes such as product development, customer care, marketing, and talent management are all interlocked in Hyper-Social organizations from the customer perspective. Indeed, you cannot divorce any one from the others and expect optimal outcomes. Now the customer can see the public interplay of these departments— if products are having problems, users will learn that from their tribes. No marketing campaign will be able to change that communication. Talent inside the company will be speaking with the customer, perhaps in a much more credible way than corporate communications is. It will take significant management to make this work well, and to ensure consistent information across all of these functions.

Another question that we urge managers to ask themselves is, "Where are the biggest gaps between your goals and what you actually hit?" Improperly managed and perceived, these misses can be some of the most damaging to a company. If it was a legitimate goal, you wanted to hit it, and you didn't, that's a loss. Worse yet, you have disappointed people—customers, employees, and investors. Direct Hyper-Sociality at those problems, and you are likely to generate new insights and tactics for your next attempt. The power to mobilize people, both inside and outside the organization, and to tap into capabilities, knowledge, and energy that you formerly missed may well turn the tide on your next attempt. Hyper-Socialize the business processes that you know are connected to reaching these goals, and experience shows that you'll stand a much better chance of success. Companies as varied as those in online retailing, video rentals, and computer networking have all taken this step to their advantage.

The Changing Role of Corporations in Business

Management should also consider the possible changes in the role of the corporation in business that Hyper-Sociality will lead to. Corporations arose in large part because the costs of coordinating internal corporate resources were lower than those of trying to coordinate external third parties. Executives should ask themselves whether this structure may change now that social media permits the coordination of marketing, support, and development activities with outside parties. Corporations may be compelled to shrink their internal functions because there will be fewer functions that need to be or should be "internal." Which functions will remain within the corporation? We agree with other researchers that a corporation's advantage in the future will depend less on the resources that the company owns and more on its capability and insights in finding and mobilizing the resources of others to add more value for customers.[6] Some of these new benefits that the corporation may deliver more effectively than individuals include shared services and economies around activities like regulatory approvals and raw materials sourcing.

Given the dynamics of how investors prefer to invest (there are certain economies that investors typically prefer, i.e., investing a large sum in one entity, rather than conducting due diligence on 20 companies and investing 1/20 of that same sum in each of those companies), corporations may be more alluring investment vehicles than individuals. This could be a long-term competitive advantage of the corporation over communities or loose affiliations in terms of raising financing, and one that management should consider exploiting in a Hyper-Social future.

It is likely that there will be a fundamental and widespread reassessment by management of the relative power and quality of the relationship between the company and its employees. Right now, many companies in many industries are dealing with the fallout from technology-driven customer choice. For instance, now that there is a surfeit of entertainment content, and much of it can be found for free, media companies are being forced to become more responsive to customer demands, as customers finally have the choice of going somewhere else for entertainment. A number of analogous technological and economic forces are giving employees greater freedom to leave unfulfilling jobs or places that fail to meet their Human 1.0 needs. As demographic trends create greater shortages of qualified employees, the need to appeal to the Human 1.0 features of their employees will become painfully evident to many companies. Those organizations that fail to make the Hyper-Social shift will be outcompeted at the most basic and important level—they will not be able to attract the best employees.

Classic core attributes of companies—buildings, factories, distribution channels, and access to the mass media—are becoming less important in the rising knowledge economy. Here, the critical factors of production are intelligence, creativity, the ability to communicate and collaborate effectively, and the ability to solve problems. The most Hyper-Social companies, those that put humans at the center of their operations and guiding principles, will appeal to these creative, thinking beings and match their interests and passions.

Thanks to social media and richer insights into how companies really work, competitors will be able to poach talent from other companies more easily. Formerly, it was difficult to determine exactly which staff engineer was turning out the best designs—recruiters would first look at the person who was leading the group and assume that he was the star. Today, each staff engineer probably has a Facebook page on which she tells and shows what she does and what she is good at, and a recruiter can find her instantly.

We consider this aspect of managerial change, the rising power of the employee, to be one of the easiest to forecast, but the one that management will probably struggle with the most. Why? Well, because in many cases it upends the status quo, where the people who make the most do so because of seniority or perceived value. Because of the transparency that social media brings, and the scrutiny that the community can bring to bear on who is really contributing what to the bottom line, the status quo might well be reconfigured. That would indeed be a wrenching change for many managers.

Alfred Chandler, in the seminal book *The Visible Hand: The Managerial Revolution in American Business*, observes, "Once a managerial hierarchy had been formed, and successfully carried out its function of administrative coordination, the hierarchy itself became a source of permanence, power and continued growth."[7]

It is also likely that management will have to realize that volunteers will figure prominently in the future of business. We've all heard the weary complaint of executives that "It's hard to compete with free," but too many people ignore the corollary to that rule: "It's wonderful to have volunteers working for your business for free." In fact, that's what we have seen proven by open-source software development, the formation and rise of Wikipedia, and online retailers' customer review sections. To realize the full potential of the volunteer effect, executives need to understand that this volunteerism can be both overt and coincidental.

Think, for instance, about the collaborative filtering that online retailers employ when they suggest that, since many other previous buyers bought a secondary battery when they bought a digital camera, you might want to buy the same battery along with the camera you are purchasing. Here, the prior customers' decision to purchase a secondary battery serves as advice of sorts, or at least a prompting, to subsequent buyers that they might want that second battery while their primary one is recharging. And as some commentators point out, in many cases you can actually position yourself to take advantage of this inherent human volunteerism.[8]

Amazon allowed negative reviews of products, a decision that most retail conventional wisdom would have opposed. Instead, Amazon sought to tap into the passion that consumers had for products and for shopping, and began developing a knowledge platform that would attract users.[9] Amazon has built a veritable Wikipedia of product reviews that rely on a user-generated model that is likely to steamroll any competitor who tries to fight back with professionally created reviews.

Similarly, we often encounter managers who shrink from Hyper-Sociality because "we won't be able to control our brand if we do that." Again, controlling the brand is an artifact of the past. Communication with the customer used to be a study in control—the company allowed out only those communications and interactions about its brand that passed muster. Now there is no opacity or control over what the customer knows or says about your brand, or how many millions of people he says it to. Today, authenticity and being able to adequately reward your customers for their attention are the scarce attributes that managers must be concerned about possessing.

As we mentioned at the opening of this chapter, all of these examples point toward the increased relevance of gifted management, don't they?

Summary

The Hyper-Social shift promises to radically affect long-standing management thinking. Often managers underappreciate the impact that Hyper-Socialization will have on their organizations, and the following questions can be used to demonstrate just how significant the shifts in managers' thinking may have to be: Are current notions of corporate control over brand and corporate communications reasonable in a world in which marketing budgets are eclipsed by the scale and reach of the Internet and the blogosphere? Is your organization optimally arranged for the flows of information that will spring up as customers and future customers interact with more touch points within the organization in real time? Do legacy views of your organizational boundaries help or hinder increased collaboration and codevelopment with customers and others outside of the organization? What sort of employees do you need to attract and develop now that customers and external partners expect more frequent, unscripted, and authentic communication across multiple communication channels?

eleven

Hyper-Social Organizations Use Different Metrics

When dealing with metrics, we need to be careful and walk a fine line between practicality and innovation. Metrics are often hardwired in companies' DNA, and it may be difficult, if not impossible, to change them or to gain acceptance of new metrics that might better reflect the actual health of your business. It is important for our purposes to look at metrics through the Hyper-Social lens and to see how companies are measuring the impact of their Hyper-Social activities on their business.

Hyper-Social companies consider tribes to be more important than market segments; they are human- and customer-centric instead of company- or product-centric, and they think about knowledge networks instead of information channels. While many companies have adopted customer-centric metrics like customer loyalty and customer equity–based metrics [focusing on the net present value (NPV) of a customer's future purchases], few have adopted tribal equity–based metrics or knowledge-based metrics. Few also truly measure the impact of word of mouth on customer equity, even though research has shown that customers who are acquired by positive word-of-mouth activity can have twice the customer lifetime value of customers who are acquired via marketing-induced programs, and that word-of-mouth customers can bring in twice the number of new customers through their referrals.[1]

Hyper-Social companies also consider their customer interaction departments, including marketing and customer service, as investments in customer equity, not as cost centers. They also consider their talent to be assets, not disposable commodities the way most other companies do. Alan Webber, the cofounder of *Fast Company*, talked to us about this phenomenon as follows: "It's my sense that in large publicly traded corporations, where the finance function and the mandate to drive up shareholder value is still the default mindset, those organizations are locked into a mental model that prohibits them from really valuing the human dimension. They want what people can contribute, but they don't want to give value to it, because it's very complicated to manage people, and it's very easy to manage numbers."

In the next section of this chapter, we explain why it is important to be practical and argue that companies should measure the impact of Hyper-Social activities on their business processes, just as they measure the impact of any other program. We will also review why companies should focus on the metrics that matter, not just the ones that they can measure easily. And finally, we will take a walk on the wild side and talk about potential new metrics that Hyper-Social organizations might want to monitor.

Be Practical: Measure Progress with Existing Metrics

It's exciting to invent new metrics that may be better at gauging the true health of your business than the ones that are currently in place; however, you need to balance that excitement with deep practicality. You see, most people who are in charge of business processes already have fixed ways in which they measure their business—and in most cases, the number of key performance indicators that they are tracking is in single digits. Chances are that if you don't report the impact of your Hyper-Social activities on these business processes using the same metrics, your programs will remain on the fringe of the organization and never become mainstream.

That is exactly what we have found in our yearly Tribalization of Business Study, where we gather information from more than 500 companies on how they measure the effectiveness of their community and social media initiatives. Many companies are struggling with how to measure the impact of Hyper-Sociality on their businesses. In what we interpret as signs of an early market, we found many companies using advertising metrics when measuring the impact of online communities—time spent on the site and number of page views. Needless to say, most of those companies are not satisfied with their community initiatives and are not making much progress on scaling their Hyper-Sociality.

In fact, we could characterize the whole social measurement space as one of mass confusion. Take a look at the results shown in Figure 11-1, which illustrate our point. We found that the top five business objectives for communities are generate more word of mouth (38 percent), increase customer loyalty (34 percent), increase product or brand awareness (30 percent), bring outside ideas into the organization (29 percent), and improve customer support quality (23 percent). The same study found that the top five business measures are greater awareness (26 percent), word of mouth (22 percent), improved brand perception (18 percent), buzz in media and the blogosphere (17 percent), and increased sales (16 percent).

You see the disconnect? Referrals, customer retention, and customer satisfaction are in seventh, eighth, and ninth place— even though increasing customer loyalty ranked as the second most important objective. And the number of new ideas and number of newly adopted ideas are in tenth and sixteenth place, respectively,

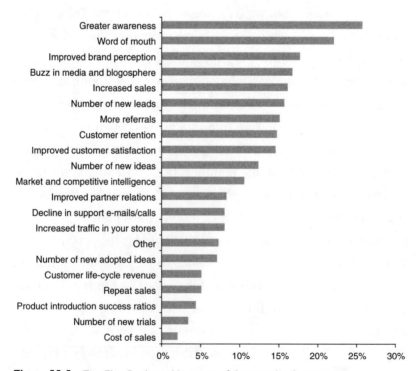

Figure 11-1 Top Five Business Measures of Community Success

even though bringing in new ideas is the fourth most important goal. And look at customer life-cycle revenue and product introduction success ratios, two measures that you would expect companies that care about customer loyalty and bringing new ideas inside the company would measure—they did not show up until seventeenth and nineteenth place, respectively.

Those organizations that are happiest with their online community initiatives are those that measure the impact of those communities the exact same way you would measure the impact of any other program on a particular business process. So, if you measure the impact of a focus group on product innovation in a certain way, or the impact of your call center on customer loyalty, then you should also measure the impact of your product innovation community or your customer support community the exact same way. Some companies, like Intuit, take this idea a step further and create centers for excellence, cross-functional teams that are funded by the different business units that derive benefits from those initiatives. If you extract funding from the various operating groups within your company, that will naturally force you to report the benefits to those groups in the same way as they measure the impact of other programs. This model is especially suited for companies that have more mature online communities, where community members start crossing organizational boundaries by giving product ideas in your customer support forums or supporting complaints in your product innovation communities.

So first and foremost, be pragmatic—by demonstrating that your Hyper-Social programs affect the various business processes that they are supposed to support, you will help those programs gain much-needed legitimacy. Once you get there, you can start looking for alternatives that best measure the long-term impact of Hyper-Sociality on your business and compare it to that of other, more short-term-focused programs.

Measure Only What Matters

In an online world, almost everything can be measured. The result: people become enamored with what they can measure, and measure far too many things. As Alan Webber, the cofounder of *Fast Company*, told us: "If you measure too many things, you might as well measure nothing." Some people become obsessive, compiling statistics that don't reflect a program's impact on their business. Many also confuse analytics with business metrics. Analytics are helpful for optimizing a particular process, like your natural search engine ranking or how to find influencers in communities, but they will rarely tell you anything about the impact of a program on your company's bottom line and future health.

Some companies measure the wrong things. In one particular case, a company set up a community whose members would communicate with one another primarily though SMS text messaging and e-mail. What did it measure to track its progress and success? Time spent on the site and page views—even though the whole effort could be successful even if people never went to the site. Needless to say, that community never became a mainstream marketing program and was eventually shut down.

When we conducted the Tribalization of Business Study, we found another anomaly in how people measure progress and success for their Hyper-Social activities. The study found, as shown in Figure 11-2, that the top five analytics being tracked are the number of

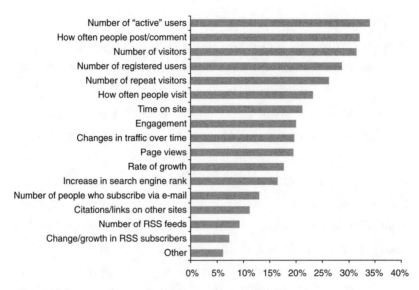

Figure 11-2 Analytics Used to Measure Community Success

"active" users (34 percent), how often people post and comment (32 percent), number of visitors (31 percent), number of registered users (29 percent), and number of repeat visitors (26 percent).

Not surprisingly, the same study found that the biggest reported obstacle to success was getting people to engage and participate (30 percent). While it is inevitable that larger communities will end up with 1 percent of their members being very active users who provide enough value for the 9 percent of somewhat active users, who together provide enough value for the 90 percent of lurkers, the largest form of participation in online communities happens to be active lurking. Active lurkers, who may make up 40 to 50 percent[2] of your community membership, are those who may take something from the community and pass it along to others using different channels, so they end up contributing to your word of mouth.

Active lurkers also include those people who visit a customer support community and find a solution to their problem without contributing to the community. Those people derive a lot of value from that community interaction, and so does your company, since they do not clog up your customer call center. Active lurkers also include those who will contact the original poster through a different channel, such as telephone, e-mail, or perhaps a face-to-face meeting, in effect continuing the conversation outside of the visible public side of the community, but not outside of the community itself. Fortunately, we found that 18 percent of the companies that participated in the 2009 Tribalization of Business Study are starting to track "lurker" metrics. It's not easy to measure the impact of active lurkers, but without some sort of measure of their activity, you could miss a lot of the value that they bring to your Hyper-Social processes—especially in a world in which the customer lifetime value is directly proportional to word-of-mouth activities.

Much of the reasoning that leads people to worry about participation levels comes from years of thinking in terms of company- and product-centricity. People look for signs of customer engagement with their brand, their product, and now their communities and other Hyper-Social programs. They have a hard time letting go of that worldview and replacing it with a human- and customer-centric worldview.

Because communities do not align properly with organizational lines or business processes, you should also, wherever possible, measure the indirect effects of your Hyper-Social programs—for example, the impact of your customer service community on your new product development process. Not only will people who participate in your customer service community give you new product ideas, but research has shown[3] that informal knowledge-sharing environments like online communities will in fact improve the effectiveness of your formal organizational processes. For example, a sales-driven customer feedback community might improve the efficiency of your formal customer service escalation process as well as that of your formal product definition process.

New Measurements through the Hyper-Social Lens

If we could develop new Hyper-Social metrics, what would they look like? Some of the newer metrics that are already being bandied around could actually be considered Hyper-Social.

Don Peppers, the coauthor of *Return on Customer* and *Rules to Break and Laws to Follow*, talks about return on customer, a metric based on customer equity. Don's take, supported by research,[4] is that not all customers are created equal and that we should focus on retaining the ones we have and attracting those with the highest potential customer lifetime value.

Retaining the customers we have is what most customer loyalty programs are focused on. Increasing customer loyalty can have tremendous benefits. When we spoke with Mark Colombo, the senior vice president for digital access marketing at FedEx, he told us that for every percentage point that the company improves its loyalty score, it adds about $100 million to the bottom line. Loyalty is important because as customers stay longer, they tend to buy more, require less help, and pay higher prices. Conceivably they also spread more buzz on your behalf, bringing in more customers through their positive word of mouth.

As we have seen earlier, the customers with the highest lifetime value potential are not necessarily those who convert to customers as a result of your traditional marketing programs. Their total lifetime value also has to include the significant percentage of additional business that will come in because of their positive word of mouth. Don Peppers also reinforced the need to consider customer referrals when calculating customer lifetime value, and he mentioned research pointing to the fact that your highest spenders are not necessarily those who buzz the most about you: "I saw an academic study recently[5] about customer referral value being separated out of customer lifetime value. What's interesting about the study was that these academics found that the highest spenders are often not the same as the highest referrers. A lot of times the customers who refer the most business to you are not spending as much. And if you don't try to at least understand the value of their referrals, you may not be treating those customers with the kid gloves that they deserve." In defining return on customer, and in favoring it over return on investment (ROI), Don argues that the number of customers you can have is finite, or, to use economic jargon, customers are the scarcity. Investments, on the other hand are plentiful, as you can always get more.

ROI is a poor indicator for measuring anything that is customer-related. Let's apply the concept of ROI to marketing programs to illustrate our point. Assume that you have a new product version, for which you develop a special upgrade price and an extra sales incentive. Let's further assume that you have done well in the past and therefore enjoy some positive word of mouth in the marketplace. You now decide to launch this product upgrade with a massive e-mail campaign and by participating in an industry trade show. What does the ROI on the e-mail campaign tell you about the efficacy of e-mail marketing in this case?

Answer: *nothing!*

The e-mail campaign could bomb because you could have the wrong offer for that audience, or because you have a sales incentive that competes with a better one, causing the channel to push an alternative product. You could have had a few of your products explode a few weeks before the campaign (it happens; remember the exploding computer batteries),[6] resulting in negative word of mouth. Or you could get 30 percent of the good leads that both read the e-mail and went to your show. How do you then determine ROI? And assuming that you can, what does it tell you?

Nothing! With so many variables, you cannot accurately predict the behavior of the whole system that is in play during a launch by understanding the individual parts. Also, the system exhibits emergent behavior, which cannot easily be measured with standard ROI metrics. Let's assume that you could find a method of measuring ROI that takes into account all of the interdependencies and variables that rule your market at this particular point in time. What would it tell you about the future performance of your marketing programs, incentives, and promotional pricing schemes?

Nothing! Because ROI is a trailing indicator, not a leading indicator.

John Hagel, a renowned business thinker, author, and the co-chair of the Center of the Edge at Deloitte, also takes umbrage with the traditional ROI. Rather than looking for the standard return on investment, he prefers instead to focus on return on information—a leading indicator. You measure this ROI both from your company's point of view and from the customer's point of view. As John says: "From a company perspective, the question becomes: How much effort and cost did I invest in acquiring information about an individual participant and how much value have I been able to generate in return, both for the participant and for me? From a customer perspective, the key question is: How much information about myself and my needs have I provided, how much effort did it require and, relative to both of these, how much value have I received in return from the information provided?"

You could, of course, extend this concept to also measure the amount of information you would need to provide a prospective buyer to induce her to make a buying decision. Two other leading indicators that John introduces are return on attention and return on skill set (the latter should really be return on talent, but return on skill set is preferable, since ROT is such an unfortunate acronym).

While many of those metrics are steps in the right direction (they are much more customer-centric than many of the older metrics, and they are also leading indicators instead of trailing indicators), they still suffer from some degree of company-centricity. They center on the interactions between the customer and the company, and the rich Hyper-Sociality that is part of any buying decision is not embedded in them.

Another interesting metric comes from marketing professor Rob Kozinets, who was also the coauthor of *Consumer Tribes*.[7] When we spoke with Rob, he talked about "share of community time" as a metric.[8] The problem with calculating share of community time is that there is a huge spread in the estimates of the number of people that participate in communities—between 100 million and 1 billion.

One of the widely adopted metrics that comes close to measuring what we're looking for is the Net Promoter Score (NPS), which is also elegant in its simplicity. NPS is based on the assumption that companies have three types of customers: promoters, passives, and detractors. You identify those people by asking them a simple question: "How likely is it that you would you recommend [Company X] to a friend or colleague?" Those who score 9 or 10 are promoters, those who score 7 or 8 are passives, and the ones who score between 0 and 6 are detractors. The Net Promoter Score is the percentage of promoters minus the percentage of detractors. So in effect the NPS has elements of loyalty, and also indicates the amount of buzzing that customers are likely to be doing on your behalf. While NPS has proved to be a great tool for many companies, it still lacks the ability to let you focus on those tribal groups that really matter. You can correlate NPS with certain aspects of the offering, but it does not give you cause and effect. As Marty St. George, the CMO at JetBlue, reminded us, "It's not because there is a strong correlation between NPS and on-time arrival that we should rip out the entertainment centers in our planes."

In a world in which most buying decisions are social decisions based on knowledge flows that happen within our tribes, and in a world in which tribal word of mouth results in much higher customer lifetime value and customer equity than traditional marketing programs, we should be able to map tribal equity and return on knowledge flows. No one will argue that the tribal equity that exists in the Fiskateers community, where people talk about how the community changed their lives, is much higher than the tribal equity that exists in a company's Facebook group where a majority of the members join because of couponing.

But how do we measure tribal equity?

Monitoring the Health of Your Hyper-Social Programs

For starters, let's look at the field of sociology, where researchers have developed a large body of knowledge concerning social capital in communities—something that is very close to tribal equity.[9] The World Bank even developed a toolkit to help measure social capital in communities.[10] The problem with those methods is their complexity. If the process of measuring becomes too complex, people will most likely fail to monitor their tribal equity adequately.

We propose two barometers for monitoring the health of your Hyper-Social programs. The first one is the Reciprocity Barometer, which measures the degree of reciprocity that exists among your community members. Just as with NPS, you could periodically gauge your communities with simple member surveys asking the question:[11] "Do you expect to give back and help others in the community?" The second one is a Trust Barometer for your Hyper-Social environments. While trust is not part of social capital or tribal equity, it results from it.[12] Trust allows knowledge to flow more freely and encourages reciprocity between strangers. A Trust Barometer could be based on a simple survey question like: "Would you base important decisions on advice that you receive from this community?" Losing trust is the last thing you want to have happen in your tribal environments. As with everything else in social spheres, if mistrust takes hold in your community, it will amplify and spread rapidly.

Just like the Net Promoter Score, the two barometers could also be used to develop scorecards: the Net Reciprocity Score and the Net Trust Score. Both of those scores will tell you a lot about the health of your Hyper-Social activities, and together with the Hyper-Social Index, they will give you a good idea of what might happen if your company were to be hit with a crisis. Companies with high HSIs may still suffer from temporary dips in their Net Trust Score or their Net Reciprocity Score, but because of their high HSI, chances are that they will quickly recover.

The ultimate question, in view of this book's topic, is whether we can turn the business metrics process into a social process. The answer to that question is yes. Many B2B companies have leveraged the wisdom of their collective sales force to forecast sales. Some forward-thinking companies, like Best Buy and Google, are taking this idea a step further and deploying prediction markets to successfully enlist the power of all their employees to predict what will happen—from store opening dates to product introduction successes.

Summary

When it comes to measurements, never forget the end goal of all business: to create a customer. Also remember to be practical, first and foremost. As Jeff Hayzlett, the CMO at Kodak, told us: "You know there are some [measurement] tools that you can use … but I'm not a huge, huge believer in them. I think that in your gut, you know what works. . . . all marketing does exist to drive sales."

Here are some other questions that you should ask yourself as people report back on their Hyper-Social activities. Do those metrics make sense? Are they in line with what we are trying to achieve? Are they in line with how we measure our business today? Do the metrics tell me anything about the social behavior of my tribes? Are we monitoring trust and reciprocity in everything we do? Are we rewarding people for the right metrics? Are our metrics customer-centric? Do we know where our future business needs to come from? Do we have a handle on the value of our talent in our business? Do we have a handle on the value of our customers in our business? Do we understand the importance of customer and tribal equity for our future?

twelve

Hyper-Social Businesses
Need Different Talent

As your organization makes the Hyper-Social shift, it is likely to require managers and employees with skills and attitudes markedly different from those that are currently in place. In Chapter 10, we looked at how the Hyper-Social company would require new managerial thinking; now we turn our attention to the qualities and skills that will be required of company employees. Our Tribalization of Business Study indicates that one of the key drivers of a successful Hyper-Social community is the quality of facilitation and moderation (see Figure 12-1), but how many companies have the ability to identify and retain the sort of people who can interact with customers on such different terms?

The skill set that the new corporate Hyper-Social superstars may well need will include comfort with social media, the ability to communicate effectively from both the corporate and the human perspective, the ability to communicate with a minimum of oversight

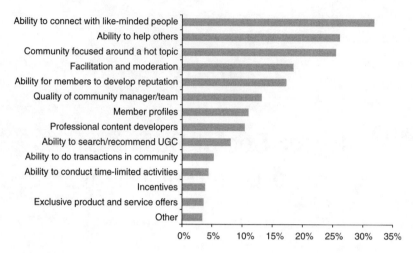

Figure 12-1 Community Features that Contribute Most to Effectiveness

and direction, the authority to speak for the business, and a sufficient depth of knowledge about the company to find customer solutions, no matter where the employee may personally reside within the organization chart. Employees who are well suited for the Hyper-Social organization also tend to be relationship-centric, open-minded, adaptable, collaborative, and comfortable with technology. Even if such people do exist at your company today, how can you identify them? And can you articulate an attractive career path for them?

The Hyper-Social shift will also challenge executives to discover or develop different skills within themselves. One key skill that successful executives will need to cultivate is the ability to continually define what business they are in. As noted earlier, with the increased involvement of the community in product development, marketing, customer service, and just about every other corporate function imaginable, savvy leaders will need to determine what the community values, and what the company can most effectively and economically provide. These managers will develop a clear view of what the organization's real mission and competencies are, and shed those investments that don't move them in that direction.

As John Hagel and Marc Singer observed in their article "Unbundling the Corporation" in 1999, when you deconstruct a company, you often discover that there are three different types of businesses working side by side by side, with vastly different economic, competitive, and talent imperatives.[1] The three types of firms-within-a-firm are

- Customer relationship businesses

- Product innovation businesses

- Infrastructure businesses

Each of these requires a different operating model, and each differs with regard to who the actual customer is. According to Hagel and Singer, as the transaction costs of working with entities outside the firm drop, leaders must decide which one of the three businesses to retain, and which two to shed. In a customer relationship business, for instance, employees must focus sharply on serving the customer, whereas in an infrastructure business, talent focuses more on optimal efficiency. Clearly, if Hyper-Sociality drives unbundling in your business, you will need to carefully consider what sort of talent you need.

Managers will need to develop frameworks for identifying and motivating passionate individuals, and endowing them with sufficient training, guidance, and then autonomy to act effectively. Passion is critical when you are dealing with tribes, and those people who have it are the ones who you want managing those relationships. As Barry Judge, CMO of Best Buy, recently told us:

> The guy that thought up Prediction Markets [a program in which employees trade virtual stocks that predict future outcomes, like sales numbers, or future events], he runs it. He happens to be running Geek Squad, but he has the passion around it so he runs it. The Loop [another market prediction tool] is run by retail operations. They have the passion for it so they run it. Typically at Best Buy one of the ideas is if you've got passion then you may be best suited to take it on regardless of what organization you're in because you have point of view.[2]

One observation from the Tribalization of Business Study is that successful managers in Hyper-Social companies are skilled at communicating with multiple stakeholders. Hyper-Social managers instinctively realize that at any moment, they may be communicating simultaneously with employees, members, customers, and business partners, and they transparently convey information to all of these people simultaneously. They are also comfortable with not having exclusive control of their marketing messages, their brand, or how they are viewed by the external world. Nonetheless, they work tirelessly to make sure that their organizations are viewed in the best light by all observers. They keep their ears to the ground, listen to what's being said about their companies, and develop systems for responding to inaccuracies (even leveraging their tribes for assistance in correcting inaccuracies). As Michael Dell, founder and CEO of Dell, observed of the Dell Hell debacle, "We screwed up. These conversations are going to occur whether you like it or not. Do you want to be part of that or not? My argument is you absolutely do. You can learn from that. You can improve your reaction time. And you can be a better company by listening and being involved in that conversation."[3]

A Shift in Which Skills Are of Most Value

A critical, albeit sometimes subtle, issue that emerges as you consider the Hyper-Social shift is that as your company becomes increasingly Hyper-Social, valuable employees may well possess skills that are very dissimilar to those that successful employees of yesteryear possessed. In the past, a great employee might work 10-hour days, executing corporate marketing campaigns expertly. Or perhaps the model employee was corporate counsel, who prided himself on never exposing the company to any risk whatsoever. Clearly, either one of those paragons of corporate success would be severely challenged in navigating the Hyper-Social shift if he expected to behave the same way.

What would the marketer do in an environment in which there were few or no formal campaigns, and every day was an unpredictable, thrilling, and sometimes disappointing conversation in real time with humans who find real flaws in the company's products? What if a willingness to endure 10-hour days wasn't good enough—would she be ready to respond to a blog over the weekend, or be savvy enough about the business to pass on critical information from the tribes to product development? Would she be able to develop new metrics for tribe satisfaction, loyalty, or lifetime client value and communicate them to the finance group as it set budgets for the coming cycle? As conversations with customers and other members of the tribe continue into the future, possibly outliving the original marketing campaign that sparked them, will she have the strategic foresight and skills to support those conversations, so that the members of the tribe don't feel that they are being ignored?

And would the diligent lawyer be able to quickly develop protocols and procedures that permitted employees to engage in product development with consumers? Could he design policies that ensured that hourly workers could blog about the company after hours without exposing the company to labor-law violations for permitting hourly workers to work "off the clock"? Could he accept the ambiguity of allowing more risk in return for a more Hyper-Social relationship with the customer, and communicate that to his superiors effectively?

Given the reality of working with social media, an organization's talent will inevitably need to engage with detractors. Detractors range from one-time complainers to protracted adversaries who maintain long-term criticism of a company or its products and its behavior. Encouragingly, however, there have been a number of cases in which online detractors, after complaining publicly and vigorously about a company's performance, have been converted to supporters. For instance, last year a Twitter user named James called out Bank of America for shoddy customer support. Because of a rapid and authentic response from the bank, James reversed himself, and publicly thanked the bank for its help.[4]

Clearly Bank of America had developed a means of monitoring such complaints and empowered a company representative to remedy the problem. But this can be a daunting challenge for companies, as it requires people who may be untrained in dealing with customers to step up and begin engaging with them. At the same time, in order to be successful, these same employees are often given the task of creating and running the systems for routing inbound information to the right decision makers, updating and refreshing company information in customer-facing online venues, understanding the dynamics of the tribe, and ensuring that a small group of commenters doesn't monopolize the conversation or keep others from contributing by intimidation and bullying.

Discussions with executives from companies that are undergoing the Hyper-Social shift confirm many of these observations and research. For instance, when we asked Ram Menon, CMO of TIBCO, about hiring marketing talent, he noted that he looks first for smart people who may have come from areas outside of marketing. What is important, according to Menon, is finding people who can "correlate and parse" information so that they can prioritize and make quick decisions. Menon further observed, "If you're a marketer who doesn't understand technology, you are a problem. So, you know, get on it real quick. Don't hire a social media agency to tell you how to do a social media strategy; do it yourself—start a blog, post things, be on Twitter, read on your own every morning what people are saying about your company and figure it out."[5]

Mozilla's CEO, Mitchell Baker, when asked about hiring into her open-source company, observed that if potential employees are too inflexible with stakeholders, it gives her pause. "If we ask, 'What do you do if someone disagrees with you? What do you do if you think something needs to happen and it seems to be slow or stopped?' And the answer is, 'Well, I tell them I'm in charge.' Bing. Even our employees rarely get told that, because I believe that many of the things that work in open-source management are also very valuable for your employees. You can try to tell an employee what to do, but if the two of you disagree the employee may be right. There's much more negotiation here, like a professional partnership."[6]

Mark Gambill, CMO at computer distributor CDW, told us how the company trains its sales talent at CDW to interact with customers, and the autonomy that salespeople are given. When CDW noticed that it was not as visible in the social media as it might have liked, it asked its sales force to begin engaging in more online conversations with buyers. "You don't want to create an employee's script such that they're very rigid, but you want to give them some perspective around what we're trying to do as a company in these different types of conversations. We have a bunch of great entrepreneurs. They'll take the bull by the horns, and they'll move out and get involved in these conversations. So, we have a lot of confidence in our sales force and coworkers to do the right thing, but we want to make sure we're continuing to give them the right tools as well."[7]

In addition, Beth Comstock, global CMO at GE, looks for digital capabilities and community- and network-building skills in her marketers.

We're sort of on this tear right now about what we're calling new world skills. . . . The big one is digital capabilities and understanding how we move more quickly. . . . There are a few others. First, this notion of simplicity, of trying to, if you will, curate an experience for a customer, help them sort of take away all the extraneous and deliver what's most valuable. That is so hard . . . . and I think our new challenge is, how do you focus and simplify? That is hard for marketers. The other thing we talk a lot about is just this notion of networks, communities, and understanding how do you better mine those for insights. How do you better create more participatory marketing?[8]

Remember that many of these conversations and interactions between employees and community members are taking place in a context in which all conversations are visible, searchable, and probably archived for perpetuity. In addition, front-line employees could well find themselves up against an army of disgruntled customers as a result of a service or product failure that is no fault of their own. And, of course, there is no real "end" to the job at the end of the workday—the conversations happen after hours, on weekends, and while workers are trying to take a vacation.

Align Your Talent with the Four Pillars of Hyper-Sociality

Given that many companies are product-centric and think of their value proposition to the client as being related to the technical excellence of their products and their features, will your employees be able to shift from product-centric to customer-centric? Talent needs to create trust, to be fair, and to put humans in the center, all the while constantly gathering insight and suggesting actions to the company. Employees must be able to deliver on the Four Pillars of Hyper-Sociality and think:

- Tribe vs. market segment
- Human-centricity vs. company-centricity

- Network vs. channel
- Social messiness vs. process and hierarchy

In addition, management needs to be aware that when the firm is dealing with humans socially, there will be a lot of "exception handling." This refers to the situations in which a human needs to get involved in a process that is typically automated because an "exception" has occurred, and a human's fuzzy logic is required. Perhaps the exception is a product return, a suggestion about how to improve a process, or a request for assistance in a difficult-to-articulate area. Your business will be generating an increasing number of messy, nonuniform interactions with customers as the pace of the Hyper-Social shift picks up. And although machines are increasingly being integrated into our workflows and our interactions, it appears that one place where they won't find a home anytime soon is in dealing with humans in a Hyper-Social context. As Don Peppers noted recently in an interview with us, judgment, creativity, empathy, and wisdom are things that computers still can't supply.

Given the Hyper-Social shift, companies will not be able to rely on programs to sway public opinion. In the past, a narrow view of customers reigned supreme: they all appeared to be the same, and one public relations or communications message would fit them all. In a networked, Hyper-Social world, you will need talent that can connect quickly, create trust, and follow up with an army of voices.

To ensure that your talent is well aligned with the Hyper-Social shift, run through the different areas of your company, and see what the talent there should look like to match the tribes. For instance, a customer service professional who spends his entire shift responding to blog posts or tweets is likely to be outgoing, conversant with social media tools, and able to communicate expertly through written words. Mark Colombo, senior vice president of digital access marketing at FedEx, noted that he looks for employees "who have the right academic skills; you want great listeners; and when you start to talk about the skills, you want someone really well-rounded with great business acumen and some strong technical skills—not necessarily the technology du jour, but strong technical skills being quantitative, and an understanding of how to leverage technology to drive business results."[9]

Barry Judge, CMO at Best Buy, when discussing how he chooses talent to speak with Best Buy's tribes, observed,

> I think there's some basic understanding of what the brand is about and there's some basic understanding of policies and then you hire the right people . . . and you let everybody participate and for the most part people will do the right thing. They won't do the right thing every time. But if you hire the right people and they're trained to some degree and have some knowledge, then in general they'll do the right thing and the brand will be better off because it will be human. So I think that's the opportunity. I think brands can become human. Especially as a retailer I think that's a critical idea.[10]

A key aspect of making a process Hyper-Social is ensuring that all the people who are interested and capable in the role are given the opportunity to engage and demonstrate their abilities. Accordingly, we suggest that employees who are interested in engaging with the tribes be permitted to self-select. Self-selection has been proven to work in cases like Wikipedia's article drafting and crowd-sourced product development, and we have observed a number of additional cases where employees in Hyper-Social organizations have effectively self-selected.

But self-selection is no replacement for training and orientation. Are your salespeople comfortable with having much more discussion about the prices, concessions, and deals they have put together with the customers? Do your employees in general know enough about Human 1.0 through formal training? One suggestion for formally training employees in this regard is to role-play various processes that involve interactions that may be unfamiliar to the employee. These may include

- Cocreating with a customer for product development
- Handling a very visible and cantankerous customer through a customer experience touch point
- Negotiating with a potential buyer through the sales cycle as other members of the tribe (and competitors) view the process

While this greater social interaction is likely to be exciting for the right talent (those who decide to engage in the increasingly Hyper-Social relationship with the customer and other stakeholders), it will be tough on other individuals, and will increasingly require facility with statistics and research. As we've shown, there is a great deal of science concerning human social behavior that needs to be considered, as well as increasing amounts of Web-based data showing tribal actions and conversations. Increased Hyper-Sociality will also require deep and up-to-date knowledge of the company's products and services by all workers, not just the marketing and sales personnel who formerly had those discussions with prospects.

Since conversations between the tribes and the companies will be taking place through new pathways (buyers conversing with product designers, support people, or marketing folks, depending on the buyers' outreach and choice of forum), employees will need to know more about the company and its products to be responsive to customers.

Talent needs to be constantly innovating and communicating those innovations to the firm through knowledge management systems or other processes. A lack of talent that can handle this new knowledge flow (process and business innovation) will be a huge lost opportunity, and the companies that do not capture these people will eventually lose ground to better-run peers. This is a perfect example of an area where Hyper-Sociality can profit both the customer and the company—make sure that your talent is improving and innovating for you in tandem with what it's doing for the customer.

Although management must focus on the attributes of the talent that will be necessary to drive successful Hyper-Social organizations, it must not lose sight of the fact that the talent will have access to unprecedented amounts of insight from customers. What will management do to ensure that this information and insight will be visible to the right people in the organization? Employee training on both data parsing and knowledge sharing is likely to be required. As we speak with Hyper-Social companies, the need for significant data analysis skills repeatedly crops up as a need-to-have element of employees' skill sets.

Other organizations are experimenting with the creation of a chief commercial officer or chief customer officer (CCO). Charged with managing all contacts with the customer across the organization, CCOs are still a relatively rare breed. Their ranks are growing, however: in 2001, there were only 5 CCOs worldwide, but in 2008, the number of CCOs had jumped to 56.[11] The Chief Customer Officer Council, a peer-advisor network where CCOs share experiences, states that the CCO "must be the ultimate authority on customers, understanding customers better than any other individual in the company and perhaps better than some customers may even understand themselves." The CCO Council cautions, however, that a CCO must have the power to create and implement customer strategy across all business units or silos, and that without this ability, "the individual's purview is limited and does not warrant the CCO title."[12]

Given the importance of understanding Human 1.0 principles such as trust, reciprocity, and fairness, and our sometimes irrational behaviors, managers might also consider consulting with behavioral economists and anthropologists as they develop their view of what sort of talent their organization needs. Hyper-Sociality, as we've seen, can bestow significant benefits on organizations, but the benefits carry with them the requirement that your people understand humans, their motivations, and their behavior in groups. Indeed, you need to come to terms with their irrationality, and how Hyper-Sociality can be at the root of that irrationality. As Dan Ariely, professor at Duke, visiting professor at MIT's Media Center, and author of *Predictably Irrational*, observed to us recently about the current global recession:

> So, the failing of the market in such a big way this year in some sense has been very good for behavioral economics. I think we understand it. Irrationality is not limited to a few people who are

making small decisions, but instead it's a huge part of the market, it's very important to understand and figure out and unless we do it, we're going to get into difficult, difficult circumstances, and repeatedly doing so.[13]

Summary

By now it should be clear that your organization will need different talent to help drive its success in a Hyper-Social world. Do you think your organization is thinking ahead of the talent curve, or is it merely recruiting the same sorts of talent it always has? Is your company thinking enough about Human 1.0 behaviors, and what sort of employees would best engage with those behaviors, or is it hiring based on evidence of past success in unrelated areas? Is your organization assessing how well employees are exhibiting the Four Pillars of Hyper-Sociality? Are decision makers taking the proper measures to ensure that those employees who are increasingly interacting with your tribes have the information, training, and authority to act in those ways that are best for both the tribes and the organization? And is your organization managing its talent so that learnings about your tribes are being captured and acted on?

thirteen

The Seven Myths of Hyper-Social Organizations

Much of the discussion up to this point has been within the context of advocacy—we have attempted to show how and why fundamental social, economic, and technological forces are combining to change the nature of companies, and how companies engage with their customers, employees, members, and business partners. We have presented all manner of evidence (behavioral science, economics, history, and logic) to make the case that the Hyper-Social shift is inevitable for businesses, and is therefore important to understand and master.

Indeed, during the course of our research, we have encountered many companies (hundreds, as a matter of fact) that have already begun the Hyper-Social shift. For many of the reasons discussed earlier, these companies have reached just the same conclusion, and have confidently and wisely begun to craft their visions of what Hyper-Social organizations might look like.

And, in the course of studying these companies in our Tribal-ization of Business research, we have determined that there is a disturbingly high rate of incidence of certain mistakes. Indeed, it almost seems as if the companies making these mistakes are reading from the same playbook, given the striking preponderance and repetition of their missteps. We've studied all the bad advice floating around regarding the Hyper-Social shift, and in doing so, we've noticed several patterns of thought. There are seven main myths on the subject that many well-intentioned companies act on, to their detriment. Several of these myths are in direct conflict with the Four Pillars of Hyper-Sociality:

- Tribe vs. market segment
- Human-centricity vs. company-centricity
- Network vs. channel
- Social messiness vs. process and hierarchy

In this chapter, we will discuss each of these myths in order to highlight and flag philosophies, attitudes, and biases that can hamper your successful Hyper-Social shift, and to provide some alternative solutions. So without any further ado, here are the seven key myths we've discovered that lead to Hyper-Social pitfalls.

Myth 1: Build It and They Will *(Continue to)* Come

The mere presence of an online venue does not automatically create a community to populate it. That's why the Internet is littered with communities that are devoid of any recent activity and blogs with no comments that were last updated months ago. You surely have seen some of these virtual ghost towns. After a while, they fail to meet the expectations of the companies that set them up, and they are usually taken down. Examples of defunct communities abound; our research indicates that "getting people to come back" is one of the key challenges companies face. There are also plenty of examples of projects that have not been taken down, even though they are clearly not experiencing much success. One such community at the time of this writing is a computer manufacturer's small business community, which has been around for years and has attracted only a little over 600 members. Another is a large bank's community, also focused on the small business market, with 4,700 members who seem to have nothing to say to one another in the forums.

Organizations make this mistake all the time—they think that if they build online communities for their target customers, people will show up and populate the forums, the blogs, and other content-related areas. What they miss is something that we reviewed in Chapter 4: the need for high-quality content. You need valuable content in order to get your communities going, and in most cases, you also need professionally developed content in order to keep them going. People are much better at reacting to existing content than they are at creating original content. Also, a typical community consists of 90 percent lurkers, and while lurkers may benefit you in some ways, as we saw in Chapter 11, they do not participate in the public forums and don't help you create content that might provide value for the rest of your members.

The "build it and they will come" vision fails to materialize for other reasons as well. Because of a number of predictable (and correctable) mistakes that are chronicled in our Tribalization of Business Study, simply "building it" does not guarantee that anyone will show up. The first key attribute of successful communities is that they tap into a shared passion. Has the company identified a passion that users will want to tap into, or is it the passions of the company (its products and services) that it wants people to tap into? The ability to help others, according to the 500 companies we polled, is the second most effective community feature. In our experience, it is a rare management team that intuitively builds in this feature from the start. Should we, the company, be able to help customers? Sure. But what about customers helping one another? Well, that's more unlikely, because then the company typically begins to worry about liability for giving wrong answers, or starts to get focused on who owns the solutions if it wants to sell them one day. Notice that the top handful of most effective community features are really Human 1.0 features, not things that a company typically thinks of when it starts to "build" a community.

This myth also includes a little bit of organizational hubris: we will build it because no one else was smart enough, or big enough, or rich enough to build it. News flash: there's a huge online ency-clopedia that, at last count in 2010, included more than 3.2 million articles in English alone, and that wasn't built by any one person or company. It was built by a global crowd, and it didn't need any company on whose behalf to build it. So think about the value you are really trying to deliver to your tribe, and then build accordingly. Maybe it is a platform for discussion, maybe it is a place to access great content, or perhaps cocreation is another option that the tribe would appreciate. Put up a lot of good content and information about the motorcycles that they love or the small entrepreneurial companies that they run, and then let your visitors add to it, change it, and take it over.

Myth 2: The "Not Invented Here" Syndrome

This is probably the second-largest cause of Hyper-Social program failures. In a typical "not invented here" scenario, company executives first read or hear about the amazing benefits that other companies have gained by leveraging social media and communities (of course, they never hear about the failures). Then they get the sense that their company is falling behind, and they "empower" their marketing team or their IT team to initiate Hyper-Social programs. The knee-jerk reaction of those who are given the task of setting up the Hyper-Social programs is to build it on their platforms—the company Web site or the e-commerce site. They never bother to do an ecosystem scan to see whether the tribes that they might want to engage with are already congregating somewhere else.

If your tribes already have a home, trying to get them to move is akin to focusing your whole go-to-market strategy on switching customers who use competitive products. It can be done if your competitor is offering subpar products, but it is rarely a successful stand-alone strategy. Similarly, trying to get an existing community to move to the site you've provided is not likely to be successful. The endowment effect, a well-documented Human 1.0 trait wherein we overvalue what we have and undervalue what we don't have, can be blamed for that stubbornness.

The independent TiVo customer support community is a perfect illustration of the not invented here syndrome (http://www.tivo community.com). While the community had thousands of fanatic users early on, TiVo never really put this amazing word-of-mouth engine at the center of its customer-facing efforts (it had more than 40,000 members in 2003, and at the time of this writing that number had grown to over 215,000). TiVo did not ignore it—some of its employees participated in the community activities, and TiVo derived many product enhancements and innovations from it. But it never built on this enviable Hyper-Social customer foundation, making you wonder whether it truly understood the power of Hyper-Sociality.

Recent developments point in a direction suggesting that TiVo probably never really got it. For some reason, it decided to set up its own customer support community (http://forums.tivo.com/pe). We estimate that this community, which is more than a year old now, has fewer than 2,000 members. The place is devoid of passion and, in a lot of ways, devoid of the social element that makes the other community so vibrant. Why did TiVo feel the need to create its own community and, in effect, compete with its most avid fans, who were doing a superb job of providing online support? Was it to have more control? Was it so that it could mine more insights from the community? If so, it clearly didn't meet its goal. Most people barely fill out their profiles, and the place clearly lacks the social interactions needed for great ideas to flourish.

If you ask your IT department to set up Hyper-Social programs, chances are that it will default to setting them up in its own environment. It's in an IT department's genes to want to control access, manage policies, protect the company from nefarious comments and malicious hackers, remain in charge of the data, and above all provide a *secure* environment for its users. It is also likely to start your Hyper-Social project the same way that many failed projects start—by first deciding on which technology to use. Technology, as we saw in Chapter 4, is not one of the four forces of increasing returns that make for successful communities. Rather than deciding on the technology to start with, companies should focus their energies on members, content, member profiles, and ease of executing transactions, as we saw in Chapter 4.

One company that avoided the not invented here syndrome early on was the $8 billion technology retailer CDW. At first it had its own customer community initiatives. Fortunately, it quickly realized that the people it was trying to reach were already hanging out together somewhere else. It closed their own initiatives and instead started engaging with the tribes where they were already hanging out. When we spoke with Mark Gambill, CDW's CMO, he told us: "So, the evolution of what we did is that we're now going to places where customers are engaging. We know where customers typically go in the small business community, and we'll tap into those existing communities and understand how to get involved with them."[1]

Sometimes your tribes will form into self-organized Hyper-Social environments, like the TiVo customer support community that we just discussed. Sometimes they will hang out in places that are hosted by vendors, as is the case with the American Express Open Forum (http://www.openforum.com), one of the few successful small business communities. If you are MasterCard or Visa, chances are that you will not want to engage in American Express's small business community. But if you are FedEx, Intuit, HP, or Staples, why wouldn't you engage with small business customers alongside American Express? Together you could provide more value to the community members. Your chances of success would also increase compared to going it alone.

Partnering is something that every Hyper-Social company should evaluate, because in most spaces, there is no room for multiple tribes with the same purpose. You see, people have limited attention, and they typically will not belong to more than one community with the same purpose. If there are multiple communities in the same space, the forces of increasing returns that we discussed in Chapter 4 will cause one of them to grow at the expense of the others, creating insurmountable barriers to getting off the ground for other similar communities. We are not suggesting that there will be only one successful small business community— on the contrary. You could have niches, such as a women-owned small business community, an independent bookstore small business community, or a small business community centered on common technology usage, like Intuit's Partner Platform. What we're saying is that unless you can further subsegment the tribe, we don't believe that you can have multiple successful independent bookstore small business communities.

Companies are increasingly looking at the possibility of partnering. In the Tribalization of Business Study, we found that many organizations considered partnering with existing communities (25 percent), complementary vendors (13 percent), or fans (20 percent). Of those that considered partnering, however, only 45 percent ended up doing it. We expect that number to grow as more dominant communities emerge on the horizon and executives start realizing that they cannot be Hyper-Social without partnering.

Myth 3: Let's Keep It Small so It Doesn't Move the Needle

Many Hyper-Social efforts are too small to make a difference to the business processes that they are supposed to support. We can think of two main reasons for this. First, some companies have a culture of using test or pilot programs before launching broadly—it's just something we have been trained to do in business for ages. The second reason why companies fail to scale is that they are chronically underfunding their Hyper-Social projects—especially from a human resources point of view.

Take the Marriott Rewards Insiders community as an example.[2] It has a little over 10,000 community members out of 30 million Marriott Rewards members—a whopping 0.03 percent participation rate. Does anyone at Marriott seriously believe that a community with a 0.03 percent customer participation rate is going to make a difference in the business? Of course not. What if Marriott were to spend 5 percent of its advertising budget on the initiative—surely there would be a lot more people buzzing about the program. Travel, of course, is a tricky space, with TripAdvisor, a division of Expedia, looming as the elephant in the room. The point we are trying to make, however, is that most large companies would not think twice before dropping millions of dollars on an ad campaign. Yet they probably hesitate when it comes to their Hyper-Social plans—even though those plans have the potential to become predictable word-of-mouth engines.

For most organizations, it gets worse when it comes to allocating human resources to those projects. They forget that if they ask their customers and prospects to spend some of their social capital with them, those same people will expect reciprocity. Of course, if the purpose of the community was to gain market insights for product innovation, they could have gotten by with fewer members. In most cases, however, that is clearly not what the communities were set up to do.

If you rely on having tens of thousands or millions of customers to achieve your revenue numbers, you need Hyper-Social initiatives that are commensurate with those numbers. That is especially true if the purpose of your Hyper-Social activity is to amplify word of mouth to the point where it makes a measurable difference in sales. Let's do a quick (overly simplified) back-of-the-envelope calculation to make our point. Let's assume that you are a retailer with 1,000 stores that average 3,000 unique visitors a week each. If you want to increase traffic to your stores by 2 percent, on a weekly basis, you need to increase traffic for all your stores combined by 60,000 visitors. On a yearly basis, you need an additional 3,120,000 visitors at your stores. How many people do you need buzzing about your company in order to achieve that?

Assuming that the average number of people you reach every year through positive word of mouth from one satisfied customer is 150 (about three people a week), and further assuming that 30 percent of those who have been on the receiving end of these referrals will actually visit the store, and that 20 percent of those who visit the store will be won over and actually start buzzing like us, we find that every year, you will drive an additional 65 people to the store. In order to drive an additional 3,120,000 people to your stores, assuming a 10 percent active participation ratio in your community, you need 480,000 community members. (Considering the complex network effects that are at work in Hyper-Social environments, this calculation is going to vary wildly depending on the assumptions at work in each instance.)

The bottom line is that you probably will need more people than you thought you would. The good news is that achieving these levels of participation is not unheard of—think of SAP with its 1.5 million developers, or the IBM developer community with its 5 million registered users. Even the self-organized TiVo support community has more than 215,000 members. If your community is too small to make a real impact on your bottom line, you might as well scrap the project and redirect your budgets to other programs. That being said, and considering the long-term cost efficiencies of community- and social media–based business initiatives, you may be better off redirecting additional resources to scale your Hyper-Social programs to the point where they can make a real impact.

An interesting way for companies to have their Hyper-Social programs become part of the fabric of the processes they are intended to support and avoid having them being stuck in the pilot stage can be learned from Humana. It incubates its Hyper-Social programs in a cross-functional Innovation Lab for a given period of time and shuts them down after that — even if they are not adopted by the business units or functional groups. That is how the company embraced a successful Twitter-based customer service program. Humana incubated it in the lab for three months, after which it was adopted by the customer service group and made part of the main customer service process, where it belonged.

Another potential issue with pilot programs is that the conditions of the pilot may in fact give you little insight into what will happen when you launch a broader program. Unlike other marketing programs, say direct-mail campaigns, where the conditions for a test program are mostly the same as those for a broader program, that is not the case for Hyper-Social programs. Smaller communities, for example, will require a lot more moderation and professional content than larger communities. So if you start small, you may have to do things in order to succeed that you will not have to do with larger programs. You could also not do them and wrongly conclude that the program will fail because the test failed.

More injurious than a company's decision to keep it small is the company's resistance to the tribe's decision to make it big. Networks, which is what tribes essentially are, tend to grow when they are successful (notwithstanding the sponsoring organization's desire to "keep it small"). These community efforts can literally be killed by their success—there are not enough people working on the organization's side to effectively manage, moderate, or facilitate the community, or the meager budgets run out before business cases can be made for greater investments. Companies may also fail to appreciate the real size of these communities because they measure only "active users." We know of cases where a community was shut down, and the until-then-invisible tribe emerged and began running the community on its own, out of the view of the formerly sponsoring organization. One such example was a large imaging company that tried to shut down one of its printer communities, only to find the community continuing to flourish as a Yahoo! group.

Myth 4: My Company Is Smarter than I Am

"Our company has plans and strategies to engage in social media," is what is usually said first. Then what usually comes a few months later is, "We don't get any comments on our corporate blog," or "Nobody seems to follow us on Twitter," or the most common one to emerge from our Tribalization of Business Study, "Nobody engages in our community."

When you engage in Hyper-Social activities, you are asking your employees, partners, customers, and prospects to invest some of their social capital with you. What they expect in return is a human, or preferably a group of humans, to engage with them in return, not some faceless corporate entity. Why would anyone want to chat with "Marriott" in the Marriott Rewards Insiders community, unless, of course, it was Bill Marriott?

Hyper-Social organizations do not agonize over what the corporate response is in a social environment—they realize that people want to interact with other people, and they allow and even encourage individual voices to engage on their behalf. They don't presume that the company is smarter than the individuals that make up the organization.

While some companies succeed, many, if not most, fail in their corporate blogging initiatives. They fail not only because they are anonymous, hidden behind the name of their company, but also because either they have nothing interesting to say or they repurpose their press releases as blog posts, convinced that some people will find them interesting. They fail because what started as a project full of good intentions is all of a sudden falling by the wayside as people get busy—failing to realize that there is nothing more uninviting than a blog that has not been updated for months. They fail because they are primarily motivated by optimizing the firm's natural search engine ranking, not because the firms want to be Hyper-Social. In fact, many of them are not social at all—they don't link to others, they don't comment on other people's posts and tweets, and they never really seek to engage people. They mostly want to broadcast their corporate-speak-laden messages.

Sometimes they fail even though they do have interesting and engaging content. Take Unica, a Massachusetts enterprise marketing management software vendor that launched a marketing thought leadership community[3] called the Marketers' Consortium. The effort included well-known marketing thought leaders, people like Elena Anderson from Forrester and Don Peppers from Peppers and Rogers, who took on the monthly rotating role of moderator. The Marketers' Consortium was closed after a little more than a year[4] for lack of engagement and ROI. What happened here? It was a well-intended effort, pretty well executed, and with prominent thought leaders who had interesting points of view. What could the company have done differently to make the community succeed?

While it is usually hard to look back and make predictions on what might have worked, one of the authors of this book actually ran a similar thought leadership community for Microsoft for three years—one that proved hugely successful. The main differences between the two programs? One was Hyper-Social, the other much less so. The Microsoft community was launched with well-known thought leaders who were also popular bloggers (instead of analysts). Those people knew how to behave Hyper-Socially, and they had tremendous respect for one another. There was a strong sense of belonging among the group members, which resulted in a true group conversation, not just a series of points of view. The contributors were so proud to belong to this group of thought leaders that they also brought their existing audiences to the project. The other main difference was that the Microsoft thought leadership community was run as an editorially independent community that was totally disconnected from the firm's corporate Web site. Perhaps if it had not been, it might have been perceived as another corporate initiative.

We frequently find the "my company is smarter than me" effect in the social media monitoring and engagement side of the business. Organizations will monitor what is being said about them, and then agonize over whether they are providing the proper "corporate" response. Did customer support reply to this installation complaint? Did PR respond to this comment about our CEO's remarks during his latest public speech? Did we get anyone from development to engage with this product idea that seemed to catch fire on a couple of fan sites last week? While customers will not perfectly align their comments, rants, and reviews with the way you are organized as a company, you should not stress over which department will engage with whom. As we've said before, people love to get attention from other people. If they get it from more than one person, no matter what department those people are from, they will love you for it—even if the information they provide is not 100 percent helpful or accurate. As long as the information is delivered in an honest and fair exchange, people will reward you with their loyalty.

Myth 5: Finding That One "Big Idea" Will Work Magic

Another frequent mistake that companies make is banking on one program to solve all their needs. It's not just companies like Wal-Mart, IBM, or P&G that cannot rely on a single solution to make a difference in their sales results. Everyone needs a balanced portfolio of programs: initiatives to increase word of mouth, improve product reviews, develop better products, and make customer service a better experience. You need to think about how to Hyper-Socialize everything that you do, including your products and services. And you need to extend Hyper-Sociality to all the platforms that your customers and prospects use, including gaming platforms, mobile platforms, car platforms, exercise platforms, and other entertaining platforms. Look at Netflix. Not only did it disrupt the movie rental business by changing the delivery paradigm, but it also leveraged the wisdom of the crowd through its $1 million Netflix Prize[5] program to design a better product offering. And it found a way to embed Hyper-Sociality within its service by offering instant movie downloads to the Xbox gaming platform and allowing seven players to watch the movie simultaneously while chatting with one another over the Xbox Voice over IP channel. Note that Netflix did not invent anything new; movie watching has always been a social process. It just extended that social process to a new platform.

Nike is another innovator in this space. Using a Nike+ sensor in your running shoe, which communicates with your iPod, your iPhone, or a special Nike armband device, Nike+ allows you to track your distance, pace, and calories burned while you run. After your run, you can upload that information and share it with your social network. You can share your goals and your training calendar and set up challenges with your friends. As the Nike site puts it, you can see who's "kicking butt and who needs a kick in the butt."[6] In effect, Nike turned what has primarily been an individual activity (most people run alone) into a worldwide social experience. The results: 35 percent of Nike+ members are new to Nike footwear, 50 percent of members use the site four times a week, and 93 percent of users said that they would recommend it to a friend.[7] Like most other successful Hyper-Social organizations, Nike has dozens of Hyper-Social programs.

And herein lies the lesson: companies that are looking for the single Hyper-Social killer app will invariably walk away disappointed.

Myth 6: It's My World, Customer; You Just Live in It

This is one of the most pernicious of all the myths because it distorts the very reason why a company might undertake the Hyper-Social shift—to profit in tandem with a more engaged group of human beings. The Hyper-Social shift should be based on the realization that your customers can now interact with you and others in the way that they always wanted to but couldn't. The reason for adopting Hyper-Sociality shouldn't be to exploit your customers in a new way, or to gain some new advantage over them. Companies that develop Hyper-Social behavior solely as a way to increase profits, thwart customers' ability to communicate effectively with others, or serve as an alternative marketing platform are missing the message here, and are committing a foul that those who are paying attention will surely detect. And since humans are hardwired for reciprocity and fairness, they will surely communicate this information far and wide. The ardor with which people pursue crusades against companies, often to their own social or economic detriment, highlights this point.

The numerous boycotts of products and companies as diverse as coffee and cigarette manufacturers over the years point to the propensity of tribes to invest heavily in effecting what they believe is fairness. The documented phenomenon of tribes taking actions against third-party surrogates when they cannot reach their intended targets directly is a cautionary tale of what may occur in the future as companies become increasingly connected, but complacent with regard to the actions of those people or organizations that are associated with them.

This distortion of Hyper-Sociality can be explicit or subtle. Some organizations view social media and the trend toward Hyper-Sociality as nothing more than an affordable way to engage in legacy business activities such as couponing, marketing, and advertising, and will act in ways that are clearly inconsistent with the Four Pillars of Hyper-Sociality. Other leaders genuinely miss the logic behind Hyper-Sociality, and view it primarily as a set of new social media tools that need to be mastered for their benefit. These managers fail to discern the radical change that Hyper-Sociality brings to communications with tribes and to the way in which their companies should operate.

From our experience, a surprising number of companies start their Hyper-Social shift for the right reasons and with the right philosophy about human-centricity, but then slide into a mindset ruled by "What's in it for my company?" rather than "What's in it for people that would make them want to hang out with my company?" Time and again we see this metamorphosis take place, and it always has an unfortunate ending for the company. We often see companies shift into a "What's the return on investment?" frame of mind, in which business is a zero-sum game and giving the customer something of value is contingent upon extracting an immediate return.

A good rule of thumb to employ against falling victim to this myth is, check your terms of use statement. Would you feel comfortable pointing it out to the community members and having them comment on it? Also, as Don Peppers, cofounder of Peppers and Rogers and author of *The One to One Future*, recently reminded us:

I think that in the era of social media you should always step back from whatever marketing policy you're considering, whatever kind of new idea you have and ask yourself, "Gee, if this became public, would it be an embarrassment to us? Would we be proud of it? Would some of our customers hold it against us?" There's a really good chance that whatever your company is cooking up will become public in today's age and if you want to protect yourself then you really have to have clean hands, not just a good alibi.[8]

Management should demonstrate a clear vision as to why its company is embarking on deeper engagement with its customers, partners, employees, and detractors alike. The message needs to be communicated clearly and often that we now operate in a Hyper-Social economy in which authenticity, fairness, and transparency are rewarded, and that our human customers must be at the center of everything we do. To do anything less is to invite this reflexive corporate grasping for advantage.

Myth 7: You Can Control Your Brand

This chestnut appears repeatedly, usually during the same conversation in which the organization that is sponsoring the community tries to justify its intention to act in an anti-Hyper-Social fashion. This is a good point at which to recall that there are a number of ways to define *brand*, but most definitions acknowledge that the customer has some input. And given the clear increase in the power of humans to discuss products, services, and their experiences with your company, it is logical that the net balance of power in brand creation and maintenance has shifted permanently to the humans and away from the corporate owner. Notwithstanding this clear logic, it is surprising how many companies cling to the belief that by resisting the Hyper-Social shift, they are somehow ensuring the health of their brand, affirming that the customer cannot be trusted with the brand and that a brand is an asset that can be safely sequestered somewhere.

This idea stands in stark contrast to what Beth Comstock, global CMO of GE, told us about her thinking about marketing today: "It's this idea of letting go. I really learned this from my NBC experience. Your customers have a lot more access to things that you don't have control over and you're never going to get that control back, so how do you make it work for you?"[9]

Believers of the myth that "you can control your brand" should recall that *brand* is an organizational abstraction, and arguably is not held in the same esteem among outsiders as it is within the corporation. Therefore, clinging to the importance of your brand, and control of it, is very company-centric, not human-centric. This fascination with control usually extends beyond the brand. It moves to realms like controlling participation, discussion, or other Hyper-Social behaviors. Eventually, it leads to companies failing to respond to detractors, for instance, in the belief that withholding attention will somehow reduce the detractors' impact. It also leads to corporate policies that limit employee blogging or use of social media within the enterprise.

We believe that those companies that are making the Hyper-Social shift are learning from their discussions with their tribes that there are a number of dynamics affecting their brand, and that they have very little control over these dynamics. For instance, research on how people buy in online communities notes that the social status of the recommenders will influence the sale. In another study, researchers showed that by giving people a greater opportunity to participate in the creation of a watch, they could boost sales of the watches. In neither case did the company's shepherding of "brand" have any impact on the sale—instead, it was the engagement of Human 1.0 behaviors that influenced the purchase.

Summary

When people within your company start Hyper-Social programs, always ask yourself whether they are grounded in Hyper-Sociality. Are we thinking tribe and not market segment? Are we thinking knowledge networks and not channels? Are we being human-centric and not company-centric?

Then also ask yourself questions related to the myths we discussed in this chapter. Are we providing enough value in our Hyper-Social efforts? Do we have enough content that is worthy of people's attention? Why would people come to us in the first place, and why would they come back? Why would they engage with one another? How will this help us? Are we doing everything we can to humanize our presence in the marketplace? Are we adequately funding and staffing our Hyper-Social projects? Do our projects have a chance to move the needle? What happens if our competitors do the same thing first and succeed? Who else would want to engage with my tribes?

part four

HYPER-SOCIALITY IS NOT JUST ABOUT MARKETING: YOUR NEW HYPER-SOCIAL ORGANIZATION CHART

fourteen

Marketing 2.0 and the Rise of the CMO 2.0

F ew people would argue against the idea that marketing is in need of great change (marketers too, for that matter). Not only are the things it used to do no longer working, but they were probably the wrong set of things to do in the first place. Let's go back to one of our favorite Peter Drucker[1] quotes: "Because the purpose of business is to create a customer, the business enterprise has two—and only two—basic functions: marketing and innovation. Marketing and innovation produce results; all the rest are costs. Marketing is the distinguishing, unique function of the business."

That boiled-down approach, of course, is not what most marketers have been doing for the past century. Perhaps that is the reason why we should start thinking of marketing as *a way for organizations to behave in the marketplace* instead of as a department. Knowing that there is little chance that most companies will toss out their marketing departments altogether, the way Ducati[2] did, and remain successful, let's instead focus on what marketing should be in view of its business purpose: creating a customer and keeping that customer for as long as possible.

Looking at this simple definition through our Hyper-Social lens, creating a customer can happen in multiple ways—the old way and the way it should have been happening all along. In the old days, we would define a market segment based on people's individual characteristics. We marketers would then target them and *interrupt* them with information blasts about our products and our brands. Next, we would *isolate* them from their tribes so that the information that they had about us came only from us, and we would work hard to *inhibit* them from talking to any other vendors. John Hagel calls these the three I's of marketing: interrupt, isolate, and inhibit.

As marketers, we never recognized that the buying process is an inherently social process that is influenced by our tribes and our status within them. Marketers never tried to communicate with their customers in a way that was reciprocal, instead just bombarding them with (sometimes useless) information through mass channels of communication. The 4P's of marketing placed all aspects of the offering (product, place, price, and promotion) squarely at the center of all marketers' programs. We developed militaristic marketing approaches: fighting the battle for the mind,[3] targeting niche markets, outflanking competitors, and developing go-to-market strategies and campaigns. Everything became hierarchical and operationalized to the point where marketing became like finance—interchangeable from one industry to the next.

Now that our customers can be Hyper-Social, those old ways of doing things no longer work. Our customers and prospects reject and mistrust the information coming directly from our companies, and they make buying decisions based on online user reviews and knowledge-based conversations within their tribes that don't involve us. Some still want to talk with us—but in a meaningful and reciprocal way, and in their social context.

John Hagel suggested an alternative approach to the three I's of marketing, one that involves the three A's of marketing: attract, assist, and affiliate.[4] In order to attract prospects, we have to find ways to add value to their knowledge-based conversations. We need to assist both existing customers and prospects by making ourselves findable and by being helpful. And wherever possible, we have to affiliate with other solutions providers to satisfy the customer's real needs, not our need for sales revenue. We believe that maybe there is a fourth A for marketers, that of being the passionate *advocate* for the customer within our company. Instead of thinking of the CMO as the chief brand advocate in the marketplace, we should think of the CMO as the chief customer advocate, who represents the voice of the customer at the executive table. Let the customers be the product and brand advocates within their tribes—that makes for a nice reciprocal relationship.

Let's now take a closer look at the different parts of marketing through our Hyper-Social lens and see what happens.

Brand Positioning Takes On a New Meaning in a Hyper-Social World

We're not suggesting that you should do away with brand messaging and positioning altogether, since you cannot control it anyway. People need to know what bucket to put your offering in, and if they can't figure it out, they won't know how to assign value to what you have to offer. TiVo ended up in that pickle, with consumers not being quite sure what category of products TiVo occupied. Was it more like a DVD player, or was it more like a computer?

Rock-solid positioning will still affect your revenue and your profits. It's important to realize that you still have a seat at the customer's decision-making table—it's just a much more crowded table, and the size of your seat has been significantly reduced. You need to develop a point of view about your positioning and try to get your tribe to accept it voluntarily. As in most social interactions, your chances of getting someone to adopt your point of view are going to increase if you involve him early on. The more say you give him in the process of cocreating your products and services, and the earlier you get him involved (preferably at the product concept stage), the more he will embrace a shared view of the brand and the product positioning. An added benefit of cocreating products with your customers is that those who are involved in the design of new products will typically pay higher prices for those products.

Marketing executives have come to understand, sometimes the hard way, that brand perception is only as good as the last interaction that the customer had with the brand. When we spoke with Mark Colombo, senior vice president of digital access marketing at FedEx, he described the challenge as follows: "In the 50s and 60s, brands used to be built on a set of attributes. Now brands are built by customers, one experience at a time, and those experiences are, obviously, more and more often online experiences." You cannot just convey a brand's promise or a product's positioning through advertising and packaging anymore; you also need to deliver against that promise across all your other customer touch points, and at any time. That idea becomes especially challenging when you have complex product distribution channels, high numbers of people involved in your service delivery, or a high level of interaction between your customers and your customer service and support center. And remember, even if you are a B2B company, most of those touch points are staffed by humans. This is further complicated by user-generated touch points that people will encounter, such as online reviews, blogs, and online communities. All those touch points can make or break your brand, product, or service promise and position. Like many other things in marketing, this idea is not something new; it's just that we used to get away with problems in this area because our customers, prospects, and detractors could not behave Hyper-Socially and hold us accountable for our actions.

The way you control a brand promise through multiple touch points is not with the elaborate process manuals that we have grown accustomed to in business. The way to do it is by embracing Hyper-Sociality and all the messiness that comes with it, and allowing all the people involved in the process to behave like humans. Some companies, such as Zappos and JetBlue, achieve this through a shared values-based culture that creates a common sense of belonging among their employees. Others, like Western Union, achieve it by becoming customer-centric to a fault. Still others, like IBM, are doing it by encouraging all of their employees to set up communities with whomever they want, wherever they want, and about anything they want.

The key to success is to embrace all four tenets of Hyper-Sociality: think tribes, knowledge networks, customer-centricity, and willingness to accept some of the messiness that comes with Hyper-Sociality.

Lead Generation through the Hyper-Social Lens

"Where are my leads, and why am I getting crappy leads from my marketing department?" If you have been anywhere near the intersection of sales and marketing recently, these are questions that you have probably heard—perhaps many times over. Many senior sales executives are still looking for a predictable flow of leads at the end of a lead acquisition and nurturing "funnel." And while many marketers have been struggling with setting expectations for predictable lead delivery for more than a decade, their sense of panic and angst about this issue has risen to alarming levels.

So what's going on?

For starters, the funnel metaphor is broken. People no longer make buying decisions in a linear fashion, going from awareness, to familiarity, to consideration, evaluation, and purchase (or perhaps they never did). Second, people are now turning to their peers, friends, and other users of a particular product for advice instead of to the company. Third, the potential number of choices that prospects can have in their product consideration set is much larger than it has ever been before, and the information sources through which those products can become part of buyers' consideration sets has grown exponentially as well.

So how should you think differently about lead generation?

First off, ditch the funnel concept, and educate sales on why the funnel no longer works. It's neat to think of our buying process as a linear and rational process, and in the corporate world, this concept has certainly paid its dues as a reliable sales and marketing management tool. The problem is that we don't buy that way—the actual process is much more social and much messier. We buy because we bought the same thing before and it feels right, we buy because the purchase is going to make us look intelligent or help us snare a better mate, we buy to increase our status, or we buy for no good reason and make up a rationally acceptable story after the fact. We try to eliminate choices from our consideration set as quickly as possible and for seemingly random reasons. And for some products, we gladly switch our consideration set at the point of purchase. Our buying decisions are emotional ones. Now, that does not look like a funnel—does it?

In a Hyper-Social world, people don't want to be sold to. They prefer to make their buying decisions as part of a social process (even if they make decisions all by themselves), and they want the company to be involved only at the last minute, when they think they are ready to buy.

That does not take away the need for the company to become part of the buyer's consideration set. However, since that set will be heavily influenced by Hyper-Social activities and touch points that are out of your control, you will need to think differently about lead-generation activities and in some cases let go of traditional ways of creating leads.

So how do you increase your chances of becoming part of a prospect's consideration set? You can use traditional marketing programs, such as advertising, direct mail, e-mail marketing, and event marketing, to increase your chances of being noticed by potential customers and their tribal mates. You can also opt to take a more Hyper-Social approach and fuel the word of mouth that happens naturally within your customer tribes by designing the information about your offerings so that it can easily become part of their knowledge conversations, and by knowing where and when those conversations take place.

The good news for marketers who want to follow this path is that most buyers leave a digital trail as they move through their buying journey. When they ask friends on Twitter, you can see it. If they ask peers in communities, you can find it. And when they read or contribute to online reviews, you can get alerts on it. By engaging with your tribes through relevant content at the right times and in the right places, you may actually find that they will grant you a seat at their table. In order for that to happen, though, you need to be Hyper-Social—to act as humans who are part of those tribes and not corporate spokespeople, be willing to help members even if that means recommending things that are not part of your company's offerings, and listen more than you talk. You want to make customers' buying journey and all the social contraptions that surround that process as smooth as possible—and since people are self-herding, you want to give them reasons to switch to your offerings rather than stay with the one that they are familiar with.

One of the authors of this book used this method to set up a hugely successful lead-generation program for a large technology vendor. We found that the people we wanted to engage with were especially active on Twitter, so we hired two people with relevant domain expertise. Our two hires were clearly identifying themselves as representatives of our client and started to be generally helpful to prospects who were looking for help. They would point them to valuable resources, sometimes on the client's Web site or community, and sometimes on competing sites. Within two months, both of them had hundreds of followers, and the program became the most successful lead-generation program that our client had seen for that product line.

If you are still on the fence in terms of whether to engage directly with your tribes and thereby amplify word of mouth or to continue using more traditional marketing programs, let's review some other evidence that may sway your vote. Research has shown[5] that people who become customers as a result of positive word of mouth have twice the lifetime value of customers who become customers because of traditional marketing programs. They also bring in twice the number of new customers because of their word-of-mouth activity than the ones who were sold to.

How is that for a no-brainer?

Now, if you decide to leverage communities as part of your word-of-mouth efforts, which our Tribalization of Business Study shows is being done by more than 40 percent of companies that leverage online communities, you also have to prepare yourself for some counterintuitive consequences. Another research project[6] found that while the overall sales of products and services increase in communities, the leaders of your online communities may actually buy less from you. Sure enough, the main culprits here are again Human 1.0 reasons, not Web 2.0 reasons. Researchers found that the people with the highest status within the communities bought less because purchasing did not add to their status anymore—they felt at ease with their status. People who had less status, on the other hand, bought more, and the buying decisions of people with no status were not influenced by the community one way or the other.

Another counterintuitive aspect of increasing word of mouth is that the impact of that increased chatter on sales will be greater if it comes from your nonloyals rather than from your most loyal customers. It's also worth noting that the same research project[7] that came to that conclusion found that while the biggest buzzers among your most loyal customers are the opinion leaders, that is not the case among your nonloyals.

Finally, we could not have a section on lead generation without talking about search engine marketing or search engine optimization techniques to improve the relevance of your content in natural searches. These techniques allow you to deliver information in an ambient and contextual way when the prospect is searching for information about products and services. It's the low-hanging fruit that should be part of any comprehensive marketing plan. Unfortunately, the increasing competition for keywords may eventually result in decreasing returns for this method as well, so marketers shouldn't get complacent and come to rely exclusively on search marketing for lead generation.

Another low-hanging fruit that is not always used effectively is to proactively engage with customers about new products and services when they interact with you through your customer service and support center. But please don't give your service reps incentives to start selling product. Train them instead to ask how people use your product and see if they can perhaps suggest better alternatives, and above all, let them be Hyper-Social when they have the customer at the other end of the line. You'll see: amazing things can and will happen in Hyper-Social environments.

Setting up a page or buying banners on Facebook or MySpace may seem like a good idea because of the targeting capabilities—and some will see it as a way to become Hyper-Social. In reality, you will find that most people will not befriend a brand's fan page

unless there is some serious incentive or heavy couponing associated with it. So while it taps into a Human 1.0 trait, it's hardly a
Hyper-Social one. Discounts and coupons affect the pleasure side
of our brain, the part that gets addicted to things and constantly
needs more of them in order to derive the same pleasure. These
incentives destroy revenue and profitability for all the players in
the long run.

Advertising May Not Survive Hyper-Sociality

Even though advertising is not a marketing process, but an activity
in support of various marketing processes (awareness creation, lead
generation, brand positioning, and so on), it is important enough
to merit its own section in this chapter. Considering the budgets
that companies are allocating to advertising, it's important to
understand how fundamental market changes will affect the role
of advertising in the future marketing mix.

Let's first take a look at advertising through the Hyper-Social lens.
Most advertising is focused not on tribes, but on market segments.
When it does focus on tribes, as much of the MINI Cooper advertising does, it strengthens the link between the social activity that
happens in those tribes and the brand itself.

Most advertising is channel-focused, meant to reach a mass
audience through mass channels of communication. Sometimes
it is focused on the networks that matter, though, and when that
happens, ads go viral. A good example of that is the Dove Evolution ad, targeted at normal-looking women rather than models,
which got 44,000 views in its first day, 1,700,000 views in its
first month, and 12,000,000 views in its first year. Many ads are

product- or brand-centric, touting the features and benefits of particular brands and products. Some are human-centric, and even reciprocal—think of the ones that entertain and make you laugh. The problem is that we often forget the brands that brought us these entertaining ads.

This brings us to one of the underlying drivers that will change the face of advertising in the future: people have limited attention, and they are increasingly tuning out brands and products. In fact, all the drivers that allowed advertising to work are undergoing deep transformations. First, the number of media outlets available to advertisers is exploding. Next, an increasing number of products are vying for our attention—which is limited and which we can increasingly direct toward where we want it. Last, the advertisers themselves are getting fed up with the diminishing returns of eyeball-based advertising. When enough companies shift from paying for impressions and click-throughs to paying for engagement, which some companies have signaled they will do, the whole eyeball-based business model that sustained traditional media will start falling apart. Underlying most of these tectonic shifts is Hyper-Sociality at work.

Moving forward, what do you think advertisers will do? The early signs of where they will focus their attention and assign their budgets are already here. Some, like Kodak, will rally around product placement on popular TV shows like *The Apprentice*. Others will extend the product placement concept to online social games, like Farmville or Mafia Wars. While doing so may deliver great results in the short term, especially for the game producers, saturation of product messages will inevitably reach its peak, and people will once again tune out the brand messages. Almost all companies will try to capitalize on the psychological "halo" effect—a Human 1.0 bias in which we project certain characteristics from a particular situation onto the evaluation of other traits of a person or brand. So if companies allow us to do good and to feel good in the context of their brand, we will automatically extend that feeling to the brand. Most corporate social responsibility programs are the result of companies trying to capitalize on that halo effect.

Some brands take this idea one step further and integrate their programs with social networks or let you participate in their socially feel-good, do-good programs. Kellogg brought its Kellogg Cares social responsibility program, focused on relieving hunger in America, to Facebook in the hope that members would join its cause—and they did, to the tune of more than 200,000 members. American Express, through its Members Project,[8] is turning part of its charitable program into a Hyper-Social process by allowing people to submit their causes and letting others vote on which ones Amex should fund. While there is plenty of research to show that people will switch to socially responsible brands and buzz about them more than others, we predict that this too will have short-lived marketing results. As more and more brands become socially responsible, making this switch will become a norm for doing business, much like product quality, and not a competitive differentiator.

Still other brands are resorting to crowdsourcing their advertising to their user base. A successful example of that concept is the network Current TV, which turned it into a semisocial process by allowing its audiences to create and vote for viewer-created ad messages (VCAMs) on behalf of its advertisers. While the use of this model may reduce the cost of ad creation and increase the likelihood that ads are more customer-centric, the end result is still eyeball-based, a broken business model.

We need a fundamental shift in how we think about engaging customers and prospects. Engagement needs to happen in a Hyper-Social context, focused on tribal networks and human-centric to a great degree. Marketers have to move past individual behavioral targeting and instead engage with their customers and prospects based on what they know about them from their social profiles. This process can happen in online customer communities, open e-commerce platforms like Amazon, or social applications like the LivingSocial Visual Bookshelf on Facebook.

Realizing that the status quo is a powerful force, and that the technology to give users full control over their social profiles is not quite here yet, we know that these changes will not happen overnight. We are also conscious of Paul Saffo's rule on change:[9] "Change is never linear. Our expectations are linear, but new technologies come in 'S' curves, so we routinely overestimate short-term change and underestimate long-term change." Thus, we believe that the future of advertising in a Hyper-Social world will in fact be far more different from what we can now imagine.

Market Research 2.0 and CRM 2.0

In Chapter 5, we talked about how market research in a Hyper-Social world will need to change, and how the data from our in-house customer relationship management (CRM) systems should be used as part of customer support more than as part of sales. Let's circle back to this topic and highlight two other issues related to capturing and managing Hyper-Social customers and prospects.

Many industry leaders will argue that the return on investment (ROI) of traditional CRM systems has been dismal at best. Combine that with the fact that the latest economic crisis has rendered much of the data in these systems obsolete (people lost their job, some switched industries, many companies "right-sized," and so on), and you realize that good ROIs for CRM investments are not on the short-term horizon. What will make a difference is if we can combine our in-house CRM data with our customer and prospect dynamic (not static) social profiles that reside in their communities and tribal hangouts. If we host those communities ourselves, it's easy to marry the two, but if we don't, getting to those profiles becomes a whole lot trickier. Either we have to rely on the people who own the community platforms to give us access to those profiles, which could be fraught with complex privacy issues, or we have to wait until the members themselves can control their profiles and decide how much of those profiles to share with us. One way or the other, the future of CRM systems will have to include a social component—some call it social CRM.

Capturing customer social profiles will give us the ability to identify who has the most influence in a community and who has the biggest megaphone. For instance, it's easy to see, on Twitter, whose announcements are "re-tweeted" by more than 100 people more often than not.

Herein lies a danger, though. The knee-jerk reaction of most marketers will be to give preferential treatment to those people, extending better pricing to the influentials or demonstrating a greater willingness to bend the rules for those with bigger megaphones. Creating special pricing for the influentials is like giving them special leadership status. In the short term, it often leads to solid gains, but in the long run, it could ruin your ability to attract new customers. You see, leadership status is something that humans covet, and when they reach it, they hoard it and sometimes bend the rules to keep it to themselves and away from others, especially newbies. When communities do not refresh their leadership, but, instead, make it hard for new members to become leaders, they start repelling new members. The long-term prognosis for those communities is always the same: a slow but certain death. This is a problem with which all too many online gaming companies are already familiar.

No one will argue that knowing who has the biggest megaphone in social media is not immensely valuable. As Pete Blackshaw, the executive vice president for Nielsen Online Strategic Services, said to us when we spoke with him,[10] "The people who typically use the customer service back channels are the same people who tend to use megaphones to express their dissatisfaction. If you do it right you can use that information to develop a so-called user contribution system, where consumers help one another and become advocates for the brand—reducing not only your customer support cost but also other costs like consumer research." What you cannot do is allow your company to become a hostage of those with the biggest megaphones by showing a higher willingness to bend the rules for them. Marty St. George, the CMO at JetBlue, is very adamant about this point. He told us that catering too much to the most influential users in the community at JetBlue not only would undermine the decisions made by the company's front-line employees, but could eventually bring down the whole values-based culture that allows the company to be Hyper-Social in the first place.

PR and Thought Leadership

In case you missed it, traditional media is under siege. As we said in the advertising section, it does not look as if the eyeball-based business will survive Hyper-Sociality. The results so far: 30,000 reporters have left the industry since 2008.[11] Combine that statistic with the ongoing increase in people who are vying for the attention of the remaining mainstream media reporters, and you end up with a pretty bleak picture. PR and thought leadership will have to change fundamentally in order to deliver the same results.

Most PR agencies have seen the writing on the wall and have jumped on the social media bandwagon. They will now monitor your online chatter and deal with social media bloggers and influencers the same way they deal with traditional journalists. The problem is that they approach these influencers as representatives of a channel, not as the leaders of their tribes. For most of the PR agencies, social media is not a platform that enables Hyper-Sociality, it's another channel through which to send free messages to prospects.

In the face of dwindling traditional media outlets, companies like Procter & Gamble, MasterCard,[12] Microsoft, IBM, and H&R Block[13] are compensating by creating their own media outlets. P&G does it both online and offline with its *Rouge* magazine,[14] while companies like H&R Block and MasterCard set up YouTube channels to run customer contests, generate consumer-generated support tips, or otherwise engage with their audiences. Both Microsoft and IBM created online publications, but with very different approaches.

Unfortunately, most of those initiatives rely on the old media models. They are company-centric information channels focused on specific market segments. Take one retailer as an example. It originally hired a team of frugal moms (there are now more than 20) who normally blog about frugal shopping, and gave them all a free video camera to record video tips on how to shop frugally. Those videos are posted on a YouTube channel, where other frugal shoppers are encouraged to upload their own video clips. Periodically the company gives away one year of free groceries to the producer of the best video clip. Now this makes for a nice marketing program—one that probably does well for the retailer.

If the company had decided to take a more Hyper-Social approach however, it may have ended up with a movement that no one could stop. It could have augmented its YouTube channel with a Twitterlike system to allow people to post their frugal finds in real time. Along the way, the company would have enabled these moms to establish status within their tribes through the number of their followers, thereby inspiring a competitive streak and probably better "content" as a result of their individual efforts to get more followers. In a tribal environment like that, you would not even need monetary rewards—the program would work on reciprocity, the glue of Hyper-Sociality.

Sony took a different approach. The company recruited a number of dads to form the DigiDads.[15] The site describes the program as follows: "Each participant will receive various Sony products on loan and will be given different assignments that capture their family experiences using the products." In a lot of ways, this approach is not all that different from sending sample products to review editors at mainstream media publications. But here again, while Sony may have ended up with a nice marketing program, it could have tapped into the Hyper-Social nature of its buyers. Some of these blogger-dads may be the leaders of real tribes (their families), but they are not leaders of consumer electronics enthusiasts' tribes. And even if Sony had identified the right tribal leaders, it did not to provide a place for these tribes to engage and form stronger social bonds in the context of its products, the way Jeep did with its online and offline communities. Instead of approaching the program with a PR mindset, the company could have taken a more Hyper-Social course.

The difference between Microsoft's approach and that of IBM, which we described in Chapter 4, lies again in the Hyper-Social approach. IBM created the Internet Evolution online magazine[16] the same way you would create a mainstream media property. Microsoft, on the other hand, took a more Hyper-Social[17] approach. It set up its FASTforward thought leadership blog, focused the blog on the Enterprise 2.0 tribe (people who are passionately convinced that Web 2.0 tools within the enterprise will forever change the way we work), and recruited the leaders of that tribe to develop original content for the community instead of traditional reporters.

The Possible Future and the Probable Future of Marketing 2.0

A majority of the Marketing 2.0 efforts that we are seeing today are timid attempts to leverage Hyper-Sociality. More often than not, they are extensions of what companies already do today. Table 14-1 gives some examples of what we are likely to see in the short term, and what could happen if those same companies were to fully understand Hyper-Sociality.

When designing social media–based marketing programs, companies have to make sure not to think of them as timid, bolt-on

Table 14-1 Potential Marketing Shifts Driven by Hyper-Sociality

What Social Media Marketing Activity Are We Likely to Encounter in the Short Term?	What Social Media Marketing Activity Should We See in the Future?
Social media "listening" campaigns to track the chatter and to identify key influencers	Social media "sensing" and "engaging" campaigns to go beyond listening, to analyze what is being said, understand what is being meant, and make that information actionable, both internally and externally
YouTube/Facebook–based incentive marketing contests around specific brands or products	Sponsored YouTube channels or Facebook groups and pages centered around fan clubs, causes, and shared passions
Corporate blogs that are (1) indistinguishable from the rest of the corporate Web site and (2) controlled by the messaging/branding "police"	Editorially independent thought leadership blogs on the industry in which the company operates, a topic about which its customers care passionately, or advocacy related to the company's markets
Company-centric or product-centric virtual communities	Virtual communities centered around the users and their shared passions or causes
Company-specific industry-based virtual communities (e.g., a small business community)	Industry-focused communities that are sponsored by multiple vendors
Product innovation– or market insight–focused communities that are nothing more than sophisticated online suggestion boxes	Product innovation– and market insight–focused communities that leverage the social, i.e., to enable true co-innovation with customers, prospects, and detractors

programs, but instead think about how to turn traditional marketing processes into socially enabled processes.

Summary

Other than customer service, marketing is probably the part of your business that is most affected by the Hyper-Social shift. It is likely that Hyper-Sociality has already invaded all aspects of your marketing activities—whether you like it or not. Hopefully your leadership team is not resisting this shift, as doing so would be futile. If you want to challenge the thinking of your team and help steer it in the right direction, make sure to ask the following questions when you review marketing plans.

Why are we still wasting so much money on advertising? How has the efficacy of our lead-generation programs changed over time? Are we thinking about all the customer touch points when we talk about brand management? How are we amplifying word of mouth? Are we having success? Are our customers embracing our position, or is there a disconnect between what we think we stand for and how they perceive us? Are we getting our customers involved in our marketing activities? Do we understand how people make buying decisions for our products, or are we hanging on to the old funnel metaphor? Are we getting our customers addicted to coupons and discounts, or are they buying for other reasons? Do we have an idea of how long customers stay with us and why they defect? How are we conducting market research? Does it really tell us something about the future? Have we allowed the Hyper-Social shift to affect how we do PR and thought leadership? Do we have the right customer information in our CRM system?

fifteen

Customer Experience 2.0

What is the value of a customer? Customers' value is multi-faceted: They buy products; they may recommend products to other purchasers, serving roles as comarketers and cosalespeople; and they may support your business model by contributing more data, information, or content (as they do with Amazon's book reviews). Loyal customers may return repeatedly and buy over and over again. With such repeat business, you have to wonder, what attracted them to come back to you in a world that is brimming with other products? Perhaps it was a marketing message that they received or a word-of-mouth recommendation. Perhaps it was a coupon or some other incentive. More likely than not, however, such return business is the result of their enjoying an exemplary customer experience.

Do you know what sort of customer experience your customers are receiving, both from your company and from other people outside your company? And are you ascribing value to your different customers correctly? Customer experience is the internal and specific response that customers have to direct or indirect contact with a company. Direct contact can be with customer service, sales, or some other area of a company. Indirect contact can include recommendations, advertisements, ease of use, and criticisms or reviews that customers see. The sum of these various touch points determines the customer experience, and an enjoyable customer experience can be used to target specific high-potential customers.[1]

Customer Service 2.0 is customer service that is socially enabled—it's where people help one another, not where corporate processes simply work toward minimizing the time spent trying to resolve customers' problems and complaints. To get to Customer Service 2.0, companies first need to fix what Pete Blackshaw, the executive vice president of digital strategic services at Nielsen Online, calls the great "conversational divide" that exists between marketing and customer service. Blackshaw believes that it is unfortunate that customer service is so frequently considered a nonstrategic part of the business, so that there is little integration among what companies know about their customers from their CRM systems, their social media strategies, the promises they make through marketing, and what actually happens in their customer service departments when service representatives talk with customers.

It is curious how many people fail to realize that Customer Service 2.0 is a strategic part of the business, not just a cost center. Customer service is the one place where customers *expect* companies to participate in the conversation, and by engaging in those conversations, companies have the opportunity to turn customer service into an extension of their sales and marketing efforts.

Just as with marketing, most early attempts at Customer Service 2.0 have been timid and have failed to take full advantage of the true potential of Hyper-Sociality in customer service. Table 15-1 gives some examples of what we are likely to encounter in the short term and what could happen.

As part of the Tribalization of Business Study, we encountered many companies that have begun creating Customer Service 2.0 initiatives. One company whose program is being copied over and over again is Microsoft, which came up with a "Most Valuable Professional" (MVP) program to reward its most helpful customers. The uniqueness of the program is that people get rewarded for their past performance, not future expectations. In fact, there are

Table 15-1 Potential Customer Service Shifts Driven by Hyper-Sociality

What Social Media Customer Service Activity Are We Likely to Encounter in the Short Term?	What Social Media Customer Service Activity Should We See in the Future?
Social media–based customer service initiatives that are nothing more than online Q&A systems or bulletin boards	Social media–based customer service initiatives that truly leverage the reciprocity reflex that makes humans Hyper-Social—i.e., the desire to help and be helped
YouTube channels with company-produced how-to video clips to help customers use the product better	YouTube channels with consumer-generated video clips on what can be done with the product
Social media–based customer service initiatives that are totally disconnected from the rest of the customer support process	A fully integrated Hyper-Social customer service environment that crosses the traditional channels as well as social media
Top-down social media customer listening initiatives with an attempt at controlling the corporate response	Distributed social media listening initiatives where employees decide what to listen to and how to respond

no expectations of MVPs in the customer support communities. Because the MVPs have in essence already shown their inclination and ability to help others, they don't need to be encouraged to do so in the future. The MVPs have self-selected themselves as helpers, and there is no requirement that they continue to do so in the future. Programs run by other organizations have set future requirements, which has led people to become competitive and to engage in aggressive tactics to become higher rated.

As we've said before, it is amazing how few companies consider their customer support and customer service a strategic part of the business. An informal poll that we conducted among 50 companies found that almost none of them was thinking of making social media investments in customer service.

It makes you wonder, "What *are* they thinking?"

Customer service is a perfect area for companies to use social media and to leverage Hyper-Sociality. After all, most people do love helping other people. Plus, it's a given that at some point in the customer life cycle, most people do need help. And when people need help, they prefer to get it from other people rather than from organizations. In fact, one of the interesting "unexpected learnings" that we uncovered while conducting our yearly Tribalization of Business Study, in which we interviewed more than 500 companies on how they leverage online communities as part of their business, is this: people actually want to help companies and one another. This reciprocity ranked second among those features that, when included in a community, contributed most to the effectiveness of the community (see Figure 15-1).

It is also ironic how many companies do not consider customer service a strategic part of their business when you realize that the

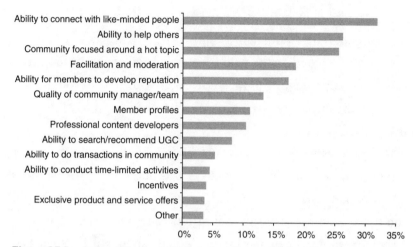

Figure 15.1 Community Features that Contribute Most to Effectiveness

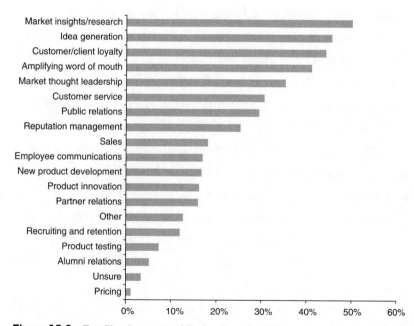

Figure 15-2 Top Five Purposes of Online Communities

biggest brand damage often occurs as the result of a poor customer service experience. Indeed, as shown in Figure 15-2, customer service was ranked sixth in the top purposes of online communities. If companies are, as they universally claim, truly focused on pleasing the customer, then customer service should be at the very top of the list.

Trying to assess how Hyper-Sociality might affect your customer service can be scary. Just ask yourself this question: What happens when nobody calls my help desk anymore? That question should prompt a series of increasingly disturbing questions: Where are customers going to get their support? What happens if they get bad advice? Am I liable if a misused product ends up injuring someone? Don't I need to protect my organization's investment in branding and product development by ensuring corporate customer service?

As we discussed in Chapter 3, Hyper-Sociality will eventually invade all aspects of customer service. It will not happen overnight, but it will happen, whether you like it or not. The drive for people to help one another is just too powerful a social force to stop. Just take a look at the popularity of social Q&As,[2] which have become the highest-trafficked areas not only on sites like Yahoo! and LinkedIn, but also on commercial sites like CarSpace. Or visit customer support boards like Dell's or Microsoft's, where you will find people helping others who seem to be putting in the hours of a full-time job—except that they are not getting paid for their efforts.[3] As we said before, the drive to help one another is caused by a reciprocity reflex—and once people realize that they can do so on a large scale, they will.

Smart businesspeople will see this trend as a positive one and tap the power of Hyper-Sociality through online communities to increase the effectiveness of their customer service departments while decreasing their costs. Visionary business leaders, on the other hand, will go a step beyond this and turn their customer service department into a revenue source rather than a cost center. These leaders are the ones who recognize that customer service is actually one of the most logical points at which to enter the most important conversations that are happening in their marketplace — those that happen between their customers. They will turn their customer service department into an extension of their marketing and sales departments, or, like Zappos, they will turn it into their sales and marketing department by empowering the customer care team to suggest alternative products. And just like TiVo or Ducati before them, they may also find their most promising new product innovation ideas that way.

Note that leveraging Hyper-Sociality in customer service is not the same as crowdsourcing your customer support activities. In some rare cases, there may be enough passion around your offering or a critical mass of users of your products to allow you to crowdsource customer service. In most cases, however, your support activities will remain at the center of the customer service community and will be amplified by that community, not replaced. Microsoft may be able to turn every single one of its support articles into a wiki and expect decent results from cocreating those support articles with its users. For most companies with fewer users, however, this could end up in disaster, with tons of inaccuracies, stale articles, or, worse, content that could expose you to liability. This is especially true in rapidly evolving markets where products are constantly being updated or upgraded, and where product variations introduce new customer support opportunities.

More so than for any other department within your company, taking advantage of Hyper-Sociality in customer support requires that your organization be allowed to behave in a Hyper-Social manner as well. If you truly want to support your customers, you need to empower your employees to engage those people where they are already gathering, and where they will be gathering next month. Sometimes that is at your organization's site, sometimes it is all over the place, and sometimes it's at a focused destination that you did not set up. The reason that this is so important is twofold: (1) people will seek help with your products from others in a variety of places, not just your customer support community, and (2) people want to be helped by people, not by faceless organizations.

While it may seem obvious that customers would seek support for your products in your customer support community, in reality, they will look for it across a multitude of sites. That is especially true for products that have complex distribution channels. When you have a problem with your shiny new Canon lens, do you look for help on Canon.com, Bestbuy.com, Amazon.com, or GetSatisfaction.com? Or do you turn to your independent photography enthusiast community, or maybe a photography Facebook group that you belong to? Such was the case with TiVo, where users set up a vibrant TiVo customer support community and ran it independently from the company. TiVo did not try to set up its own customer community and lure people away, which many companies might have attempted to do for the sake of controllable knowledge management—i.e., access to people's profiles, ability to mine the content, ability to generate reports, and so on. Instead, it engaged people where they were already hanging out, and turned the existing community into a real competitive advantage.[4]

Another company that allows its organization to behave Hyper-Socially in order to provide better customer support is Best Buy. An employee developed a very simple social media monitoring tool, called Spy,[5] that can easily be configured by any individual within or outside of the company. Spy scours the Internet in real time, looking for the terms that the user has defined—perhaps about a product, or perhaps about the company itself. Spy has no workflow system in the background to dictate what information is important or to whom it must be reported, nor does Spy produce the sophisticated reports that you can bring to your staff meeting every week. Instead, managers encourage employees to download the little application, monitor what they think is important, and engage where appropriate and without embarrassing the company. This program has been hugely successful in fostering awareness of the conversations about the company that are taking place. Best Buy realized that in order to take advantage of Hyper-Sociality in customer support, you need to behave Hyper-Socially yourself. Best Buy has since increased its commitment to Hyper-Social customer support by introducing Twelpforce on Twitter, where volunteers and Best Buy employees alike answer users' calls for help.

We are probably witnessing a change in mindset among customers as well, with customers' first thought being to reach for a search engine or social media tool and look for DIY solutions to their problem with a product. As a result of the increasing willingness of customers to get involved in problem solving, figuring out Customer Support 2.0 should be top of mind for all companies. The increasing tendency of products and services to have a software component, often updated remotely by the seller (consider MP3 players, GPS devices, and consumer software), will additionally contribute to the expectation of continuing and proactive after-sales care.

Moving toward Hyper-Social Customer Service

Organizations can take a number of actions to begin moving toward Hyper-Social customer service. First, all departments where the customer may go with complaints or questions—and these include sales, product development, and marketing—should be included in the information flow. All of the employees in these departments should be allowed to listen and to go where they need to go, both online and within the company, in order to engage in conversations with consumers. Super-users among the tribes should be cultivated, and resources should be devoted to the Customer Service 2.0 initiative so that content is curated to the extent possible. Super-users probably have important insights into how products and services can be improved, and hold positions of authority with their tribes, so their insights need to be communicated both internally and externally. Adding social Q&A functionality is likely to be well received, and customer service should determine whether customer experience goals, including customer satisfaction, repeat sales, and referrals, are being realized, and what sort of course corrections are warranted by the user feedback. Customer service should also be primarily responsible for making sure that findings are circulated to all stakeholders, and that return on investment (ROI) calculations are both appropriate and circulated to the appropriate decision makers (lest the initiative be shut down because of inadequate returns). For instance, if more loyal customers are being created through Hyper-Social customer service, a value should be ascribed to this enhanced loyalty, and then it should be communicated in terms of ROI.

Management must be thoughtful and innovative about incentives and metrics when it comes to customer care. Too many companies seem to develop metrics that encourage customers to leave the site or get off the phone as quickly as possible. Similarly, using "time on site" or highest number of page views (which we have seen companies measure in the Tribalization of Business Study) as a metric in the customer care realm is probably inappropriate as well. When Customer Care 2.0 becomes Hyper-Socialized, it will include employees outside of the formal customer care group. A salesperson, for instance, might find herself jumping into a conversation with a customer who is having trouble, and given her deep product knowledge and passion, she will probably be able to develop solutions to the customer's concerns. But if one of those solutions is a used or refurbished product with lower profit margins or a lower price point, will the salesperson be put in the position of pitting her financial performance against what is best for the customer? Has the company properly aligned her goals and incentives so that she doesn't feel conflicted about suggesting the lower-priced used product, or does the company instead demand that she reach a certain sales quota? Properly thinking through scenarios like this will be a critical process for companies that wish to manage the transition to Hyper-Social customer service successfully.

The best way to attract and retain customers in an increasingly noisy and competitive world is probably to be as helpful as possible, both before and after the purchase. This implies an emerging requirement for customer care people in your company: to enable greater flows of knowledge between your customers and *all* of the people who can help them with their problems. Implementing social Q&A features, like those mentioned previously, is a strong step in the right direction. You will also have to develop platforms of resources, people, and institutions that are preidentified and accessible to your customers so that they can get more value from your products and services than from those of your competitors.[6] The SAP Developer Network, where SAP users can gather to ask questions and help others, is one such example. This Hyper-Social customer care platform is so effective that the average response time for posted questions is about 17 minutes, and about 84 percent of the problems raised are resolved.

When the company has structured its systems to support Hyper-Social customer service, it can work beautifully, as Ram Menon of TIBCO recently told us:

> Well, the first thing we did is create a dedicated community for our customers where they had all those things: they had friends, they could post confidential information, they could share information.
>
> . . . We had this large travel firm post an issue with their production implementation of TIBCO. Normally if they called us for support, they would call tech support and the kind of support we provide costs us $1,000 a call. And within 20 minutes another architect at a big financial services' firm actually told him how to solve it and sent him a piece of code on this behind-the-moat kind of website.
>
> So, the thing you learn from that is, you created a community and the community helped each other and saved us money, but at the same time provided a positive experience for people within the TIBCO system to work with each other."[7]

Other companies, such as Kodak, report monitoring Twitter and then disseminating the top 20 or 30 complaints that crop up to different points in the company on a daily basis.[8] Mark Colombo, senior vice president of digital access marketing at FedEx, noted to us recently that using a listening platform that permits the company to immediately engage online with people who are having problems is having a profound impact on customer loyalty. Indeed, Colombo says that customers who have had a problem resolved to their satisfaction are actually more loyal than consumers who have never had a problem!

> And when someone does have a negative experience, we can jump into that post that is going on, and offer that customer support and help, where we can actually turn someone from being a negative word-of-mouth into positive word-of-mouth marketing. And what we have found, even on our loyalty work, customers who've never experienced a problem have lower loyalty than customers who experienced a problem that was resolved to their satisfaction.[9]

Colombo explained that FedEx's research indicated that optimizing key "customer touch points" contributed to loyalty. These touch points include a combination of brand and transactional experiences. FedEx data show that every point by which the company can improve its loyalty score translates into about $100 million added to the bottom line.[10] Moreover, Colombo notes that his research shows that if you try to solve people's problems, and you can't, as long as you were fair in trying to do so, the customer will continue using your services and promoting the company.[11]

Clearly there is an enormous opportunity for Hyper-Social companies to manage the customer relationship better. Indeed, customer relationship management (CRM) systems are the organization's attempt to develop a memory of its customers—to become more Hyper-Social. The customers already have a memory—indeed, they will recall past misdeeds and punish corporations for not doing what they consider to be fair.

It's important that you develop an accurate picture of your customer and develop better rapport with that customer in order to enhance the customer's true lifetime value. As some commentators note, customers are becoming the scarce resource in today's world, because of the plethora of products and services available on a global level.[12] The balance of power has shifted from the producer to the customer. As a result, you will need to leverage every touch point with that customer to ensure a superior customer experience, and to tap into both that customer's value as a buyer today and tomorrow and that customer's role as an advocate and an unpaid sales agent.

Summary

In a Hyper-Social world, your present and future customers interact with your organization in countless new ways. They are likely to be discussing your products and services on many different blogs, enthusiast Web sites, and social networks. They are evaluating your marketing promises, what your products actually provide, and how your organization resolves the differences between the promises and what was delivered. The tool that companies mainly use today to manage customer interactions is their CRM system. But is your

CRM tool capturing only purchasers' information, direct touch points, and complaint info? *Does it help you develop more trust in your company within your customer?* Does the tool include insight into where the customers came from—word of mouth, marketing campaign, or referrals? Does your system include information about what each person is saying about your company, brands, and products, and does it include information about what he's saying about your company on social media? Does it capture information on whether that person is a super-user, or otherwise helpful to other customers? And is the information being used to better help the customer? Or is the new information being used in an organizational system of sales rewards and measurements that were better suited for a previous era and are dangerously out of synch with present Hyper-Social customer care expectations?

sixteen

Sales 2.0

The sales function is one of the most studied, dissected, and carefully managed parts of the corporate machine. Modern businesses have long focused psychology, mathematics, game theory, and sophisticated software on sales, and have dramatically added science to what many consider to be an art. Curiously absent, however, has been a strong focus on how people purchase in groups; for most of recent history, sales has been a one-on-one game.

Accordingly, as we consider the implications of the Hyper-Social shift for the corporation, one of the locations that will experience a strong impact is the sales function. One of the fundamental changes to consider is that sales is no longer a one-on-one phenomenon; when you're trying to sell to social beings within a communicating group, the other members of that group can trump all of your sales and marketing efforts, and the group has a long memory for prior exchanges. Moreover, trust among members of the group (who in most cases have self-selected one another as members of the same tribe) is high, and this can be either a wonderful boost or a terrible impediment during the sales cycle.

It is unclear at this point how the relative importance of the corporate sales force will change. Will more of the sales function be ceded to the tribes? Will sales become irrelevant—won't buyers just fill in online forms when they want to order? How will salespeople deal with the perfect transparency of pricing that the community will impose? Historically, transparency on matters of pricing, terms, and incentives has not been encouraged or appreciated by salespeople.

On a positive note, prior to the Hyper-Social shift, sales were based on the sales "funnel"—many potential sales entered at the wide end, but only a few actual sales emerged from the narrow end. Ostensibly, the sales cycle should be more efficient and perhaps shorter when the tribe can communicate in real time on matters of interest and price. Since it is typically to the salesperson's advantage to spend as little time as possible on a sale, and therefore to shorten the sales cycle for whatever she is selling, this narrowing of the funnel could well be a positive development.

In addition, as SAP learned when it began selling developer kits to its developer tribe, customers who could not profitably be sold to in the past can now become customers when the tribe is doing the selling. Selling software to small developers in a one-off fashion was apparently unprofitable for SAP, but when it could qualify sales leads via its tribe, those individual customers suddenly became profitable customers.

Moreover, arguably the two greatest frustrations of salespeople, trying to sell the wrong product at the wrong price, could be ameliorated by the Hyper-Social shift. If the tribe participates in product development and pricing discussions as well, then sales-people should never find themselves in the position of trying to push a poorly priced product to a customer who has no interest.

Many of the changes driven by the Hyper-Social shift may well also prove to be boons to the salesperson. Faster innovation cycles, an explosion of choice in a global marketplace, and varying levels of trust in unfamiliar vendors may make the informed and familiar salesperson a preferred resource for helping consumers to make the right choice. Given the increased visibility that sales will have to the rest of the tribe, salespeople will be driven to seek enduring relationships rather than to exploit buyers with "quick hits" that maximize short-term profit, but tarnish that salesperson's repu-tation forever. As a result, salespeople will be able to capitalize on economies of scope, deriving more and more revenue from those buyers with whom they've worked successfully in the past.

If social media and coordinating technologies like the Internet result in lower coordination cost between players in the mar-ketplace, we may see an "unbundling"[1] of the corporation in the near future. Unbundling refers to the ability to disaggregate an organization into disparate functions, such as customer rela-tionship management, product innovation, and infrastructure subfirms, when the costs of coordinating these functions outside the organization are lower than the costs of coordinating them within the same company. This unbundling may result in sales-people beginning to serve a more important coordinating role, helping to source interlocking, complementary products from dif-ferent vendors that deliver the required functionality.

The increased incidence of products that require ongoing services (software upgrades, tweaks to keep products in regulatory compliance, and so on) may well transform the salesperson into a relationship manager who is expected to continue delivering even after the product has been sold. This expansion of the sale past the actual payment will also be driven by social media that permits buyers to continue to question the value of the sale long after it has been technically consummated. Conventional product recalls have typically involved major defects that affected many clients. Since the salesperson is likely to be the most immediate beneficiary (or victim) of a satisfactory (or unsatisfactory) sale, she will be the person who is most invested in ensuring that problems are resolved to the satisfaction of the tribe.

If this seems like a lot more work for the same sale that could have been finalized privately over a dinner in a smoky restaurant 10 years ago, consider the benefits. Salespeople will have a better idea of what consumers want, as consumers will talk about what they're buying, how much they paid, and what they think of the competition. Moreover, when the salesperson has satisfied them, they are likely to transmit this information far and wide, ensuring follow-up sales from other members of the tribe.

Let's take a closer look at how Hyper-Sociality can affect your sales activities. The most important conversations in a Hyper-Social business environment are no longer the ones that you have with your customers, prospects, and detractors—they are the ones that are taking place *among* them.

Now that they can, people will increasingly make their buying decisions based not on information coming from your marketing or sales department, but on information coming from their friends, their peers, or people in their tribes who are recognized as experts. People trust recommendations from friends more than any other source of information. Illustrating this trend, recent consumer research[2] shows that more than 50 percent of U.S. electronics consumers now rely on Web-based research to narrow the choice of brands rather than following the advice of the sales staff when choosing among products in stores. The same research predicted that by 2010, 80 percent of customers purchasing insurance products will do so based on information that does not come from the insurance companies.

How Sales Is Changing

If people make buying decisions based on recommendations from other people within their tribes, that means that you have to change the way you create and distribute branded content. You will also need to change the way you get people's attention and the way you sell to them.

Let's start with content.

You may be frustrated that only about 20 percent of the content developed by your marketers is actually used during the sales process. In a Hyper-Social world, you should brace yourself for worse. If you continue to develop corporate-speak-laden materials and lengthy product-centric white papers, nobody will use your content to inform his buying decision. Remember, the most important conversations are those among your customers, prospects, and detractors. What you need is content that has a high likelihood of becoming part of those conversations. That content needs to be findable, shareable, retellable, and, most important, valuable and compelling. In short, it needs to be "social-mediafied." While you can no longer control the message about your products and services, you can arm your champions to tell their story about your products and services within their tribes.

Are you interrupting people to get their attention? Stop wasting your money—that is no longer going to work. The dynamics of Hyper-Sociality will make interruption marketing increasingly ineffective and cost-prohibitive. To draw from our previous example again, you used to go to parties where nobody knew one another, and now you go to parties where there are strong social cliques. When nobody knows one another, it's easy to start a conversation or interrupt an existing one to start a new one. When there are strong social cliques present, you can stand in the presence of a group that is having a conversation for minutes without anyone even acknowledging your existence. That is exactly what Hyper-Sociality has done to your ability to have conversations with your audiences. In the past, the members of your audience had no way of communicating with one another in a scalable way, or to form tribes. So it was easy for you to interrupt them and pass along your information (and in many cases, to develop very bad habits in the process). Now, your customers have found one another and formed strong networks. Combine that with the fact that most people no longer trust the information that comes from you, and you can stand there all day waving your arms, only to find out that not one person will acknowledge your presence.

The same is true for sales. In a Hyper-Social world, and from your perspective, your goods may increasingly be bought and not necessarily sold. People will make most of their buying decisions by talking to other people within their tribes and will get you involved only in the later stages of the buying process—when they are ready to acquire the product or service that you are offering. Increasingly, the conversations that they have with others are happening in public — they can be monitored, they can be mined for insights, and they can be joined. So your salespeople need to become much more consultative, and to be available when and where questions arise within those consumer tribes. When marketing author Geoffrey Moore says, "sales IS social networking," he hits the proverbial nail on the head.[3] Sales should have been viewed in such a way all along, but it hasn't been, and that's why it needs to change. From now on, you will need to earn people's attention; you cannot just buy it anymore.

Of course, nobody can predict the full extent of Hyper-Sociality's impact on your sales team. You will need new talent, new systems, new metrics, and new sales management practices. You will also need to consider how the sales world has changed, and what the likely opportunities of a Hyper-Social firm look like. Sales used to be largely one-to-one, and to be heavy on educating the customer through catalogs, brochures, and documents. Indeed, the more complex the product or the more crowded the competitive set, the greater the amount of information needed to teach the customer how to use the product, how it solves their problem, and how it is better than the competitors' products. Historically, sales has been a matter of matching demand with hidden, restricted, or dispersed supply (consider the collectible, real estate, and auction markets, for instance). Salespeople often used information inequality to their benefit as well; they typically knew much more about what they were selling than the buyer knew about what he was purchasing. The ancient statement *caveat emptor* earned its longevity through centuries of validation.

The relatively recent introduction of the Internet has changed much of this opacity and evened the information gradient between buyer and seller. Indeed, new technologies have changed the matching of supply and demand so fundamentally across so many industries that to many it seems as though the salesperson's role is an endangered one. Given the ascent of powerful search platforms on the Internet, it appears that much of what salespeople used to do has been made irrelevant or marginalized. Sales positions in areas as different as commodity products and stock trading have been eliminated, adding support to the thesis that the golden age of the salesperson has ended.

But, just as technology and innovation have taken away from the sales profession, they have also brought new benefits. As our technical and communications systems have come to rely more on common standards and protocols (as opposed to the proprietary, closed platforms of yesteryear), the number of products that are available from multiple suppliers has exploded. The sheer number of brands (and brand extensions) has proliferated to what many consider a ridiculous extent.[4] Globalization has added so many more products and choices for any purchase that the sheer scale of choice can slow or paralyze a potential buyer's inclination to purchase. In addition, firms are increasingly buying more critical corporate functions as a result of outsourcing and seeking business efficiencies. The rise of practices such as "cloud computing" is emblematic of the new corporate behavior of decoupling important business processes from their physical or legacy businesses, and allowing a vendor to perform those functions at a lower cost and/or higher level of performance.

Thanks to social media, salespeople now have a rich new source of information about their customers and targets. As social media is increasingly adopted by organizations, salespeople will have unprecedented access to information about the target company, its issues, and the humans there who will be the actual buyers of products and services. The tribes that these people belong to will also provide insight into the philosophies, interests, concerns, and preferences of buyers. Organizations will need to learn how to learn from salespeople. Indeed, the sales force is increasingly privy to the sequence of events that noncustomers pass through prior to becoming customers. Will their own organization be aware of what its salespeople are learning? How will this information from the sales force be captured and communicated to other groups, such as product development, customer support, or knowledge management? Since human relationships become more important in Hyper-Social environments, won't salespeople hold the keys to the kingdom, as they are the people who are trusted by the people who buy?

So, applying our view that business processes are generally improved by becoming Hyper-Social, what might happen to the sales function in the process? Social media can certainly help buyers make these sorts of difficult or high-risk purchase decisions, but you are relying on, among other things, your ability to adequately educate the community on the particulars of your technical requirements. Moreover, you may want to be circumspect in what you communicate to the community; given how critical these purchases could be to your company, you may decide that it is unwise to post these plans on a publicly available blog for competitors to see.

Perhaps, then, it would be better, from the Hyper-Social user's perspective, to have someone who is more knowledgeable than she is, and who is dedicated to providing value over an extended relationship, inserted into the sales process. This person, who is deeply aware of the buyer's specific and often idiosyncratic needs, and who has a vested interest in the long-term satisfaction of the potential buyer, is the sort of person the salesperson of the future may be.[5]

Also, this process that we're describing assumes that the potential buyer has the time and inclination to even determine that he wants to buy. As the complexity of business solutions increases, as a result of collapsed cycle times and technological advances, buyers will find it increasingly difficult to scan the environment and match new solutions to present or emerging business issues. This proactive creation of solutions is another example of the critical role that salespeople will have going forward, and one that should increase the trust relationship they have with their buyers.

The defense industry, for example, has long been characterized by sales professionals who work closely with buyers to understand how a complex system can be conceived, built, and then configured. Typically called a "diagnostic" sales model, it requires the salesperson to act almost as an outsourced company executive, who needs to consider the buyer's complex and unique interests, and then suggest a combination of her products (and perhaps the products of others) that will satisfy the buyer's needs. Such a diagnostic system puts great demands on the salesperson: She must have a deep knowledge of the customer's business, external factors, purchase systems, and the product's relationship to the company's business goals. She must juggle this constant learning about the customer with the need to hit sales numbers and to develop new leads. This is an area in which her employer can add unique value by providing the salesperson with the ability to learn even more than she could on her own through skills training and access to knowledge flows that she would not have access to as an individual.

An additional force that is at work in redefining the salesperson's role is the transition from a "push" model of sales to a "pull" model that commentators feel is afoot.[6] Given the unprecedented number of products available, some theorize that the old model of pushing products is untenable. Instead, assisting clients in pulling appropriate solutions to their complex problems will become another value that salespeople add to the ecosystem.

Another issue to consider is the ever-increasing costs of sales in most organizations. Burgeoning costs associated with travel, lodging, and entertainment—along with increasing concern about carbon emissions—will reduce the attractiveness of a salesperson's actually being on the road more in the future. Leveraging Hyper-Sociality and using social media, Web conferencing, and social networks is potentially a superior replacement of these costs in many cases, permitting organizations to shift easily to more of an "inside sales" organization, and enabling sales professionals to do more with less during this recession of historic scale.

Emerging technologies, such as online virtual worlds like Second Life, also have the potential to bring more Hyper-Sociality to the sales process. We can only imagine how these virtual environments, which are much more interactive and social than static text or graphics pages, will even further enable the interaction between buyer and seller. Aside from the obvious parallel to real human interactions, the rich graphical environment will also permit rich product demonstrations, tutorials, and troubleshooting of complex products.

Shifting to Sales 2.0

Research indicates that declining sales effectiveness was top of mind for CEOs as we entered the present global economic recession. Other data suggest that it is taking longer for sales professionals to get up to full productivity, and that the top-performing 10 percent of sales companies had the very highest level of Internet use.[7] Based on all these indicators, Sales 1.0 is clearly not working as well as it once did, and a Hyper-Social shift, where buyers and sellers connect in tribes via social media, is a possible solution. Some of the most effective processes could include team selling and best practices sharing between salespeople and other business functions (such as customer support and marketing). Will your organization be able to lead this shift to Sales 2.0, or merely observe it?

Preliminary research indicates that there is a large gap between the promise that organizations see in Hyper-Social sales and what their ability to execute on that promise has been. For instance, looking at Figures 16-1 and 16-2, we see that although more than 20 percent of respondents in our 2009 Tribalization of Business Study identified "increasing sales" as a key business objective of their online communities, less than 10 percent of respondents believed that they had successfully achieved that objective.

Clearly, the process of Hyper-Socializing sales can be successfully implemented, but a significant number of those that attempt it fail to enjoy the desired outcome of increased sales. There are a number of factors that we believe will improve the Hyper-Socialization of sales functions going forward, and that will require organizational attention.

First, it is important to recognize that as the sales process is made a social process, it is likely that new salespeople will be created. Perhaps they will be the developers of related products who steer potential customers to a company via referrals. Perhaps product development or customer service staffers will show a strong aptitude for selling the product, and for matching it with

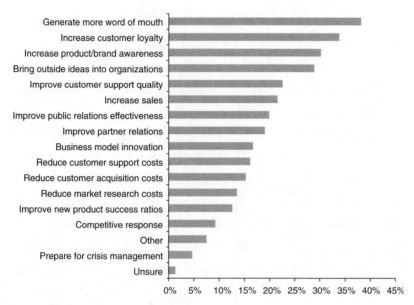

Figure 16-1 Business Objectives of Communities

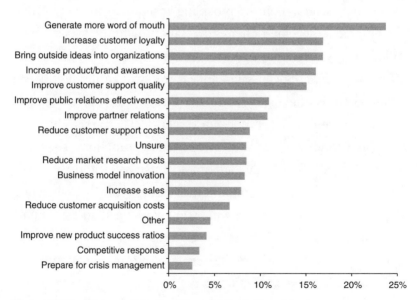

Figure 16-2 Business Objectives Successfully Achieved

the proper client and client problem. We know that developer communities like the SAP Developer Network help to generate interest and product sales. Perhaps the new salespeople will be satisfied customers who tell other members of the tribe about their good experiences and the value that they received. The challenge for the organization will be to identify these new salespeople and provide them or buyers with additional information or support.

In addition, it is likely that the Hyper-Social shift in sales will drive the need for developing new metrics (instead of just simple sales numbers). Perhaps the salespeople may be measured in part on their net contribution to knowledge flows by populating knowledge management systems with client information, identifying the people in the tribe who are most likely to refer business, or identifying those who are most likely to buy in the future. Organizations should consider how to reward salespeople for assisting in product development or providing insights to marketing that can be used to develop richer conversations with the tribes.

The organization needs to consider other potential issues raised by a Hyper-Social sales shift as well. Since product development, marketing, sales, and customer service are all equally connected with the customer in a Hyper-Social market, the organization cannot divorce any one of these functions from the others and expect optimal outcomes. Since sales and the other functions will be having more conversations with the tribes in a Hyper-Social market, the organization will need to coordinate these more frequent conversations more carefully in order to bring value. Organizations will need to leverage information technology and knowledge management systems to permit employees to see all interactions with employees in sales, product development, customer support, and marketing, and to learn from colleagues' interactions with the tribe. Indeed, customers and other members of the tribe may be having simultaneous conversations with multiple parts of the company. Such conversations almost never took place in the past in most companies. Now your knowledge flows and interactions with the client must be informed by what you just said to him today or what a different business function said to him a month ago. If a customer was speaking about product features with one of your colleagues in marketing this morning on a social network, and you are now helping him with a support question via Twitter, the onus is on you and your information systems to know that, and to know that the person is also an MVP in your support community. Anything less will demonstrate lack of interest in providing value, will hurt authenticity, and will be a harmful touch point in the series of contacts that build the customer experience and enable sales.

Summary

As the Hyper-Social shift continues, the sales function will likely undergo tremendous change. One critical change will be that fewer sales will take place one-on-one between a buyer and a seller; because of Hyper-Social behavior and social media, organizations will find themselves increasingly selling to people who reach out to tribes for guidance and information. As a result, sales terms, concessions, and prices are likely to be known not only by the buyer, but by her tribe as well. Is your organization developing salespeople with the right skills to close sales in such an open, transparent marketplace? Are your organization's sales compensation plans structured to ensure the optimal use of your salespeople as information sources and external emissaries, or are they rewarded solely for closing a sale? Is your organization carefully considering how the sales force could be empowered to provide even greater value outside of the actual sale?

seventeen

Product Development 2.0 and Innovation 2.0

The cofounder of Sun Microsystems, Bill Joy, has been quoted as saying that there are always more smart people outside your company than within it. With the Hyper-Social shift that we are witnessing right now, it's important to know that those smart people outside your company can help you design and develop your company's latest products and services.

Some of the most immediate and exciting applications of how Hyper-Sociality can change your company are in the areas of product development and innovation. Indeed, there has been a significant amount of recent experimentation in this realm, and the astute businessperson need not look far to see how his peers are using tribes to improve, reconfigure, or completely replace product development and innovation. The actual tactics used span a wide spectrum, from users innovating new features to people outside the company being paid to solve thorny problems, to companies receiving virtually all their product ideas from people outside the company. And it's not only products that we see tribes influencing—business models are also being improved by opening up corporate processes to the tribes and socializing these processes. Companies are using Hyper-Social innovation to improve product development, business models, and corporate processes.

Product Development 2.0

Let's look first at how Hyper-Sociality is affecting product development. Intuitively, businesspeople know that successful product development, and creating innovative goods and services for the customer, is one of the core goals of most companies. Products that the user desires and that are differentiated from those offered by the competition drive profits and pricing power. Few people want to sell a commodity, a me-too product that is distinguished only by price. Any manager worth her salt wants to develop the new mousetrap for which the world will clamor, and to have the associated pricing power.

Unfortunately, successful product development in the conventional sense has proved to be notoriously difficult to get right. The majority of new products that are introduced fail, and those that work tend not to be followed up effectively with similar hits. And, for the reasons explored by Clay Christensen in his series of books on disruption theory, companies' incentive plans, corporate structure, and product development and introduction processes are geared more toward regularly giving present consumers "improved" products that are designed more to support existing profitable businesses than to provide customers with what they truly want.

The Hyper-Social shift promises to dramatically reform product development in fundamental ways. First, there are new inputs to consider. Product development today is often an insular process of passing best estimates of customer desires through a proprietary corporate process of determining what can be provided profitably and in conformance with distribution, competitive, regulatory, and strategic constraints. R&D and marketing typically are part of the product development process, and a snapshot of customer demand is periodically checked to see how the new product comports with that screen shot of customer demand. Depending on the competitive nature of the industry and the products that are being created, the specifics of product development vary widely. As Table 17-1 details, however, companies in most industries that have been socializing the product development process have met with great success.

As these companies show, the social humans who are the target consumers of your products and services often are very happy to participate in product development (or to "cocreate"), and can be quite good at it. What we see from the marketplace, however, is that companies are following more of a gradual approach toward tribe-based product development. When we surveyed hundreds of companies for our 2009 Tribalization of Business Study, we found that the top five corporate purposes of online communities were

- Market insights/research (50 percent cited this as a top five purpose of their online community)

- Idea generation (46 percent cited this as a top five purpose of their online community)

- Customer/client loyalty (44 percent cited this as a top five purpose of their online community)

Table 17-1 Examples of Hyper-Social Product Development

Name of Company	Aspects of Hyper-Social Product Development
Threadless	T-shirt company produces only designs developed by the community
Intuit	Community of users generates ideas for new features in popular tax preparation and accounting software
InnoCentive	Community of problem solvers is linked with problems; large companies such as Colgate-Palmolive submit problems, and more than 120,000 experts submit solutions
Chumby	Consumer computer device whose final design and function is determined by external developers and hackers
IdeaStorm	Dell Web site that solicits users' ideas on new features for Dell products
Neuros	Consumer electronics company that receives 50 percent of product development ideas from open-source software community
Kodak	Developed simplified exposure settings on new digital camera on the basis of user recommendations
Cisco	I-Prize competition sought ideas from external marketplace on where the next $1 billion Cisco market opportunity might lie
Procter & Gamble	Developed program to solicit the assistance of outside experts in solving product issues
Mozilla	Community of product users has written more than 40 percent of the software code in the Firefox browser

- Amplifying word of mouth (42 percent cited this as a top five purpose of their online community)

- Market thought leadership (35 percent cited this as a top five purpose of their online community)

Only 17 percent of the companies surveyed cited new product development as a top five purpose of their corporate-sponsored online communities, however. And only 7 percent cited product testing as a top five purpose of their online communities.

We believe there are several reasons for this subordination of product development to more conventional marketing activities in corporate online communities. First, since the marketing function is most likely to be the sponsor of online corporate communities,[1] it's logical that marketing goals would be the primary drivers of those communities. In addition, at this early point in the Hyper-Social shift, companies may be merely porting their prior marketing activities to a new platform—that online place where the tribes are congregating. Many of the executives who are in charge obviously have not made the next conceptual leap to moving product development to the tribes as well. As we discuss in Chapter 10, relinquishing that degree of control to the consumer or to non-customers (and possibly to other functions within the company) frequently challenges management.

Another outcome of product development moving to the tribe is that cycle times are likely to contract sharply, as the community of interested users, fans, and detractors will provide its input immediately and constantly until its comments have been acknowledged (ideally, from the vantage point of the community, by affecting the next iteration of the product or service). Given this dynamic, present product development cycles, which are keyed more to the time of year, what the competition is doing, or technological innovations that enable product innovation, will have to yield to a much better driver: what the customers are asking for in highly visible online forums.

Also, given the networked nature of Hyper-Social product development, companies will need to develop alternative methods for determining when a product is finished or when it is complete. As Susan Lavington, senior vice president of marketing at *USA Today*, recently told us about the product development process with readers at her newspaper:

> We're in constant evolution. It doesn't have to be perfect, it doesn't have to have all the bells and whistles when we launch it and we're just going to keep working on it and improving it. That's something that we did embrace in our early years and continue to try to embrace and get to that idea of we're in "constant beta," and that's just the way life is these days.[2]

Another likely impact on product development will be how companies organize themselves to create new products or enhancements to existing ones. It's not unimaginable either that in-house R&D or product development will dramatically shrink, or that they will grow to include people with new skill sets. Corporate researchers who formerly spent most of their time researching what the purchaser might want in new products will have new roles as that information is generated in real time through interaction with the tribes. Internal groups that have had the task of forecasting future demand and manufacturing needs would similarly undergo significant change as customer demand becomes increasingly visible and quantifiable.

Yet another change that we can expect in product development will be the emergence of completely new products from perhaps noncommercial locations. Take the open-source phenomenon, for instance, where passionate but unpaid computer programmers write professional-grade software that is then made available for free use and further development by others. Product development may well take place elsewhere (for instance, in the open-source community) and drive immediate and substantial opportunities for your company to develop associated products for markets that someone else has identified and pioneered!

Hyper-Social product development could also serve a critical marketing function, reaching people who are inclined to buy the product or who participated in its creation, and those who became interested in the product through their membership in a tribe. Deloitte's 2009 State of the Media Democracy Survey indicates that 63 percent of American consumers learned of a new product for the first time while they were online, and 51 percent say that they purchased a product because of an online review. If these people were allowed to participate in the product development process as well, imagine what that could do to improve your commercial prospects. As Barry Judge, CMO of Best Buy, noted in a recent discussion with us, "I think you can really turn consumers on because they'd love to be part of the creation, not just getting feedback on what you created. We have to figure out how to turn that on."[3] Dan Ariely, behavioral economist and author of the book *Predictably Irrational,* echoes this when he observes that one of the best ways to get more and better ideas from people is to let them see what other people are building on top of their ideas.[4]

One of the key revelations here, however, is that by adopting a Hyper-Social approach to product development, you are opening product development to smart people everywhere, not just in your company. As prescient executives have noted, no one company will ever employ the majority of the world's smartest people. Hyper-

Social product development won't be a panacea for everything that ails corporate product development groups, but it could be one of the most potent tools for product development to emerge since disruption theory.

Possible Drawbacks

A fair point to raise at this juncture is whether the voice of the communities or the crowd will provide *better* information, as opposed to just *more* information. Although we are early in the process of having users materially contribute to product development, and we don't have a lot of data to rely on, we do see that many of the ideas cannot (for various good reasons) be incorporated into new products. For instance, Caroline Dietz, manager of Dell's IdeaStorm, notes that product ideas from the online community have to make business sense. "When we're making decisions on what to do with these ideas, whether or not it plays into our long-term strategy definitely plays a role. . . . A lot of times there may be something that's a customer demand, but it may not serve our entire customer population."[5]

Another fair issue to flag here is that even though a winning idea may bubble up from the new participants in product development, the size of the market associated with that innovation may not be within the range of potential revenues or profits that the company typically requires. Beth Comstock, GE's chief marketing officer, recently observed that new product ideas sometimes don't match up with the size of the opportunity that an organization of GE's scale requires. Some of these ideas can go on to success, however, if GE attaches them to a larger platform of related products, or if it partners with smaller enterprises that can bring such smaller innovations to market profitably.

Perhaps this portends a new era of partnering between larger and smaller companies, or the emergence of a hybrid model in which a company suggests the basic platform for a new product, based on what can be produced at a certain price point and with a given technological level. Then the crowd will polish it and enhance it with those features and nuances that only a smaller crowd of specialized users would require. And perhaps others will then market the product and continue improving it, leaving manufacturing and distribution to those commercial enterprises that have special expertise or scale advantages in those areas.

In addition, it is arguable that truly breakthrough products cannot be produced effectively through a Hyper-Social committee, so to speak. As Henry Ford wryly noted, if he had given people what they wanted, he wouldn't have created the automobile; he would have produced a faster horse. But this issue doesn't point to the failure of Hyper-Socializing product development. Rather, it points to the company acting in a different capacity—as an innovator, rather than as a manufacturer or distributor. Indeed, the rise of Hyper-Social product development is likely to present companies with a critical question that is bound to keep executives busy for the next few years: What business are we in? Are we a product development company, privy to certain little-known technological developments that will enable new products that our customers would never imagine possible, or are we experts at delivering products at the lowest cost? Or are we experts at customer development and customer relationship management, and we will leave product development and manufacturing to others? This atomization of the complex modern corporation, driven by the new lower costs of communication and coordination conferred by digital technologies and the Internet, is an increasingly likely outcome for many companies.

Innovation 2.0

So, it is clear that product development and innovation will be dramatically affected by the Hyper-Social shift. And it is encouraging that some executives, like Kristin Peck, the senior vice president of worldwide strategy and innovation at Pfizer, are asking themselves the right question: "When we thought about innovation, we asked ourselves, 'how do we make it more social?'" But in addition to changing the structure of the product development team and perhaps the R&D team, what other impacts will making innovation a social process have on the organization and its ability to innovate?

As noted earlier, enabling new innovation processes will spur companies to reconsider exactly what business they are in. For instance, a vendor of witty T-shirts might realize that it's in the business of product innovation; since it is using crowdsourced designs, it can perfectly predict what its customers want. Why, then, would it continue to produce products, ship them, and handle returns as well? Wouldn't it be better to offload those functions to someone like Amazon, and focus all its resources on what it does best (assembling and polling its tribes)? This "unbundling" of the corporation is likely to accelerate as various corporate functions become less important or superfluous because of the interaction with tribes.

The changing nature of product development and innovation may well alter other key corporate functions. For instance, in a situation in which the tribes are influencing product design, the organization becomes more of a filter and reality checker (i.e., can that product ever be built profitably?) than a raw innovation house. The firm requires more researchers and more number crunchers to cycle through the possibilities, and fewer creative folks in-house to generate the ideas. It may also require more financial types to position the company with investors and to model capital needs so that it can raise additional funds to bring cocreated products to market.

And if these changes in product innovation occur, will the organization be nimble enough to respond to the collapsed cycle times, negotiate the new codevelopment relationship with its tribes, and make the significant changes in its inventory management and sales channels? The company's leaders should start thinking about the vested interests of those functions that may be challenged, and what sorts of obstacles they might pose.

Competitively, how will the company capture information and insight before competitors who are lurking in the community are able to appropriate them? How will companies compete on innovation in the future when they are all speaking with, or perhaps cocreating with, the same communities? Developing value propositions and other strategies that attract and retain the most creative tribes will clearly become critical to successful companies.

Companies will also need to avoid thinking that this interaction with passionate cocreators translates only into new product ideas; the interaction might also lead to deeper appreciation of customer frustrations with existing products or corporate processes, culminating in improved customer experiences with the company, its products, and its brands.

Indeed, cocreation can yield many other positive outcomes as well. Not only will products potentially be more aligned with what customers want, but quality can be higher because having more people with a vested interest in the product will ensure that bugs are detected and cured early on and easily. By opening up organizational boundaries and allowing people within the company to interact with people outside of the company, new perspectives and creative juices will begin to flow. New information flows will begin bubbling up between formerly disconnected humans, and teams can begin learning from formerly undiscovered resources, both within and outside the enterprise. These new information flows may create new value for customers or turn into new revenue streams for the company.

As cocreation with noncompany individuals grows, wise managers will give employees greater freedom to self-select the projects that they want to work on. Leaders will also experiment more frequently with new products, services, and processes, running an open laboratory of sorts where the customer is free to experiment and to vote on what the company should tweak or bring to market. Since innovation is more likely when different disciplines are seated at the same problem-solving table, visionary leaders will permit formerly separate groups and tribes to work on the same project and problems, eroding corporate silos, which are more suited to the slow-moving marketplaces of yore. Historically powerful corporate groups that are intent on maintaining the status quo will be kept at bay by those forward-thinking leaders who look to customers and prediction markets as arbiters of what the company should be creating or selling. Managers will realize that they are in fact now managing *for* creativity, not trying to *manage* creativity.

Vibrant cocreation with the customer, and the emergence of volunteers who provide invaluable insight into how to improve product and service offerings, will ultimately affect the culture of the company. That much-sought-after *human-centricity* that we discuss in Chapter 6 stands a much greater chance of taking root and flourishing within this sort of corporate culture as management and employees begin to see the virtuous cycle that can be created by an engaged customer sharing value with a Hyper-Social company.

Summary

Hyper-Sociality provides an elegant solution to Bill Joy's insightful observation that "there are always more smart people outside your company than within it." By leveraging your organization's tribes, you may improve and spur product development and innovation. The increased cocreation with customers and business partners may itself lead to business model innovations, and to the organization's realization that it should focus on certain activities and disengage from others. Is your organization taking the necessary steps to permit Hyper-Social product development and innovation? Is it listening to the tribes and giving them the tools, information, and feedback needed for effective innovation? Is your organization anticipating internal conflicts that might arise as a result of Hyper-Social innovation, and developing systems that reward both employees and customers for participating in Product Development 2.0? Who will own these jointly created products, and what will your organization's core business look like five years from now?

eighteen

Talent 2.0

Given the discussion up to this point about Hyper-Sociality, and about how important social interaction is to humans, it shouldn't be surprising that "human capital," the people who actually make up companies, is increasingly crucial to the proper functioning of the organization. Indeed, CEOs and other top executives routinely and regularly remind us that their people are their top priority, the chief reason that their companies have been successful, and that people are the only assets that really matter. And deep down, we all know that this is true—buildings, products, and patents are not the assets that directly generate value. These assets might appear to be the drivers of revenue and success, but all of them are abstractions of human intellect, creativity, and collaboration. They are the artifacts that humans leave behind when they're done creating. Through various proportions of inspiration, perspiration, and dedication, humans create things and information that they and others can use, or put to work.

But if you've watched organizations at work for the past 100 years or so, they seem to have forgotten these apparently self-evident truths. We saw recently that in the face of a global recession, one of the first ways in which companies cut costs was by thinning the human ranks. It is curious, and telling, that the cost-reduction lever that is pulled first is often the one attached to human capital. If companies still haven't grasped the importance of their human assets, the Hyper-Social shift will bring it to the forefront. As a company undergoes the Hyper-Social shift, the abilities and activities of its human capital need to change as well. In many cases, companies also need to readjust their view of what skills and talents their employees should possess, how they should ideally manage those employees, and how they can recruit and develop those employees more effectively. In addition, managers must become more aware of how their internal talent management philosophy will need to evolve in order to mesh with the increased Hyper-Sociality that is sweeping over the marketplace.

Prevailing in the race for the talent that will excel in the coming Hyper-Social economy requires the engagement of not only the human resources department, but the entire leadership team. This is because effective reengineering of talent will require a rewrite of many of the firm's operations, structures, and strategies. Indeed, commentators have stressed the need for taking a new view of talent in this emerging networked, dynamic, and increasingly social economy.[1] As leaders begin to prepare for the shift to Hyper-Sociality, they must consider whether employees with skills that were developed and selected 10 years ago will be able to interact with users in real time, communicating transparently and authentically, using new social media tools. Do these employees have the depth of knowledge about all of the company's offerings, and how these might be tailored and delivered to delight a vocal tribe of customers that may stretch around the globe? Are these employees sufficiently trained in what they can bind the corporation to, and aware of where in the company they need to go to convey customer insights and find what they need to develop adequate responses to the demands they are seeing from the market? Are they passionate about the products that they produce and the people who consume them? An organization's answers to these questions will indicate how closely its human capital philosophy is aligned with the evolving Hyper-Social shift.

Indeed, Susan Lavington, senior vice president of marketing at *USA Today*, cited some of these challenges in a recent conversation with us:

> And I empathize with them [*USA Today*'s journalists] when they've been asked to keep up what they're doing in print, but now have this really 24/7 community that they are in charge of and people want to talk to them on a regular basis and curate and bring content in and point out the latest happenings. . . . They're passionate about their beats, they're passionate about the content that they create. So, finding other people who are passionate about it too has been very rewarding for them.[2]

As information technology becomes increasingly ingrained in corporate functions, it will become harder for rigid, rules-based software systems to react to unexpected, human-driven exceptions to what the programmers anticipated. How many existing customer relationship management, supply-chain, or pricing systems were designed to react to customers by providing real-time feedback? How many of these systems' designers even contemplated allowing users to access them from different departments, silos, or business units (as will surely be the case in a Hyper-Social company)? One way of improving the flexibility of installed IT systems has been to overlay social networking technologies that permit humans to respond to these unanticipated events and to share best practices on how salient information can still be captured in the installed, existing IT systems.[3]

Our Tribalization of Business Study indicates that the traits of those humans who are interfacing between companies and their tribes are critical to the effectiveness and success of these communities. Indeed the quality of the "facilitation and moderation" and the "quality of community manager/team" were cited as numbers four and six, respectively, of the factors contributing most

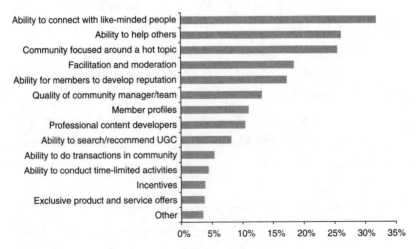

Figure 18-1 Community Features that Contribute Most to Effectiveness

to community effectiveness as can be seen in Figure 18-1. These factors placed higher, in fact, than incentives or exclusive product and service offers!

Talent Management and Employee Relations

Because of their typical command-and-control legacy, many businesses today are expert at disseminating information, policies, and communications *downward*. Where they are more challenged, however, is in moving information from the rank and file *upward*, or moving information *sideways* between different groups or silos. Indeed, suggestion boxes, peer reviews, 360-degree reviews, and anonymous reporting hotlines are all different means of moving information in a fashion that from the corporate perspective is unnatural. No formal mechanisms previously existed to move information upward or sideways—these fixes had to be created to move information in previously unimaginable ways. Communication channels, both formal and informal, have long existed in organizations, but they are likely to see dramatic changes in the near future. As social media become more entrenched, talent will begin to collaborate socially and based on skills, rather than by top-down mandate or within the traditional boundaries of the corporate world.

Since a large part of talent management involves identifying and building on skills and improving weaknesses, Hyper-Sociality will dramatically improve companies' talent development. Best practices will be better shared, high performers will be able to teach others, nodes of excellence will be easier to identify, and the tendency to hoard knowledge or expertise will be counteracted by the human bias toward reciprocity.

For instance, IBM has developed an internal employee directory called "BluePages" that permits the matching of people looking for career advice with other IBM employees who have the required knowledge or experience. The Web-based system attracted more than 3,000 employees in less than two months, and permits global employees to "see" fellow employee profiles across the entire IBM organization to find advice on everything from promotions to how to innovate.[4]

Another example of the way Hyper-Sociality is changing talent management is the appearance of tools such as Rypple at companies ranging from software developers to restaurant chains. Rypple permits employees and bosses alike to post 140-character requests for feedback on their performance ("How was my presentation this morning?"), and to quickly see a composite of all anonymized responses from their colleagues.[5]

Transparency in Talent Management

Other factors are at work in bringing greater Hyper-Sociality to talent management. One key driver is the increased use of quantitative methods to determine the specific value that individual workers deliver to the corporate bottom line. Building on the analytic rigor already employed by the finance and operations functions, where every asset or process is carefully evaluated, human resource professionals are beginning to assign value to people within an organization. Various systems are used to study corporate communications systems and networks to determine which employees seem to produce valuable contributions, are cited most by other employees, have been most successful in the past, or share common attributes with other identified high performers.

Where individual employees rank in this analysis could be used to determine who gets raises and who gets laid off. Although this might appear Orwellian, it is interesting that the software algorithms closely mimic very human-sounding ways of assessing another person's value as a team member. Indeed, it's arguable whether such a transparent system based on member input would provoke a Hyper-Social backlash.

Moreover, as Jeff Howe notes in his book *Crowdsourcing*, the community is extraordinarily good at gauging the output of other community members and identifying talent,[6] and this could reduce the all-too-common example of the terrible employee who, through flattery, office politics, or managerial inattention, rises within the organization. Such careless advancement of unqualified employees could be sharply reduced by the community's vigilant analysis.

These new systems for using social data to determine the value of employees can also be used to retain employees. One such system creates profiles of good employees who have left in the past, indicating what their skills, relationships, and educations looked like. The system then identifies similar employees who might be at risk of leaving the company.

How Will Hyper-Sociality Affect Recruiting?

The Hyper-Social shift will have a profound impact on how talent is recruited into (and sometimes alongside of) companies in the future, and how the firm retains that talent. Given the fact that many companies court volunteers who are technically not employees to assist the companies in reaching their business goals, perhaps "recruiting" needs to be expanded from its conventional sense of applying only to employees to include other people who help the company achieve its business goals (regardless of whether they are employed by the company). But before we look any further at these changes, let's look at the state of recruiting today.

In contemporary service and information companies, human capital is arguably the enterprise's most important asset. When knowledge is the key input, and the massaging of information is the key process of an enterprise, buildings, production lines, and physical inventories become less important than human intellect and talent. This alone is a challenging shift from the past, when monolithic, hard-to-replicate fixed assets were often the most important to an organization. It is also a stark shift from when employers recruited people to do specific, well-defined tasks that persisted relatively unchanged over time. Today's employees need to evolve as technology and the competitive environment change rapidly. Indeed, given this need to be chameleonlike in what one can do and what one's skills are, it's not surprising that one of the key aspects that workers today look for in their employment is the ability to develop their skills and talents.

Indeed, commentators like John Hagel, John Seely Brown, and Lang Davison point out that

> Compensation and benefits packages are surely important. But the opportunity to develop professionally consistently outranks money in surveys of employee satisfaction. Only by helping employees build their skills and capabilities can companies hope to attract and retain them. Talented workers join companies and stay there because they believe they'll learn faster and better than they would at other employers.[7]

Consider the backdrop against which this recruiting reality exists. Cultural changes over the past 30 years have given employees the freedom to job-hop without recrimination, and new technologies have freed people to work anywhere and to expand the set of potential employers for which they can work. The rise of double-income marriages provides either spouse with an income-generating safety net of sorts that enables him or her to leave an undesirable job.

As tribes exert increased influence on companies and drive change across enterprises, from product offerings to marketing practices to organizational structures, recruiting individuals who are able to navigate these shifting tides will become top of mind for corporate leaders. But today's companies aren't structured or habituated to encourage workers to develop the new skills and capabilities that they desire. Many companies may have formal training programs, but few have the flexibility or structures necessary to make workers feel that they are learning and developing faster than they could elsewhere. Because of siloed organizational structures and inflexible internal policies, workers are often specifically limited in terms of which information and resources they can access, and which other humans they can collaborate with. Given management's realization that good product development ideas may well come from outside the organization, it is probably only a matter of time before more companies rethink their policies to allow employees to reach outside of the enterprise and to collaborate with others (regardless of their employment status).[8] Such a shift will likely require management's reassessment of what sort of training and education employees will need to understand what proprietary knowledge and information should stay inside the organization, and what should be more freely shared.

Therefore, organizations that give workers the ability to alter processes so that they can solve problems and provide value more effectively in a Hyper-Social world will stand a greater chance of retaining those employees and attracting more like them. Companies that permit employees to self-select tribes that they would like to work with internally on projects are likely to appeal to Human 1.0 traits, and increase the satisfaction and performance of those employees. Much as companies need to learn to listen to their Hyper-Social customers, they need to recognize that their present employees are either attracting or repelling future recruits by what they say and do regarding their employer. Giving present employees the freedom, tools, and guidance to ensure their continual improvement is truly a win-win proposition from a recruiting perspective; it just remains to be seen how many companies are able to reconfigure their internal policies and habits to foster this sort of employee development.

As John Hagel noted in a recent discussion with us, this desire of employees to be challenged and to develop may have profound implications for corporate strategies going forward. Since it stands to reason that workers will develop fastest in companies that are growing the fastest, companies that pursue slow-growth strategies will find themselves at a competitive disadvantage when it comes to attracting the right talent.

> I would argue that training programs at best are maybe 10% of the talent development opportunity, that most of the talent development occurs in the day-to-day job environment, work environment. Your challenge as an executive is to figure out how you can reconfigure that work environment to develop talent much more rapidly.

Ultimately you'll have to rethink strategy. One example is if you are really committed to talent development, you have to pursue a high-growth strategy. If you are pursuing a low-growth strategy, you will not develop your talent as rapidly as people who pursue high-growth strategies.

So, it's important to shift your focus on the strategy dimension, how you organize the company and how you define and execute the operations of the company. If you do talent development as your key priority, all of that starts to change.[9]

Recruiting Volunteers

Another recruiting disruption that is being driven by the Hyper-Social shift is the increased ability to work with volunteers in a fashion that is tantamount to their being employees. Perhaps *recruiting* is an imprecise term for this emerging practice, but there is clearly an opportunity to use tribes to recruit supporters and helpers who want to help, but who don't want to be full employees.[10]

Recruiting professionals within organizations will also need to recognize that because of the increased and ongoing communication with Hyper-Social stakeholders, a company's recruiting is likely to become more of a continuous conversation, not just an episodic event driven by an open position. How will your organization match existing talents and emerging needs faster than your competitors? Are you working with the various business functions to anticipate the skills you will need? Are you opening up the process of developing job descriptions more widely, making it more of a social process where future colleagues are given the opportunity to weigh in on needed skills and what the role entails? Given that more than 30 percent of the companies we studied in the Tribal-ization of Business Study use only a part-time person to manage their online communities (arguably the most Hyper-Social job in any company today), we suspect that comprehensive descriptions of the type of employees that are needed to moderate online com-munities, for instance, are nonexistent in the majority of firms.

Notwithstanding these compelling reasons for using a more Hyper-Social mindset for recruiting thinking, only 23 percent of the companies surveyed by Deloitte in the 2009 Ethics & Workplace Survey used social networking for recruiting purposes. Our 2009 Tribalization of Business Survey found that only 13 percent of the more than 400 companies polled ranked "recruiting and retention" in the top five purposes of their online commu-nities, and that human resources was involved in the creation of corporate communities only about 6 percent of the time.

There is emerging scientific research that indicates how a Hyper-Social organization should manage talent, and it not only provides management with significant insight into how employees should be managed for optimal performance, but also sheds light on how external groups (such as tribes) may react to an organiza-tion's policies and actions. As David Rock notes in "Managing with the Brain in Mind," "Although a job is often regarded as a purely economic transaction, in which people exchange their labor for financial compensation, the brain experiences the workplace first and foremost as a social system."[11] Using functional magnetic res-onance imaging scans of human brains and other tools, researchers have recently conducted a significant amount of analysis into how humans' ingrained social nature affects how they perform at work and how they respond to managers' and coworkers' actions.

Rock has put together an acronym, SCARF, that captures those factors that affect humans the most in the workplace: status, certainty, autonomy, relatedness, and fairness. Simply put, any workplace developments that reduce an employee's status in the workplace, certainty, autonomy, relatedness to those around him, or sense that the organization is fair will cause him to exhibit a threat response. This threat response is expressed differently in different individuals, but it typically includes feelings of distress that impair analysis, creativity, and problem solving.[12] In essence, the threat response impairs the skills most important to knowledge workers and those dealing with a dynamic environment.

This brain research is important because it provides a scientific rationale for the Hyper-Social nature that we see humans exhibit, and because it demonstrates that the brain is really a social organ that is deeply affected by social interaction. Using these new tools, we can see the actual physical impact that social interaction, positive and negative, has on the brain and on our resulting behaviors.

Looking at these five SCARF factors that are critical to human happiness in the workplace, we can see how Hyper-Social companies should best interact with their Human 1.0 employees and tribes. Why do people contribute their valuable time and effort to developing open-source software or writing product reviews? Perhaps because it raises their status with others in the tribe. Why do people form tribes? Maybe it is because the other members of their tribe are humans with whom they feel a high degree of relatedness. Why do talented employees seek out one another across organizational silos and self-assemble into teams for certain projects? Because it allows them to exercise autonomy, which, in simple terms, makes their brains feel good.

Unfortunately, most organizations still consider their talent rational, economic beings who can be motivated by pay, bonuses, and policies. How likely is your organization to use scientific research like this to structure jobs and reward systems, and to acknowledge the social aspect of workplace dynamics? How likely is your organization to use these principles when dealing with your tribes? Which one of your competitors will begin to do so before you do?

Summary

In order to become more Hyper-Social, companies will increasingly need to recruit, retain, and develop employees who can consistently apply the Four Pillars of Hyper-Sociality. Those employees who prove to be especially adept at managing a Hyper-Social business will be in great demand, and will enjoy great power in relation to the companies that are trying to recruit them. Will your organization be able to move beyond outmoded practices that view employees as interchangeable cogs, and begin identifying and retaining those employees that permit your organization to excel in a Hyper-Social marketplace? What is your organization doing to identify these sorts of employees, and what is it doing to learn from them? Is your organization allowing these talented employees to choose the projects and teams for which they have an affinity, and ensuring that they continue to develop so that they don't go to greener pastures? Has your organization realized that employees view their work experiences through a social lens, and that workplace policies that undermine employees' status, autonomy, and feelings of fairness have dramatic physical impacts on them?

nineteen

Knowledge Management 2.0

Throughout this book, we have discussed how the Hyper-Social shift will affect each organization and its stakeholders in the areas of management thinking, marketing, the customer experience, sales, product development and innovation, talent management, and leadership. Although we have looked at nearly all of the important processes that can be Hyper-Socialized, we have omitted one key area: how organizations develop and share knowledge. Generally known as *knowledge management*, this organizational process not only will be affected by many of the changes we've discussed, but will optimally drive these changes further, and spread Hyper-Sociality throughout organizations.

We are well aware of the ongoing disputes about the function and structure of "knowledge management" as it was understood in the first decade of the twenty-first century; in the interests of not getting mired in the debate, we will use the term *knowledge management* to encompass the systems and practices that organizations use to capture, communicate, and leverage both explicit and tacit knowledge.

As we've noted elsewhere in this book, the one perfectly predictable future state of companies undergoing the Hyper-Social shift is that they will be absolutely inundated with conversations. These conversations are going to provide data, and also *require* data from disparate organizational functions, to create authentic, valuable, and engaging exchanges between customers, employees, and business partners. One person or even one team of people in marketing, for instance, will not be able to manage the knowledge flows that are going to begin, nor should it, as the knowledge is likely to have wider utility across the organization.

On the most basic level, the Hyper-Social shift will have a dramatic impact on all sorts of employee communication going forward. First, the Hyper-Social shift is an enabler of communication and knowledge sharing that couldn't easily take place in the past. Top-down communication has always been easy for the corporation; communication upward has always been harder (and more filtered). Communication from side to side within the enterprise, or across silos and divisions, has been harder still. Yet because of the massive platform for participation that social applications present, a rich dialogue can now take place with equal ease across all organizational dimensions.

This communication pays off in many ways that are not obvious. First, knowledge sharing and customer service increase when people can identify fellow human resources and access them in real time. Companies like Best Buy have discovered that employees can create powerful tools like prediction markets by leveraging the communication tools and the social nature of their coworkers. Other Best Buy employees have created idea-evaluation tools that permit coworkers to vote on new ideas and suggest their own.

Enhanced communication has other critical impacts, though, in addition to improved customer service, better business analytics, and improved knowledge sharing. Another key outcome is the sharing and reinforcing of the beliefs, attitudes, and behaviors that define a company's culture. This culture-shaping role, which it is often the responsibility of people at the top of the organization to communicate downward, can now be reinforced through a multitude of touch points between the employees and their coworkers every day.

Knowledge Management and Tribes

To succeed in satisfying the Four Pillars of Hyper-Sociality, companies are going to need to scale up their knowledge-sharing and information-processing systems dramatically. In order to deal with the messiness of speaking out in the open with customers, partners, and detractors, organizations are going to need to understand in real time, and across silos, functions, and geographies, what the tribe is talking about, asking for, and suggesting. Given the breakdown and/or blurring of the formal communication channels that existed prior to Hyper-Sociality, the organization will find itself needing knowledge about customers and products outside of the usual contexts, and then conversing with them in a way that is up-to-date and authentic, and geared more toward the tribe's interests than the company's.

To be truly human-centric, organizations are going to need to know their customers or business partners intimately, and to be held to the standard of fairness and authenticity that humans expect every time. And to be really tribe-sensitive, the company is going to be expected to understand the tribal context for each customer. It won't be enough to know that the customer is a 40-year-old male who has ordered from your company before. The organization will be expected to have a social CRM system in effect: to know that the customer is also a respected member of an important software development group, and that he has strong views on open-source software, for instance, that he blogs about frequently.

Knowledge Management Technology

Implementing new information technology systems to provide the infrastructure needed to engage in Hyper-Social conversations with stakeholders will probably be the instinctive corporate response. If the organization doesn't add a social layer to every aspect of this system, however, it is likely to fail. This has been the Achilles' heel of technology-enabled knowledge management systems for decades. They typically were designed by nonusers; were rigid in their taxonomy and functions; were geared not to human use, but rather to corporate goals; and didn't match any of the Human 1.0 behaviors we've seen. All too often, knowledge management systems were created with a predetermined and inflexible view of how information *should* flow within the organization, where it *should* be created, and who *should* have access to it. Human 1.0 principles, like the tendency of people to help one another, to seek status in the eyes of their tribe, and to accurately determine which information is really useful, were ignored, to the detriment of the organization that could be using that squandered knowledge.

Some companies are now moving in the right direction, however. IBM, for instance, has dramatically altered its legacy knowledge management technology and approach. As Bryant Clevenger, global leader for the IBM Global Business Services knowledge strategy, states:

> We undertook a massive overhaul of the technology and approach we use for knowledge management, moving from a centrally managed, linear, taxonomy- and repository-based system to one that leverages the best of Web 2.0, including social software, user participation, and key market-driven concepts like sponsored links. We see this as a shift from "knowledge management" to "knowledge sharing."[1]

Best Buy has adopted a more user-driven open collaboration and knowledge-sharing infrastructure as well, one that appears to be very different from what most would call a traditional knowledge management system:

> We have 150,000 employees in the field; the best ideas are going to come from people close to the customer. So we've been working hard at moving from a top-down hierarchical organization to one that's much flatter, an organization that plans their bottoms up and tops down.
>
> We also have a tool called the *Water Cooler*, which enables conversations on topics around the company to happen organically. It's business focused and there can be chats, our COO has chats all the time on the *Water Cooler*.
>
> We have something called *The Loop*, which is, if you're not familiar with Red Dragon, a capability where people put ideas on

The Loop and other people can vote on the ideas and improve the idea. People can also invest in the ideas and then the best ideas essentially are highlighted and emerge and move forward.

Another tool we have is called *Prediction Markets* which is sort of a stock market for ideas, everybody is given fictitious money when they participate and they trade stocks that are about ideas— how many gift cards are we selling a month, will our Geek Squad warranty product be successful, will we open a store in China by a certain date. And what that's intended to do is flush information out that may be in the system that people don't know about. Somebody who is working on the China opening at a mid-level of the company might have a good insight, for instance.

And then lastly, we have something called *Blue Shirt Nation*, which was formed; it was the first of our tools. Two guys in the company . . . they built this in their basements, a social website like MySpace, where Blue Shirts, what we call our employees, could go and talk about whatever they want to talk about. That initiative was not company sponsored. Over time they were able to get additional funding and add features and essentially lots of different kinds of topics are out there but they don't have to be business related. That is the difference from the *Water Cooler* tool, which is very business related.

So you see we have a number of different tools. Collaboration and transparency are key elements of creating better work and part of how we think we'll build better trust both with employees and with consumers.[2]

Best Buy's less structured, user-driven knowledge-sharing platforms are intriguing and instructive for a number of reasons.

First, we see the users defining the specifications and building and then adopting the tools they need to do their jobs better. The organization accepts the cocreation with its employees and provides funding, but there is little other overt control. There are no hierarchical delineations—people at all levels appear to be engaged in creating and using the tools. People are not participating or contributing because they are being told to; they are participating because it is rewarding. The rewards are the Human 1.0 sort that we've seen elsewhere—people enjoy the status of being smart, like helping others, and are developing their customer-serving skills. In addition, they are probably reciprocating the favors and goodwill that they receive regularly from their colleagues.

And since the users have helped to design and construct the tools, the likelihood of their adopting them is far higher than in the conventional case, where knowledge management tools are thrust upon an unsuspecting user base. Also, given the fact they these tools are very social, they will be familiar, and similar to the tools that the employees probably use on their days off.

Researchers looking at online communities have begun to ascribe value to lurkers, those people who observe conversations or access information, but typically do not actually participate or contribute. These researchers' insights, drawn from Hyper-Social communities, are providing new perspectives that indicate that these lurkers might actually provide great value as disseminators of the knowledge that they pull from the community. Tellingly, legacy knowledge management systems would probably view lurkers as freeloaders who are of little value to the organization; looking at them through the Hyper-Social lens, however, it can be seen that they are valuable members of the knowledge community, and probably pollinators of information beyond the formal community.[3]

The Future of Knowledge Management

So where does the Hyper-Social shift take knowledge management? Probably it will take it to the wider acquisition and sharing of information, as opposed to the management of it. Building on our learnings from earlier chapters, Knowledge Management 2.0 will allow the people closest to the information to decide what needs to be captured, what is valuable, and what is missing that needs to be captured going forward. Messiness will be accepted, and top-down processes will be minimized. Knowledge management users not only should be allowed to cocreate the information that is fed into the system, but also should be collaborators who decide how the knowledge-sharing process should work, and how it needs to change to be more valuable.

As Georg von Krogh and his collaborators note in their book *Enabling Knowledge Creation: How to Unlock the Mystery of Tacit Knowledge and Release the Power of Innovation,*

> Restricting the knowledge-worker category to certain types of professional employees will stifle a company's capacity to unleash the full potential of its human resources. Knowledge creation might occur in the close interaction between an untrained salesperson and a new customer, for example, or when a service technician together with his team finds a new solution for manufacturing a product, or a young assistant with a computer hobby might propose new ways

to present the company on the World Wide Web. In other words, knowledge work is a human condition, not a privileged one.[4]

Others have commented that it's a rare company that understands the importance of "informal improvisation"—let alone respects it as a legitimate business activity. John Seely Brown, an author and the former director of Xerox's Palo Alto Research Center, notes, "Innovation is everywhere, the problem is learning from it."[5] Few companies currently know how to learn from this so-called local innovation, but Hyper-Socialized knowledge management can remedy this problem to a large degree. Capturing this informal improvisation is often not even on the radar screens of the people who structure conventional knowledge management systems. A social system needs to have the flexibility to capture these improvisations and make them useful to others who are trying to crack the same nut. Although it may seem radical from a conventional knowledge management perspective, something as simple as an unstructured wiki that provides a repository for such improvisations clearly goes a long way toward enabling learning from them.

On a similar note, there are likely to be knowledge flows that are not being captured today, but that, if captured, would provide significant value to the organization and its customers. For instance, conventional CRM systems capture a wealth of data about known customers through their direct touch points with the organization (i.e., orders, calls for help, complaints, and delivery information). As we discussed earlier, however, equally important customer touch points are occurring in social media, where customers are discussing your products with their tribe, writing product reviews, listening to other users' comments, or seeing a competitor's advertisement.

The bulk of these incredibly useful touch points are not being captured because there is no present knowledge of them or interest in capturing them on the organization's part. Shouldn't we be capturing these insights in a knowledge flow somewhere? Giving the front-line employees in the same online communities a knowledge management system that is plastic enough to be altered so that it can capture this knowledge would clearly provide great value to both the employee and the company, as well as the customer. And since such a system would provide value to all parties (customer, employee, and organization alike), it would have a much higher likelihood of being used.

Hal Varian, chief economist at Google, says that because data are now free and ubiquitous, the scarce factor "is the ability to understand that data and extract value from it"[6]–so much so, that Varian says that the "sexy job" of the next 10 years is going to be statisticians. While we might object to that characterization of statistics, we agree with Varian's highlighting of the importance of analysis, or creating knowledge from the increasing amounts of data that are being created. Opening up information-gathering processes to more participants and cocreators, which is what Hyper-Socialization does, will only exacerbate this torrent of information that needs to be converted into knowledge.

A quick and dirty substitute for such data analysis may be the much less precise analysis at which the human brain excels, augmented by simple technologies. For instance, "social Q&A" systems are likely to become increasingly important and popular, as they deliver knowledge, remember queries, act asynchronously, and tap into users' sociality. Social Q&A tools are probably as powerful as they are because they are so humanlike. The software mimics the way many humans seek an answer—no Boolean logic is required. Users articulate their lack of knowledge in terms that they know will be familiar to others with an equal or greater degree of knowledge in that area ("Does our Product X work with Product Y from Competitor Z?") and then trust that human reciprocity will prompt someone to provide them with insight. Like a human, the social Q&A tool will remember queries that were asked in the past, and when similar queries or answers arise, it will link these individuals to a tribe of people who are obviously interested in the same topic. Social Q&A tools accomplish a valuable aspect of knowledge sharing: turning potential ties between problem solvers into actual ties.

Notwithstanding the obvious benefits of making knowledge management Hyper-Social, we appear to be early in the migration, and companies are likely to raise a number of objections to Hyper-Socializing knowledge management. Organizations have balked, for instance, at improving knowledge-sharing tools for fear of creating legal liability or making litigation discovery easier for adversaries. Others have resisted opening up knowledge management systems to wider participation for fear that information will leak outside of the organization.

Since knowledge management's functionality and features will be driven by humans who are trying to engage with and satisfy other humans, it is likely that legacy firewalls surrounding information will fall. Most organizations have walled off critical CRM information, pricing, and profitability information from employees in areas such as customer care or product development. It is wholly likely and logical that some day in the Hyper-Social future, the humans in customer care or product development will speak with or cocreate with these customers, and that knowing more about a specific customer will be critical to interacting most effectively with that individual. Formerly restricted "need to know" information will now have a wider group of employees (and perhaps business partners) who need to pull from it.

Management's guidance and messaging on how important knowledge sharing is, and its proper use, should be explicit. Rather than mandating knowledge sharing or tying it to compensation, leadership should consider what needs to be done to knowledge management to create user "pull" instead of managerial "push." It is also likely, given the Hyper-Social shift, that knowledge management will eventually open up the walls to people who were formerly "outsiders" and not considered part of the conventional knowledge management user base. Based on an observation by Beth Comstock, global CMO of GE, we may already be there:

> I think marketers' next hurdle is a knowledge management one—where we have to figure out how you start to harness the data that exists so that you know your customer better than they know themselves and so that you can understand and intuit and feed them back data that's going to make them even smarter. I think it's an opportunity for marketers to ask, "How do we then increase that knowledge and help our customers make smart decisions and help them go after their performance?" So, I think that's the way we're seeing customers starting to change, that they have more of an appetite for data and we have access to more data connected to what we offer.[7]

In effect, hasn't SAP's Developer Network become an externalized knowledge management system as well, where critical product information is shared between the company and the users? Indeed, SAP is leveraging Hyper-Sociality to improve its problem solving and knowledge sharing, goals that are squarely in the province of traditional knowledge management.

Management must not lose sight of the fact that talent will increasingly have access to unprecedented amounts of information from the world outside of the organization. What will management do to ensure that this external information and insight will be visible to the right people in the organization, and be used in tandem with organizational information in the best and highest fashion? Although this indicates the need for improved information systems, employee training on both data parsing and knowledge sharing is likely to be required, as is a fundamental reconsideration of why and how people share knowledge within the organization. Applying Hyper-Sociality may well be a large part of the solution.

Summary

Increasing Hyper-Sociality within an organization will drive both the creation of new knowledge about customers and products and the need for new knowledge management tools and policies. Organizations that harness Human 1.0 traits (like reciprocity and the desire to look smart in front of our tribes) effectively, and that put user needs before rigid organizational policies, will create powerful, sustainable new ways for the company to better serve its customers.

Many organizations are still a long way from Hyper-Socializing their knowledge management systems and policies, however. Are your organization's knowledge management systems rigid, or are they flexible in terms of where knowledge should come from or who should have access to it? Do your knowledge management systems capture local innovation effectively and share it more broadly across your organization? Is your organization leaving critical knowledge about customers, competitors, and products on the table because the system is not configured to capture that knowledge? Is your organization still trying to figure out how to persuade people to use, or contribute to, your present knowledge management system? Would your organization ever consider opening up internal knowledge management systems to business partners or customers? Your answers to these questions will help you to begin assessing how Hyper-Social your knowledge management is, and what you can do to improve it.

twenty

Business 2.0
and Leadership 2.0

ecause Hyper-Social organizations are not just the sum of
their Hyper-Social parts, let's take a more holistic view of your
business. In Chapter 8, we discussed the importance of letting go of
certain hierarchical structures and fixed processes and embracing the
messiness that comes with Hyper-Sociality. You don't need to do away
with hierarchies, as some pundits would have you believe, nor do
you have to fear that social media will destroy them—it won't. Communities of people, what we've been calling tribes, will form among
your employees, customers, prospects, and detractors. Sometimes
they will form within the hierarchies you have, and sometimes they
will form outside of them. Some will be bound by the work contract
that they have with your company, but the truly powerful ones will be
based on a social contract that they have with one another.

These tribes will generate knowledge based on whatever it is
that binds them together. Sometimes that knowledge will be good,

as when the binding force is a shared passion to wow the customer or change the future, and sometimes that tribal knowledge will be toxic, as when the binding force is a shared disrespect for your company's management. You need some form of management structure to facilitate the flow of knowledge between these different groups or tribes. When you put it in place, however, you must find the right balance between self-organization and defined management structures. If your management hierarchies are too rigid, knowledge can get trapped in the groups in which it originated. If you do not have enough formal structures, knowledge flow might happen, but the result can be a big chaotic mess. The only knowledge flow that you don't have to worry about is the flow of rumors. With or without your help, they will find a way to flow, because, being Human 1.0, we are preprogrammed to tune into the rumor mill. We developed this skill as a survival mechanism against freeloaders who might otherwise undermine the proper functioning of our large-scale reciprocal societies.

Unlike traditional organizations, which are mostly directed and managed, Hyper-Social organizations have both a directed component and an emergent component—and each needs to be evaluated in the context of the other. While traditionally directed businesses can be analyzed as the sum of their parts, emergent systems cannot. Complexity theory, the science that studies the behavior of complex emergent systems, teaches us that if there are not enough connections between the parts of the system, it becomes chaotic and unpredictable. If there are too many connections or too many rules between the parts, the system freezes up. We believe that the analogy holds true for emergent Hyper-Social businesses—if there is too much structure, the system will freeze, and if there is not enough, you will end up with chaos. The key to success in systems that have an emergent component is to operate at what complexity theorists call "the edge of chaos."

Hyper-Social organizations have to think differently about their business. They cannot just focus on the parts; they need to consider the whole as well. They also have to think differently about the leadership skills that will get them there. In the next sections, we will review how Hyper-Social leaders should think differently about their business and what it takes to be a successful Hyper-Social leader.

Business 2.0 Is Hyper-Social

In the old days, most companies considered their purpose to be providing products that would fulfill a customer need and to have those customers pay for it. Innovation focused on the features of those products and the processes required to get them to market. It was a very proprietary view of the world. Later, companies came up with product platforms, and that became a big breakthrough in terms of product innovation and business innovation. We could now reuse product components (e.g., a car chassis), processes (e.g., manufacturing processes), and design (e.g., engine design) across multiple brands, and we could reuse software components across multiple applications. In doing so, we were able to reduce learning curves, achieve economies of scale, and bring new products to market faster.

However, such thinking was still based on a very proprietary view of the world. More recently, product platform has come to mean product extensibility through application programming interfaces (APIs) and standard form factors, allowing vendors to bring out solutions that let outside companies develop products for those platforms. Facebook, Twitter, and even more proprietary platforms such as SAP are good examples of that. They allow other application developers to build add-ons for their products. Others can be found in the aerospace and automotive spaces, where fixed form factors enable third parties to develop accessories and replacement parts for the products coming from those vendors. Those new product platform–based innovation models are much more Hyper-Social, as they allow others to participate and co-create value in your ecosystem.

Most recently, we have seen companies start thinking about business model platforms instead of product platforms. Think of Amazon. It did not set out to build an electronic book retailing business; it built a new business model platform that could accommodate just about anything. Netflix can be thought of as a business model platform innovator as well. While it has not yet leveraged this platform itself, thredUP uses a similar business model platform in an attempt to disrupt the consignment business (http://www.thredup.com).

A number of cloud computing offerings have become business model platform innovators in their own right. Take Intuit's Partner Platform, which we mentioned in Chapter 13—it allows any application, no matter where it is hosted, to be integrated with other applications and delivered to small businesses. Successful business model platform innovators also leverage Hyper-Sociality by having open platforms that allow third parties to participate and cocreate value in their ecosystem.

Hyper-Social Business Platforms

During our innovation analysis, we wondered whether there might be a new wave of business innovators on the horizon, innovators who not only would leverage Hyper-Sociality as part of their business model, but would actually build their business on top of a Hyper-Social platform. Sure enough, when we looked at business innovation through our Hyper-Social lens, we were in for some interesting surprises. Threadless, a T-shirt manufacturer that produces only T-shirts designed by its customers and prospects, is one such business. Threadless has Hyper-Sociality at the heart of its business model—it's the human customer platform that powers its business. Without it, there would be no Threadless. In a lot of ways, Zappos is also a Hyper-Social business innovator. It did not design some fancy new e-commerce platform to sell products more effectively. It put its people and its culture at the center of its business model, in effect building the company on top of a true human employee platform. Rite Solutions, an information technology company that provides engineering services to both government and commercial customers, is definitely built on a Hyper-Social employee platform. Billing itself as an "employee-centric" organization, it based its business model on the simple principle of having "meaningful" relationships with employees rather than the more transactional relationships that most companies have with them—a paycheck in return for the right skills and behaviors to get a job done. At Rite Solutions, Jim Lavoie and Joe Marino, the cofounders, also ask themselves whether employees belong in their company, and whether they are important, resulting in employees caring about the future of the company. They don't stop there, they ask for their opinions and trust all of them—resulting in employees thinking about the company's future. They are recognizing their employees and listening to them, causing them to contribute to the company's future. And they make sure that people have fun, become part of the F.E.W. (Friends Enjoying Work), and feel relevant through proper rewarding—not just monetary, but also social rewards—resulting even in alumni to continue to contribute to the company's future.

Hyper-Social platform innovators didn't appear just yesterday. Similar to the way Hyper-Sociality has been around in pockets of business since people (mostly geeks) started using bulletin boards and UseNet groups, business models based on Hyper-Social platforms have also been around. For open-source projects like Linux, the Hyper-Social developer community is at the core of the business model. It's what the business is built on. Some well-established companies, like IBM, have transformed themselves by embracing open-source software—and by proxy the Hyper-Social platforms on which it was built. It is worth noting that IBM went through a very challenging experience when it donated large chunks of its proprietary code base to projects like Linux and Apache, and in turn embraced those open-source solutions and processes as its own. Some would argue that without this experience, IBM could not have evolved the way it did, but no matter what you think, the end result is that not only did it weather the storm, but it emerged with tremendous advantages over other vendors who were still trying to sell proprietary software along with their hardware.

Even though Hyper-Social business models have been around for a while, we are still effectively in the Cambrian period of

Hyper-Social business model innovation—a period that is seeing an explosion of alternative innovative business models, not all of which will survive. Many strange mutations will appear, and many will fail or be limited in their capabilities by the narrow blinders that traditional business thinking instilled in us. We will see variants of open-source principles applied not just in software applications, but also in physical goods. Take Free Beer (http://www.freebeer.org) as an example. The beer is actually not free, but home brewers can download and use the recipes for free—as long as they reciprocate by making their modifications available to the open-source community. It is only those who produce commercial products based on the recipes who ultimately pay royalties.

Even car manufacturing has attempted using open-source principles. OScar (Open Source car) is a German project (http://www.theoscarproject.org) that has been percolating since 1999. The Society for Sustainable Mobility (http://www.osgv.org) has over 150 engineers working on the Open Source Green Vehicle. Its first car, the Kernel Crossover, which is a contender for the Automotive X Prize, even borrows terminology from software open-source projects. In a lot of ways, the X Prize Foundation (http://www.xprize.org) fuels Hyper-Social platform innovators. The teams that assemble in projects to compete for those prizes are all motivated by much higher aspirations than having a job, a paycheck, or even access to the prize money (most do, in fact, spend much more than the value of the prizes). They are motivated by things like changing the future of spaceflight, saving the earth, uncovering the mysteries of life, and other grand dreams that allow humans to perform at much higher levels than they would under standard market contracts.

Other Hyper-Social platform innovators include companies like Dopplr, Visual Bookshelf, and Last.fm. These companies give their users the ability to share their travel, books, and music in a social context. Some, like Cambrian House, used the concept of marketplaces to bring together open-source business model innovators and open-source developers. At Cambrian House, crowdsourcing and open innovation principles were used not only for the development of the applications, but also to vet ideas and business plans. Unfortunately, Cambrian House did not make it in its original incarnation, as it could not get a high enough level of activity on the site. This could be because marketplaces mix market contracts with social contracts, which, as we saw in Chapter 4, behavioral economist Dan Ariely warned us against. Those companies that got off the ground in the Cambrian House marketplace used a community-based ownership structure to ensure that all community members got their fair share of the company. In a lot of ways, it offered a refreshing alternative to the advertising-based monetization schemes that everyone else seems to embrace.

Innovative business models built on Hyper-Social platforms are tricky for a number of reasons. You need some control, but you cannot wield too much power. You need some structure, but you cannot have hierarchies that are too rigid. That makes for interesting choices. Will you act as the benevolent dictator or rely on the wisdom of the majority? What happens if your wisdom of the majority becomes the tyranny of the minority? You see, in order for these projects to work, they truly need to operate at the edge of chaos. And, yes, that means that they are always on the brink of either devolving into chaos or freezing over. Business models based on Hyper-Social platforms also need high levels of participation, which does not happen naturally in large communities. Lurkers, who typically make up the largest participation group in your online communities, become more like freeloaders in Hyper-Social platform–based companies than they do in other online environments, where they actually deliver a lot of value.

Leadership 2.0—By the People, for the People

Hyper-Social organizations need different types of leaders from those in traditional organizations. In most cases, there is a real symbiotic relationship between the Hyper-Social leaders and their tribes—not only do they influence one another, but they often define one another. Before going over the characteristics of successful Hyper-Social leaders, let's look at Barack Obama's presidential campaign. Presidential candidate Obama was a classic case of a Hyper-Social leader, and you do not have to agree with his political views to understand the transformative power of that leadership style.

In an interview with NPR's *On the Media*, Marshall Ganz,[1] who designed organizational systems for the Obama campaign, talked about how Obama volunteers were motivated and coaxed to promote their candidate and to recruit other volunteers:

> What we helped them understand is that the first thing they need to learn is how to articulate their own story, in other words, what is it that moved them to become involved and engaged, because it's from their own story that they're going to be able to most effectively engage others. So when people leave, they leave equipped to do that. That's sort of the foundational piece.

And in the initial series in California, we launched 200 teams in two weekends that, with the support of four staff people, built that operation out there to the point where it could make 100,000 phone calls a day. This is like an investment in civic assets, in local communities that no political campaign has done for years.

The right benefited from being rooted in social movements, which do this because that's what social movements do. They translate values into action; they bring people in to work together. But on the progressive side, everybody had become marketers. Everybody'd been marketing their cause or marketing their candidates as if it was another bar of soap, transforming people from citizens into customers.

What we did was bring the citizenship back in and put the people back in charge, and then put the tools in their hands.

For us, the biggest difference in how the campaign empowered volunteers is not bringing the citizenship back, it's about realizing the power of letting people be themselves—about trusting them to be human. The message becomes much stronger when people tell it as part of their personal stories, and what motivated them to join the cause, rather than by regurgitating the marketing talking points about the cause. And as this story shows, it is much harder to defeat a Hyper-Social movement than it is to defeat a strong hierarchical command-and-control-based organization.

Eight Characteristics of Hyper-Social Leaders

In our travels to understand Hyper-Sociality, we found eight characteristics of successful Hyper-Social leaders. Not surprisingly, great thinkers on the topic of leadership and management—people like

Peter Drucker and Warren Bennis—came up with some of the same characteristics decades ago. That is because good leadership in Hyper-Social environments, just like good marketing and many of the other behaviors that we discussed in this book, is what leadership should have been all along.

They Behave like Humans and Demand that Their People Do Too

Hyper-Social people cannot behave like corporate automatons. When people engage with your company, they want to connect with other people—not faceless entities. In addition, as the Obama candidacy has shown, a story is much more powerful when people can be themselves instead of following a corporate script. Let them tell their own stories instead of retelling the corporate story. In order for people to behave like actual people, leaders need to do the same and treat their employees with respect—just like Zappos, where employees treat one another as family, or W. L. Gore, where all associates agree to behave according to the following principle: "Fairness to each other and everyone with whom we come in contact."

Proponents of Leadership 2.0 do not suffer from what Warren Bennis[2] calls the Hollywood syndrome, an arrogant and misguided belief that power is more important than talent. They understand the negative impact that power-related status symbols may have on the way people behave in companies.

They Ditch the Rule Books and Embrace Values

As we discussed earlier in this chapter and also in Chapter 8, controlling the brand experience across multiple human touch points does not happen with the help of corporate rule books. It happens through values-based cultures that people buy into. As we've seen from the JetBlue example, the ability to predict how people will behave based on a shared set of values is much more powerful than having a policy manual that covers every possible scenario.

Sometimes you have to supplement your values with policies or guidelines, but those who do this successfully always end up with policies and guidelines that are simple to understand and easy to live by. If your employees ask your legal department for clarification, you know that you have the wrong policies and guidelines.

If you still doubt whether rule books are good management tools, listen to the sages of modern management thinking. Most employees whose jobs have not been eliminated by automation or foreign outsourcing are likely to be knowledge workers, and according to Peter Drucker, "Knowledge workers cannot be managed." And when Warren Bennis thinks about great groups (i.e., tribes), he says: "But whatever their appearance they are always rule busters. People in great groups are never insiders or corporate types on the fast track; they are always on their own track."[3]

Proponents of Leadership 2.0 lead, they don't manage. They understand the language of their culture and help create it. And as Alan Webber, the cofounder of *Fast Company*, told us about new leaders: "We're seeing a change from leaders who have all the answers to leaders who know the best questions to ask."

They Live Their Values

It's not enough to have values; you also need to live by them. At Ritz-Carlton, there is the Gold Standard, a set of values and philosophy by which the company operates. When employees join the company, they go through a rigorous training and even get certified in the Gold Standard. But that is not all. Every single day, every one of the 25,000 Ritz-Carlton employees talks about the meaning of one of the elements of the Gold Standard with other employees for 10 or 15 minutes. That is true for the executives as well as front-line employees. This constant reinforcement of values is very important in companies. Dave Logan, the author of *Tribal Leadership*, reminded us of what happens when you do not do that: "Without that reinforcement of shared values, the knowledge or the visceral connection that we have to our values evaporates and then all we have, in order to get things done, is our political will. So, we start forming factions and coalitions and we start using spies and networks to get things done rather than, again, an inherent trust and belief that we're all fighting for the same thing."[4]

That is, of course, in sharp contrast with many companies, which spend considerable resources developing values, missions, and beliefs, only to live by some other rules. No company that we're acquainted with has ever crafted a mission statement that vows to anger, disappoint, or annoy its paying customers. A look at public social media or a search engine, however, will show that some companies are routinely and consistently doing just that. Judging from a quick Google search, there are approximately 147,000 instances of people complaining that an airline "sucks," notwithstanding the company's stated desire to make every flight "something special."

They Trust Their People and Create Trusted Environments

Without trust, Hyper-Sociality and business break down. Trust is what creates customer loyalty, trust is what reduces transaction costs, and trust is what speeds up buying decisions. You cannot expect your customers to trust you if you do not trust your employees—it just won't happen. You have to trust your employees to do what's best for the customer and thus what's best for the company. Let them engage with people who are having problems or complaints in the marketplace. Empower them to own and solve customer problems the way Ritz-Carlton does. At Ritz-Carlton, whoever runs into a customer issue owns the problem (even if it's not that person's job). Employees also have the discretion to spend up to $2,000 of the company's resources to fix that customer problem (without any authorization from higher-ups). Most companies require signatures for anything over $50 (or was it $5?)—how can you expect your customers to trust your employees if you do not trust them?

Did you know that 54 percent[5] of companies block access to outside social networks and e-commerce sites? What is going on here? Recent studies[6] have found that people who are free to surf and engage in "workplace Internet leisure browsing" are more productive than those who aren't. So why do companies feel the need to play Big Brother when it comes to surfing habits at work? Most people will do better if they are not micromanaged. Again, how do you expect your customers to trust your employees if you don't?

They Embrace Transparency

Transparency is the other side of the trust coin. You cannot have trust and no transparency. And it's best to have that transparency extend to your partners and customers. Zappos, the online shoe and fashion retailer, permits suppliers to access much of the data that Zappos's buyers see. Zappos's CEO, Tony Hsieh, acknowledges that although competitors might also see the data, that risk is outweighed by the fact that another 750 people can suggest improvements to the business.

Paul Levy, the current CEO of Beth Israel Deaconess Medical Center, a large Harvard-affiliated research hospital in the Boston area, is another big believer in transparency. In a recent interview we had with him, he said: "And—little did I know that by actually publishing our numbers, virtually in real-time—that transparency itself would become a major management tool that would encourage our people to do even better than they had hoped to do in the first place. It was a way of holding ourselves accountable that I hadn't really understood. So I like to joke that I invented a new management tool called transparency."

They Embrace Diversity

Diversity is key to creating vibrant environments with little risk of groupthink and echo-chamber effects. And when we talk about companies that embrace diversity, we don't just mean gender, racial, and cultural diversity; we mean intellectual diversity—attracting people who will approach the same problem from totally different angles. As Alan Webber[7] told us when we spoke with him: "You have to marry idea people with implementation people. You have to marry word people with picture people. Left brain and right brain—all of those combinations have to be at work for you to have the organization that really reflects the rapid changes that are going on in the world. And you've got to be able to adapt." Most companies that are also great innovators seek out diversity; they don't just let it happen. Companies like Ritz-Carlton, which we mentioned earlier, build diversity right into their recruiting plans.

Now, if you are doing well at marrying the right people to the right projects, chances are that people who embrace diversity will seek you out—diversity seeks diversity. As Warren Bennis said, "Great groups often tend to attract mavericks."[8] You just have to recognize it when such a person walks in the door.

They Never Compromise on the Quality of the People They Surround Themselves With

You have heard the story before: A people love people who are smarter than they are, and so they will hire other A people. B people feel threatened by people who are smarter than they are, and so they will hire C people. The C people, of course, know that they are total frauds in the job and will surround themselves with unnecessary processes and procedures to hide their incompetence and protect their job. That, of course, is what chokes innovation and eventually kills companies. Just as with diversity, you need to be constantly on the lookout for this to ensure that it does not take hold in your company. The last thing you want to do is to compromise on the people you surround yourself with. Not only will it be demoralizing for the good people around you, but it could allow an otherwise healthy culture to deteriorate into a *Dilbert*-like environment in no time.

When we spoke with Dave Logan, he described how easy it is to get a group to degrade itself to a level 2 in Tribal Leadership, which is where the *Dilbert*-like behaviors happen. He also described how IDEO avoids the possibility of having people not hire someone because they feel threatened by him: "I think of IDEO up in Palo Alto, the way that they hire someone is you get lunched—that's a verb—by about 11 people and the 11 people have to largely agree that the candidate, let's say it's me, that Dave has the right values, that Dave is one of us. And they probably wouldn't be interviewing me if they didn't think that I had the technical ability. So, they're really looking at culture fit when they do those interviews. And so, if there's one person there who's threatened, they're probably going to have ten people outvoting them."[9]

True tribal leaders are constantly on the lookout for the next-generation leaders, and they do that not just in the context of their companies, but in the context of their industry as a whole. Here again, the wise management thinkers figured this out a long time ago. Warren Bennis used to say: "Great groups are inevitably forged by people unafraid of hiring people better than themselves."[10]

They Let Go of Control

If you want your people to behave like grown-ups, you will need to let go of control and stop treating them like children. In a recent interview we had with Jeff Hayzlett, the CMO at Kodak, he described the letting go of control as follows: "As a parent it's tough sometimes to let go. And that's a good example. As a marketer I have to do the same thing. I have to treat it like my children. How do I know when to let go?"

Ram Menon, the CMO at TIBCO, ran into the issue of letting go of control when he decided to turn the sales process into a social process. This decision was a response to the realization that there was no way for marketing to support all of TIBCO's different customer configurations with the appropriate marketing materials. So the company created a sales community, in which salespeople help one another to modify the marketing materials to meet the needs of specific customers. When faced with the issue of control of the marketing content, Ram described his fears as follows:[11] "When I started, I had the average marketer's fear. I put together a positioning for the company and nobody's going to change that because that's going to create problems. . . . [O]ver the course of time I realized one size doesn't fit all in this market when you're selling complex products."

In this Hyper-Social age, change happens with increasing speed and complexity. The only way you can be agile enough to respond to these changes and leverage them to your advantage is by letting go of control and empowering your employees to do what they think is right for the situation. If you have to wait for information to go up the hierarchy and decisions to flow back down, chances are that you will have missed the opportunities that presented themselves to you or, worse, be hit with a crisis that could cost you dearly.

Summary

When it comes to thinking about Business 2.0 and Leadership 2.0, you really need to ask yourself and your team some tough questions. Have we challenged ourselves hard enough in evaluating everything we do? If we could restart the company tomorrow, what would it look like? If we could redo the culture, what would we come up with? If we could elect new leaders, would they be the ones that are leading us now? Are we treating our employees the way we would treat family? Are we putting the customer at the center of everything we do when we provide guidelines to our employees, or are we focusing mainly on our organizational interests?

epilogue

Your Hyper-Social Future

O f course humans will continue to evolve, and they will do so in sync with the culture that surrounds them. And yes, our environment (online and offline) will affect our future, both culturally and from an evolutionary biology point of view. However, those changes won't happen over the course of one or two generations; they will occur over the span of thousands of years. So for the foreseeable future, we are stuck with the Hyper-Social Human 1.0 in business.

As this book comes to a close, we wanted to have some fun by venturing out and making wild predictions about that future. We would not call ourselves prognosticators, and we have no grand illusions that any of our predictions will come to pass. The purpose of this exercise, however, is not a vain one; rather, these predictions may determine certain changes that you could force your organization to go through. By envisioning bold scenarios for the future, you might see paths to get there that have interesting stops along the way—stops that might provide you with valuable competitive differentiators.

So let's get started making some bold predictions, and hopefully we'll have some fun along the way. You can submit your own bold predictions, and discuss others, on www.hypersocialorg.com.

Hyper-Social Brokers in a Consolidating World

As communities proliferate, we will inevitably reach a point where there will be too many of them, both internally and externally. At IBM, there are already more than 10,000 internal communities. Many of them may be redundant, set up by people who don't bother to check whether communities with similar interests might already exist. Most of us won't belong to multiple communities with the same topic, since we have only limited time and attention to spare. So what is going to happen to all of this overabundance? The answer: consolidation.

Ultimately, some communities will become like ghost towns, while others will become magnets that attract all the members and all the value. The "owners" of those communities, fans or vendors, will become Hyper-Social brokers for access to the members of their community. This new Hyper-Social role will be a tricky one, and one that many will misuse. You see, access to members is a valuable commodity, tremendously so, and the "owners" of those communities will be hard-pressed to monetize this newly found wealth. Some will do it the right way and respect the privacy of their members, the way Amazon and others have done it before them. Some will abuse the trust that exists within their communities, resulting in increased transaction costs for all the members and a potential mass exodus.

Those who can find the right balance in being Hyper-Social brokers for their communities in a way that provides value to both the members and those who seek access to them will find themselves in charge of assets that have unbelievable value and that can provide significant long-term competitive advantages—clearly a scarcity in today's business environment.

The Backlash from Having Too Many Ideas

It's happening already. Companies that are getting their internal and external tribes involved with their business run the risk of being overwhelmed by their feedback. Look at the Dell IdeaStorm community:[1] 13,104 ideas and more than 88,000 comments; look at the My Starbucks Idea community:[2] more than 80,000 ideas. How do you manage that many ideas? How much does it cost to review and triage them, even if you count only the ones that the community deemed popular? How many ideas can you implement in your next-generation product or service offering? How much does the cost of processing this user-generated content compare to hiring a team of really smart people to come up with the same number of implementable ideas?

You can just see it happening. Companies will get overwhelmed by the amount of feedback they get from their tribes. At some point, they will no longer be able to participate appropriately in those user-generated knowledge flows (remember that our Tribalization of Business Study showed that a majority of companies have only one person dedicated to their Hyper-Social activities, if they have any at all). Tribal members will perceive that lack of participation as a lack of reciprocity and become disillusioned. At the same time, the numbers people, who still dominate most companies, will start questioning the costs of it all.

So where does this scenario lead us? To many Hyper-Social failures on the horizon.

How do you fix it? By adding structure and process.

Remember what we said in Chapter 8? Too much process and structure, and your organization will freeze up; too little, and you will end up with chaos. The same is true for all your Hyper-Social activities. You need to add some process and structure to all of them in order to get them working. Don't just have an open-ended idea community; add some structure in there, the way Pfizer does with its internal social innovation process[3] — with most of its innovation communities being centered around "collaborative problem solving" or directed innovation. Or the way Dell decided to complement its IdeaStorm suggestion box with Storm Sessions. As Erin Nelson, the CMO at Dell, said when we talked with her:[4] "So, while we still have that large IdeaStorm suggestion box that will continue to be really valuable, we've incorporated now what we've called Storm Sessions. And it's a means to, actually, further drive, kind of, period-in-time feedback and business value, and the overall IdeaStorm experience. What we do is we actually identify specific topics at specific times, and, I'll tell you, the person who has the hardest job in Dell right now is the arbiter of whose questions get to be put out." Adobe has a more radical approach to providing a "heartbeat" to its innovation communities: it periodically kills them, summarizes what happened, and restarts with fresh communities after a short hiatus.

In the future, we will see a lot more structure in Hyper-Social environments, either vendor-directed or self-directed. It won't be anything like the vertical top-down structures that we have in most organizations today, but more of a fluid, frequently changing, horizontal set of structures. The companies that understand this dynamic today will have a leg up on their competitors.

The Unbundling of the Organization as We Know It Today

John Hagel predicted it in the 1990s[5]—the unbundling of the corporation. Organizations would break up into infrastructure players, customer aggregators, and fast, agile product innovators. We may have finally arrived at this one. With the inevitable consolidation of Hyper-Social environments and the role that Hyper-Social brokers play in controlling access to their members, the advent of cloud computing, and the ongoing trend of outsourcing all nonessential work, we may in fact be witnessing the unbundling of the corporation.

Product and service innovators won't have to worry about customer segmentation and targeting anymore, as most customers will be self-segmented into tribes, and access will be dictated by the Hyper-Social brokers of those tribes. We will see product and service innovators who also "own" Hyper-Social environments. In order for such endeavors to succeed, they will have to acknowledge the inherent conflict of interest that lies in that dual role, and keep a wall between church and state. It is like having doctors own a hospital. Doctors are supposed to be the patient advocates, and the hospitals are driven by profitability. When the doctor owns both, one part of the equation stops working. Companies that own both will have to have a customer advocacy group that is independent of the group that is measured on product or service revenue.

And the New Curators Are . . .

You . . . all of you! If we are indeed witnessing the end of traditional media models and advertising as we know them today, who will play the role of information curator? "All of us" has to be the answer—but how?

Wikipedia may provide a model for the future of information curators, but there are also many failures in the area of crowd-based content creation. Self-organized publishing models like Slashdot and Kuro5shin have not replaced mainstream publishing yet, nor have they even come close to threatening the existing models. The "We are smarter than me" project, a crowd-based book publishing project that was cosponsored by the MIT Center for Collective Intelligence, ended up hiring writers to write the book.[6] Even InnoCentive, a crowd-based scientific problem-solving environment, isn't all it is heralded to be. It's hard to rely on the crowd to curate good content.

Organizations, however, have the wherewithal to pay for professional content curators, and while in the old model, they hired them for their own purposes, we expect more and more companies to hire them as a service to their tribes. The tribes will participate in being curators, but with professional curators as the catalyst, they will have a much higher chance of success.

Endnotes

Chapter 1

1. Jonathan Haidt, *The Happiness Hypothesis: Finding Modern Truth in Ancient Wisdom* (New York: Basic Books, 2006), p. 42.
2. Jon Kleinberg, "The Convergence of Social and Technological Networks," *Communications of the ACM*, November 2008, p. 2, http://www.cs.cornell.edu/home/kleinber/cacm08.pdf.
3. The 2009 Edelman Trust Barometer, http://www.edelman.com/trust/2009/.
4. Vernon Smith, *Rationality in Economics: Constructivist and Ecological Forms* (Cambridge, UK: Cambridge University Press, 2007), pp. 247–250.
5. Dan Ariely, *Predictably Irrational: The Hidden Forces That Shape Our Decisions* (New York: HarperCollins, 2008).
6. Ori Brafman and Rom Brafman, *Sway: The Irresistible Pull of Irrational Behavior* (New York: Broadway Business, 2008).
7. Clay Shirky, *Here Comes Everybody* (New York: Penguin Press, 2008), pp. 1–14.
8. Francois Gossieaux, "CMO 2.0 Conversation with Erin Nelson, CMO at Dell, and Manish Mehta, VP of Social Media and Communities," March 4, 2010, http://www.cmotwo.com/2010/03/04/cmo-20-conversation-with-erin-nelson-cmo-at-dell-and-manish-mehta-vp-of-social-media-and-communities/.

Chapter 2

1. Bernard Cova, Robert Kozinets, and Avi Shankar, *Consumer Tribes* (Amsterdam: Butterworth-Heinemann, 2007).
2. Francois Gossieaux, "CMO 2.0 Influencer Conversation with Rob Kozinets," May 7, 2009, http://www.cmotwo.com/2009/05/07/cmo-20-influencer-conversation-with-rob-kozinets-marketing-professor-at-york-university-and-author/.
3. Robert Boyd and Peter J. Richerson, *The Origin and Evolution of Cultures* (Oxford, UK: Oxford University Press, 2005), p. 256.
4. 2009 Edelman Trust Barometer, http://www.edelman.com/trust/2009/.
5. "Homophily," Wikipedia, http://en.wikipedia.org/wiki/Homophily.
6. Martin Lindström, *Buyology: Truth and Lies about Why We Buy* (New York: Broadway Books, 2010), p. 20.
7. Dave Berreby, *Us and Them: Understanding Your Tribal Mind* (New York: Little, Brown and Co., 2005), p. 313.
8. "Dunbar's number," Wikipedia, http://en.wikipedia.org/wiki/Dunbar%27s_number.
9. "Affinity group," Wikipedia, http://en.wikipedia.org/wiki/Affinity_group.
10. Thomas Gilovich, *How We Know What Isn't So: The Fallibility of Human Reason in Everyday Life* (New York: Free Press, 2008), pp. 90–91.
11. David Court, Dave Elzinga, Susan Mulder, and Ole Jørgen Vetvik, "The Consumer Decision Journey," *McKinsey Quarterly*, June 2009, http://www.mckinseyquarterly.com/The_consumer_decision_journey_2373.

Chapter 3

1. Francois Gossieaux, "CMO 2.0 Conversation with Christa Carone, CMO at Xerox," Feb. 2010, http://www.emergencemarketing.com/2010/03/03/cmo-2-0-conversation-with-christa-carone-cmo-at-xerox/
2. Deloitte's State of the Media Democracy Survey, 4th ed., http://www.deloitte.com/view/en_US/us/Industries/Media-Entertainment/article/0c89 5e8354495210VgnVCM100000ba42f00aRCRD.htm.
3. David Court, Dave Elzinga, Susan Mulder, and Ole Jørgen Vetvik, "The Consumer Decision Journey," *McKinsey Quarterly*, June 2009, http://www.mckinseyquarterly.com/The_consumer_decision_journey_2373.
4. Francois Gossieaux, "CMO 2.0 Influencer Conversation with John Hagel," July 9, 2009, http://www.cmotwo.com/2009/07/08/cmo-20-influencer-conversation-with-john-hagel-co-chairman-of-the-center-for-the-edge-at-deloitte/.
5. Clay Shirky, *Here Comes Everybody* (New York: Penguin Press, 2008).

Chapter 4

1. John Hagel III and Arthur G. Armstrong, *Net Gain: Expanding Markets through Virtual Communities* (Boston: Harvard Business School Press, 1997).
2. Clay Shirky, *Here Comes Everybody* (New York: Penguin Press, 2008), p. 239.
3. American Express Open Forum, http://www.openforum.com/.
4. Nikolous Franke and Frank Piller, "Value Creation by Toolkits for User Innovation and Design," *Journal of Product Innovation Management* 21 (November 2004), pp. 401–415.
5. Dan Ariely, *Predictably Irrational: The Hidden Forces That Shape Our Decisions* (New York: HarperCollins, 2008).
6. Francois Gossieaux, "CMO 2.0 Conversation with Rob Spencer, Chief Idea Management Officer at Pfizer," September 22, 2009, http://www.cmotwo.com/2009/09/22/cmo-20-conversation-with-rob-spencer-chief-idea-management-officer-at-pfizer/.

Chapter 5

1. Francois Gossieaux, "CMO 2.0 Influencer Conversation with Dan Ariely, Author and Professor in Behavioral Economics at Duke University," May 24, 2009, http://www.cmotwo.com/2009/05/24/cmo-20-influencer-conversation-with-dan-ariely-author-and-professor-in-behavioral-economics-at-duke-university/.
2. Gary Marcus, *Kluge: The Haphazard Evolution of the Human Mind* (Boston: Houghton Mifflin, 2008), p. 67.
3. Francois Gossieaux, "CMO 2.0 Conversation with Mark Colombo, SVP Digital Access Marketing, FedEx," May 4, 2009, http://www.cmotwo.com/2009/05/04/cmo-20-conversation-with-mark-colombo-svp-digital-access-marketing-fedex/.
4. James H. McAlexander, John W. Schouten, and Harold F. Koenig, "Building Brand Community," *Journal of Marketing*, January 2002, pp. 38–54.
5. Michael Frank, "Test Drives: 2003 Honda Element," *Forbes.com*, January 6, 2003, http://www.forbes.com/2003/01/06/cx_mf_0106test.html.
6. Francois Gossieaux, "Fiskars + Fiskateer Community," October 9, 2008, http://www.cmotwo.com/2008/10/09/fiskars-fiskateer-community/.
7. McAlexander et al., "Building Brand Community."
8. Bernard Cova, Robert Kozinets, and Avi Shankar, *Consumer Tribes* (Amsterdam: Butterworth-Heinemann, 2007).
9. Bernard Cova and Veronique Cova, "Tribal Marketing: The Tribalisation of Society and Its Impact on the Conduct of Marketing," revised paper for *European Journal of Marketing* Special Issue, "Societal Marketing in 2002

and Beyond, Visionary Marketing," January 2001, http://visionary marketing.com/_repository/wanadoo/cova-tribe-2001.pdf.

10. Dan Ariely and Jonathan Levav, "Sequential Choice in Group Settings; Taking the Road Less Traveled and Less Enjoyed," *Journal of Consumer Research* 27 (December 2000), p. 279, http://www.predictablyirrational. com/pdfs/groupvar.pdf.

11. Sheena S. Iyengar and Mark R. Lepper, "When Choice Is Demotivating: Can One Desire Too Much of a Good Thing?" *Journal of Personality and Social Psychology*, 2000, Vol. 79, No. 6, pp. 995–1006.

12. Michael M. Tseng and Frank Piller, *The Customer Centric Enterprise: Advances in Mass Customization and Personalization* (Berlin: Springer, 2003), p. 15.

13. Martin Lindström, *Buyology: Truth and Lies about Why We Buy* (New York: Broadway Books, 2010).

14. Gossieaux, "Conversation with Dan Ariely."

15. Jason Oke, "Pre-Testing," Leo Burnett Toronto blog, May 14, 2007, http:lbtoronto.typepad.com/lbto/ads/

16. James Manyika, "Google's View on the Future of Business: An Interview with CEO Eric Schmidt," *McKinsey Quarterly*, November 2008, http:// www.mckinseyquarterly.com/Googles_view_on_the_future_of_business_ An_interview_with_CEO_Eric_Schmidt_2229.

Chapter 6

1. Lenny Mendonca and Robert Sutton, "Succeeding at Open Source Innovation: An Interview with Mozilla's Mitchell Baker," *McKinsey Quarterly*, January 2008.

2. Clive Thompson, "Clive Thompson on Social Networks and the Wrath of Moms," *Wired*, October 20, 2008.

3. Rolex Forums (http://www.rolexforums.com) is a vibrant online community of Rolex wristwatch fans. A very small percentage of the conversations there have to do with the actual performance of the watches; instead, the majority of the conversations involve people helping one another find and buy watches, not pay too much, or not be swindled by a watch counterfeiter. Contributors often proudly include photos of their watches and themselves, and list all the watches they own. The forum also specifies the number of posts they've contributed and when they joined the community.

4. See V. Kumar, J. Andrew Petersen, and Robert P. Leone, "How Valuable Is Word of Mouth?" *Harvard Business Review*, October 2007, http://hbr. org/2007/10/how-valuable-is-word-of-mouth/ar/1, for a discussion of the value of customer referrals. See also Julian Villanueva, Shijin Yoo, and Dominique M. Hansens, "The Impact of Marketing-Induced versus Word-

of-Mouth Customer Acquisition on Customer Equity Growth," *Journal of Marketing Research* 45 (February 2008), for research on the efficacy of word-of-mouth marketing as compared to conventional advertising.

5. Grant McCracken, *Chief Culture Officer: How to Create a Living, Breathing Corporation*, (Basic Books: New York, 2009)

Chapter 7

1. Martin Lindström, *Buyology: Truth and Lies about Why We Buy* (New York: Broadway Books, 2010), p. 37.
2. "Conveyor Belt Advertising at Grocery Store," YouTube, July 2008, http://www.youtube.com/watch?v=oYf1g8QACUI.
3. Robert Berner, "I Sold It through the Grapevine," *BusinessWeek*, May 29, 2006, http://www.businessweek.com/magazine/content/06_22/b3986060.htm.
4. Kelly D. Martin and N. Craig Smith, "Commercializing Social Interaction: The Ethics of Stealth Marketing," INSEAD Business School Research Paper No. 2008/19/SIC, February 2008, http://ssrn.com/abstract=1111976.
5. Thomas Gilovich, *How We Know What Isn't So: The Fallibility of Human Reason in Everyday Life* (New York: Free Press, 2003), p. 91.
6. Francois Gossieaux, "CMO 2.0 Influencer Conversation with John Hagel," July 9, 2009, http://www.cmotwo.com/2009/07/08/cmo-20-influencer-conversation-with-john-hagel-co-chairman-of-the-center-for-the-edge-at-deloitte/.
7. "Emerging Best Practices: Social Media Monitoring, Engagement & Measurement," Beeline Labs, http://www.beelinelabs.com/downloads/social-media-monitoring-engagement/.
8. Francois Gossieaux, "CMO 2.0 Conversation with Susan Lavington, CMO at USA-Today," (April 15, 2009), http://www.cmotwo.com/2009/04/15/cmo-20-conversation-with-susan-lavington-senior-vice-president-of-marketing-at-usa-today/.

Chapter 8

1. Patrick Cohendet, "On Knowing Communities," Draft Paper for the Conference "Advancing Knowledge and the Knowledge Economy," January 2005, http://advancingknowledge.com/drafts/Cohendet-knowing%20communities.doc.
2. Francois Gossieaux, "CMO 2.0 Influencer Conversation with Dave Logan, Senior Partner, CultureSync," July 27, 2009, http://www.cmotwo.com/2009/07/27/cmo-20-influencer-conversation-with-dave-logan-senior-partner-culturesync/. *See also* Dave Logan, John King, Halee Fischer-Wright, *Tribal Leadership* (New York: HarperCollins, 2008).

3. Francois Gossieaux, "CMO 2.0 Conversation with Beth Comstock, CMO at GE," March 6, 2009, http://www.cmotwo.com/2009/03/06/cmo-20-conversation-with-beth-comstock-cmo-at-ge/.
4. "Practically Radical: Richard Antcliff at BIF-5," http://www.business innovationfactory.com/iss/video/bif5-richard-antcliff.

Chapter 10

1. For persuasive arguments that the discipline of management is not advancing as quickly as it should be, see Gary Hamel and Bill Breen, *The Future of Management* (Boston: Harvard Business School Press, 2007), and Gary Hamel, "Moon Shots for Management," *Harvard Business Review*, February 2009, http://hbr.harvardbusiness.org/2009/02/moon-shots-for-management/ar/pr.
2. Deloitte's State of the Media Democracy Survey, 4th ed., http://www.deloitte.com/view/en_US/us/Industries/Media-Entertainment/eb265fbf87595210VgnVCM100000ba42f00aRCRD.htm.
3. Scott Thompson and Rajiv Sinha, "Brand Communities and New Product Adoption: The Influence and Limits of Oppositional Loyalty," *Journal of Marketing* 72 (November 2008), p. 67.
4. Francois Gossieaux, "CMO 2.0 Influencer Conversation with Porter Gale, CMO at Virgin America," May 15, 2009, http://www.cmotwo.com/2009/05/15/cmo-20-conversation-with-porter-gale-cmo-at-virgin-america/.
5. Hamel, "Moon Shots for Management."
6. John Hagel and John Seely Brown, "From Push to Pull: Emerging Models for Mobilizing Resources," June 2008, p. 15, http://www.deloitte.com/view/en_US/us/Insights/centers/centers-center-for-edge/1e77742bdaa12210VgnVCM100000ba42f00aRCRD.htm.
7. Alfred D. Chandler, Jr., *The Visible Hand: The Managerial Revolution in American Business* (Cambridge, Mass.: Belknap Press, 1977), p. 8.
8. Scott Cook, "The Contribution Revolution: Letting Volunteers Build Your Business," *Harvard Business Review*, October 2008, http://hbr.harvardbusiness.org/2008/10/the-contribution-revolution/ar/pr.
9. Spencer Ante, "How Amazon Is Turning Opinions into Gold," *BusinessWeek*, October 26, 2009, p. 47.

Chapter 11

1. Julian Villanueva, Shijin Yoo, and Dominique M. Hansens, "The Impact of Marketing-Induced versus Word-of-Mouth Customer Acquisition on Customer Equity Growth," *Journal of Marketing Research* 45 (February 2008), pp. 48–59.

2. Masamichi Takahashi, Masakazu Fujimoto, and Nobuhiro Yamasaki, "Active Lurking: Enhancing the Value of In-House Online Communities through the Related Practices around the Online Communities," CCI Working Paper 2007-006, MIT Sloan School of Management Working Paper 4646-07, April 1, 2007, http://ssrn.com/abstract=1041261.

3. Masamichi Takahashi, George Herman, Atsushi Ito, Keiichi Nemoto, and JoAnne Yates, "The Role of an Online Community in Relation to Other Communication Channels in a Business Development Case," CCI Working Paper 2009-002, MIT Sloan School of Management Working Paper 4731-09, April 9, 2009, http://cci.mit.edu/publications/CCIwp2009-02.pdf

4. Michael Trusov, Randolph E. Bucklin, and Koen Pauwels, "Effects of Word-of-Mouth versus Traditional Marketing: Findings from an Internet Social Networking Site," *Journal of Marketing* 73 (September 2009), pp. 90–102.

5. V. Kumar, J. Andrew Petersen, and Robert P. Leone, "How Valuable Is Word of Mouth?" *Harvard Business Review*, October 2007, http://hbr.org/2007/10/how-valuable-is-word-of-mouth/ar/1.

6. "Dell Announces Recall of Notebook Computer Batteries Due to Fire Hazard," U.S. Consumer Product Safety Commission press release, August 15, 2006, http://www.cpsc.gov/cpscpub/prerel/prhtml06/06231.html.

7. Bernard Cova, Robert Kozinets, and Avi Shankar, *Consumer Tribes* (Amsterdam: Butterworth-Heinemann, 2007).

8. Francois Gossieaux, "CMO 2.0 Influencer Conversation with Rob Kozinets," May 7, 2009, http://www.cmotwo.com/2009/05/07/cmo-20-influencer-conversation-with-rob-kozinets-marketing-professor-at-york-university-and-author/.

9. Sarah Cummings, Richard Heeks, and Marleen Huysman, "Knowledge and Learning in Online Communities in Development: A Social Capital Perspective," Institute for Development Policy and Management Paper No. 16, 2003.

10. The World Bank Social Capital Measurement Tools, http://web.worldbank.org/WBSITE/EXTERNAL/TOPICS/EXTSOCIALDEVELOPMENT/EXTTSOCIALCAPITAL/0,,contentMDK:20193049~menuPK:994384~pagePK:148956~piPK:216618~theSitePK:401015,00.html.

11. Charla Mathwick, Caroline Wiertz, and K. O. De Ruyter, "Social Capital Production in Virtual P3 Community," *Journal of Consumer Research*, April 2008.

12. Fabio Sabatini, "Social Capital as Social Networks. A New Framework for Measurement," Working Paper, Dipartimento di Economica Pubblica, Università Degli Studi di Roma la Sapienza, August 2005.

Chapter 12

1. John Hagel and Marc Singer, "Unbundling the Corporation," *Harvard Business Review*, March 1, 1999, p. 134, http://harvardbusiness.org/product/unbundling-the-corporation/an/99205-PDF-ENG.
2. Francois Gossieaux, "CMO 2.0 Conversation with Barry Judge, CMO at Best Buy," October 23, 2008, http://www.cmotwo.com/transcripts/2008/10/23/transcript-cmo-20-conversation-with-barry-judge-cmo-at-best-buy/.
3. Jeff Jarvis, "Dell Learns to Listen," *BusinessWeek*, October 17, 2007 http://www.businessweek.com/bwdaily/dnflash/content/oct2007/db20071017_277576.htm?chan=top+news_top+news+index_top+story.
4. For select portions of the exchange, see http://twitter.com/MrComplicated/statuses/2010036172; http://twitter.com/BofA_help/status/2020510447; and http://twitter.com/MrComplicated/status/2044151738.
5. Francois Gossieaux, "CMO 2.0 Conversation with Ram Menon, CMO at TIBCO," June 8, 2009, http://www.cmotwo.com/2009/06/08/cmo-20-conversation-with-ram-menon-cmo-at-tibco/.
6. Lenny Mendonca and Robert Sutton, "Succeeding at Open Source Innovation: An Interview with Mozilla's Mitchell Baker," *McKinsey Quarterly*, January 2008.
7. Francois Gossieaux, "CMO 2.0 Conversation with Mark Gambill, CMO at CDW," July 20, 2009, http://www.cmotwo.com/2009/07/20/cmo-20-conversation-with-mark-gambill-cmo-at-cdw/.
8. Francois Gossieaux, "CMO 2.0 Conversation with Beth Comstock, CMO at GE," March 6, 2009, http://www.cmotwo.com/2009/03/06/cmo-20-conversation-with-beth-comstock-cmo-at-ge/.
9. Francois Gossieaux, "CMO 2.0 Conversation with Mark Colombo, SVP Digital Access Marketing, FedEx," May 4, 2009, http://www.cmotwo.com/2009/05/04/cmo-20-conversation-with-mark-colombo-svp-digital-access-marketing-fedex/.
10. Gossieaux, "CMO 2.0 Conversation with Barry Judge."
11. Anne Fisher, "Newcomer to the C-Suite: The CCO," *Crain's*, August 24, 2009, p. 25.
12. Chief Customer Officer Council, http://www.chiefcustomerofficer.com/site/defining-the-cco.aspx.
13. Francois Gossieaux, "CMO 2.0 Influencer Conversation with Dan Ariely, author and Professor in Behavioral Economics at Duke University," May 24, 2009, http://www.cmotwo.com/2009/05/24/cmo-20-influencer-conversation-with-dan-ariely-author-and-professor-in-behavioral-economics-at-duke-university/.

Chapter 13

1. Francois Gossieaux, "CMO 2.0 Conversation with Mark Gambill, CMO at CDW," July 20, 2009, http://www.cmotwo.com/2009/07/20/cmo-20-conversation-with-mark-gambill-cmo-at-cdw/.
2. Marriott Rewards Insiders, http://www.marriottrewardsinsiders.marriott.com/index.jspa.
3. Unica, the Marketers Consortium, http://www.crmproject.com/documents.asp?d_ID=4386.
4. Carol Meyers, "Requiem for a Blog," *Marketer's Consortium*, September 24, 2007, http://unicashare.typepad.com/share/2007/09/requiem-for-a-b.html.
5. Netflix, http://www.netflixprize.com/.
6. Nike, http://inside.nike.com/blogs/nikerunning_news-en_US/2009/11/20/welcome-to-the-mobile-nikepluscom.
7. Nike+ Online Community, http://www.freshnetworks.com/case-studies/driving-online-word-of-mouth.
8. Francois Gossieaux, "CMO 2.0 Influence Conversation with Don Peppers, Author and Co-Founder of Peppers and Rogers," December 7, 2009, http://www.cmotwo.com/2009/12/07/cmo-20-influencer-conversation-with-don-peppers-author-and-co-founder-of-peppers-and-rogers/.
9. Francois Gossieaux, "CMO 2.0 Conversation with Beth Comstock, CMO at GE," March 6, 2009, http://www.cmotwo.com/2009/03/06/cmo-20-conversation-with-beth-comstock-cmo-at-ge/.

Chapter 14

1. "Peter Drucker," Wikipedia, http://en.wikipedia.org/wiki/Peter_Drucker.
2. Jaap Favier, "Ducati Killed Its Marketing and Prospers," *Forrester Report*, November 28, 2005.
3. Al Ries and Jack Trout, *Positioning: The Battle for Your Mind* (New York: McGraw-Hill, 2000).
4. *Fast Company* Staff, "The 3 I's versus the 3 A's," *Fast Company* blog, June 8, 2006, http://www.fastcompany.com/blog/fast-company-staff/fast-company-blog/3-versus-3.
5. Michael Trusov, Randolph E. Bucklin, and Koen Pauwels, "Effects of Word of Mouth versus Traditional Marketing: Findings from an Internet Social Networking Site," *Journal of Marketing* 73 (September 2009), pp. 90–102.
6. Ranghuram Iyengar, Sangman Han, and Sunil Gupta, "Do Friends Influence Purchases in Social Networks?" Harvard Business School Working Paper 09-123, May 21, 2009.
7. David Godes and Dina Mayzlin, "Firm-Created Word-of-Mouth Communications: Evidence from a Field Test," *Marketing Science* 28, no. 4 (July–August 2009), pp. 721–739.

8. American Express Members Project, http://www.membersproject.com/about/past_projects.html.

9. Stewart Brand, "Paul Saffo, 'Embracing Uncertainty: the Secret to Effective Forecasting,'" Long Now blog, January 14, 2008, http://blog.longnow.org/2008/01/14/paul-saffo-embracing-uncertainty-the-secret-to-effective-forecasting/.

10. Francois Gossieaux, "CMO 2.0 Conversation with Pete Blackshaw, EVP Nielsen Online Strategic Services," May 8, 2009, http://www.cmotwo.com/2009/05/08/cmo-20-conversation-with-pete-blackshaw-evp-nielsen-online-strategic-services/.

11. Michael Bush, "As Media Market Shrinks, PR Passes Up Reporters, Pitches Directly to Consumers," *Advertising Age*, October 26, 2009, http://adage.com/article?article_id=139864.

12. Francois Gossieaux, "CMO 2.0 Conversation with Larry Flanagan, CMO at MasterCard," March 1, 2010, http://www.cmotwo.com/2010/03/01/cmo-20-conversation-with-larry-flanagan-cmo-at-mastercard/.

13. Francois Gossieaux, "CMO 2.0 Conversation with Paula Drum from H&R Block," September 25, 2008, http://www.cmotwo.com/2008/09/25/cmo-20-conversation-with-paula-drum-from-hr-block/.

14. Procter & Gamble, *Rouge* magazine, http://www.rougemag.com/US/Default.aspx.

15. Sony, DigiDads program, http://www.sonyelectronicscommunity.com/sony/dads/.

16. IBM, Internet Evolution, http://www.internetevolution.com/.

17. Microsoft, FASTforward blog, http://www.fastforwardblog.com.

Chapter 15

1. For a customer rating model based on customer satisfaction, see Christopher Meyer and Andre Schwager, "Understanding Customer Experience," *Harvard Business Review*, February 2007, p. 117.

2. Social question and answer (or "Q&A") sites are Web sites where visitors can post questions, answer others users' questions, and give opinions on the value of the answers being provided. Examples include Yahoo! Answers and Amazon's Askville.

3. For a description of how an unpaid customer can assist other telecommunications customers, see Steve Lohr, "Customer Service? Ask a Volunteer," *New York Times*, April 29, 2009, p. 4.

4. Interestingly, TiVo has since formed a sponsored customer support site.

5. Available at http://spy.appspot.com/find/best%20buy.

6. Francois Gossieaux, "CMO 2.0 Influencer Conversation with John Hagel," July 7, 2009, http://www.cmotwo.com/2009/07/08/cmo-20-influencer-conversation-with-john-hagel-co-chairman-of-the-center-for-the-edge-at-deloitte/.

7. Francois Gossieaux, "CMO 2.0 Conversation with Ram Menon, CMO at TIBCO," June 8, 2009, http://www.cmotwo.com/2009/06/08/cmo-20-conversation-with-ram-menon-cmo-at-tibco/.

8. Francois Gossieaux, "CMO 2.0 Conversation with Jeff Hayzlett, CMO, Kodak," January 30, 2009, http://www.cmotwo.com/transcripts/2009/01/31/transcript-of-cmo-20-conversation-with-jeff-hayzlett-cmo-kodak/.

9. Francois Gossieaux, "CMO 2.0 Conversation with Mark Colombo, SVP Digital Access Marketing, FedEx," May 4, 2009, http://www.cmotwo.com/2009/05/04/cmo-20-conversation-with-mark-colombo-svp-digital-access-marketing-fedex/.

10. Ibid.

11. Ibid.

12. Francois Gossieaux, "CMO 2.0 Influence Conversation with Don Peppers, Author and Co-Founder of Peppers and Rogers," December 7, 2009, http://www.cmotwo.com/2009/12/07/cmo-20-influencer-conversation-with-don-peppers-author-and-co-founder-of-peppers-and-rogers/.

Chapter 16

1. For a discussion of the concept of "unbundling" a corporation into discrete functions, see John Hagel and Marc Singer, "Unbundling the Corporation," *Harvard Business Review* March 1, 1999, http://harvardbusiness.org/product/unbundling-the-corporation/an/99205-PDF-ENG.

2. David Court, "The Evolving Role of the CMO," *McKinsey Quarterly*, August 2007, http://www.mckinseyquarterly.com/Marketing/The_evolving_role_of_the_CMO_2031.

3. Clara Shih, *The Facebook Era: Tapping Online Social Networks to Build Better Products, Reach New Audiences, and Sell More Stuff* (Crawfordsville, Indiana: Prentice Hall, 2009), p. 61.

4. For an examination of the relentless creation of new products and brands in our society, see Lucas Conley, *OBD: Obsessive Branding Disorder: The Business of Illusion and the Illusion of Business* (New York: Public Affairs, 2008).

5. Geoffrey James, "Knowledge Review: Selling Gets Complex," *Strategy+Business*, Autumn 2009.

6. John Hagel and John Seely Brown, "From Push to Pull: Emerging Models for Mobilizing Resources," June 2008, p. 15, http://www.deloitte.com/view/en_US/us/Insights/centers/centers-center-for-edge/1e77742bdaa12210VgnVCM100000ba42f00aRCRD.htm.

7. See Anneke Seley and Brent Holloway, *Sales 2.0: Improve Business Results Using Innovative Sales Practices and Technology* (Newark, N.J.: Wiley, 2009).

Chapter 17

1. According to the 2009 Tribalization of Business Survey, 18 percent of online communities are managed by marketing; only 3 percent are managed by the product development function.
2. Francois Gossieaux, "CMO 2.0 Conversation with Susan Lavington, Senior Vice President of Marketing at *USA Today*," April 15, 2009, http://www.cmotwo.com/2009/04/15/cmo-20-conversation-with-susan-lavington-senior-vice-president-of-marketing-at-usa-today/.
3. Francois Gossieaux, "CMO 2.0 Conversation with Barry Judge, CMO at Best Buy," October 23, 2008, http://www.cmotwo.com/transcripts/2008/10/23/transcript-cmo-20-conversation-with-barry-judge-cmo-at-best-buy/.
4. Francois Gossieaux, "CMO 2.0 Influencer Conversation with Dan Ariely, author and Professor in Behavioral Economics at Duke University," May 24, 2009, http://www.cmotwo.com/2009/05/24/cmo-20-influencer-conversation-with-dan-ariely-author-and-professor-in-behavioral-economics-at-duke-university/.
5. Michael Prospero, "R&D as We Know It Is Dead," *Laptop*, April 2008, p. 113.

Chapter 18

1. See DeAnne Aguirre, Laird Post, and Sylvia Ann Hewlett, "The Talent Innovation Imperative," *Strategy+Business* Autumn 2009, and John Hagel, John Seely Brown, and Lang Davison, "Getting Better All the Time: Becoming a Talent-Driven Firm," in *Talent Reframed: Moving to the Talent Driven Firm* (Aspen Institute: Washington, D.C., 2009).
2. Francois Gossieaux, "CMO 2.0 Conversation with Susan Lavington, Senior Vice President of Marketing at *USA Today*," April 15, 2009, http://www.cmotwo.com/2009/04/15/cmo-20-conversation-with-susan-lavington-senior-vice-president-of-marketing-at-usa-today/.
3. Hagel et al., "Getting Better All the Time."
4. Steve Hamm, "Match.com for Mentors," *BusinessWeek*, March 23 & 30, 2009, p. 57.
5. Jena McGregor, "Job Reviews in 140 Keystrokes," *BusinessWeek*, March 23 & 30, 2009, p. 58.
6. Jeff Howe, *Crowdsourcing* (New York: Crown Business, 2008), p. 115
7. Hagel et al., "Getting Better All the Time."
8. A NASA employee reports that even government agencies are experimenting with permitting workers to self-select the projects that they would like to participate in: "Practically Radical: Richard Antcliff at BIF-5," http://www.businessinnovationfactory.com/iss/video/bif5-richard-antcliff.
9. Francois Gossieaux, "CMO 2.0 Influencer Conversation with John Hagel," July 7, 2009, http://www.cmotwo.com/2009/07/08/cmo-20-

influencer-conversation-with-john-hagel-co-chairman-of-the-center-for-the-edge-at-deloitte/.

10. Steve Lohr, "Customer Service? Ask a Volunteer," *New York Times*, April 29, 2009, p. 4.

11. David Rock, "Managing with the Brain in Mind," *Strategy+Business*, Autumn 2009, p. 59.

12. Ibid., p. 61.

Chapter 19

1. Luis Suarez blog, posted April 15, 2009, http://it.toolbox.com/blogs/elsua/traditional-knowledge-management-systems-adapt-or-die-31166.

2. Francois Gossieaux, "CMO 2.0 Conversation with Barry Judge, CMO at Best Buy," October 23, 2008, http://www.cmotwo.com/transcripts/2008/10/23/transcript-cmo-20-conversation-with-barry-judge-cmo-at-best-buy/.

3. See, for instance, Masamichi Takahashi, Masakazu Fujimoto, and Nobuhiro Yamasaki, "Active Lurking: Enhancing the Value of In-House Online Communities through the Related Practices around the Online Communities," CCI Working Paper 2007-006, MIT Sloan School of Management Working Paper 4646-07, http://ssrn.com/abstract=1041261.

4. Georg von Krogh, Kazuo Ichijo, and Ikujiro Nonaka, *Enabling Knowledge Creation: How to Unlock the Mystery of Tacit Knowledge and Release the Power of Innovation* (Oxford, UK: Oxford University Press, 2000).

5. John Seely Brown, "Research That Reinvents the Corporation," *Harvard Business Review*, August 2002, http://hbr.harvardbusiness.org/2002/08/research-that-reinvents-the-corporation/ar/pr.

6. "Hal Varian on How the Web Challenges Managers," *McKinsey Quarterly*, January 2009, https://www.mckinseyquarterly.com/Hal_Varian_on_how_the_Web_challenges_managers_2286.

7. Francois Gossieaux, "CMO 2.0 Conversation with Beth Comstock, CMO at GE," March 6, 2009, http://www.cmotwo.com/2009/03/06/cmo-20-conversation-with-beth-comstock-cmo-at-ge/.

Chapter 20

1. Bob Garfield, "Marshall Ganz Interview," *On the Media*, NPR, (November 7, 2008), http://www.onthemedia.org/transcripts/2008/11/07/04.

2. Warren Bennis and Patricia Ward Biedeman, *Organizing Genius* (Reading, Mass.: Perseus Books, 1997), p. 210.

3. Ibid., p. 22.

4. Francois Gossieaux, "CMO 2.0 Influencer Conversation with Dave Logan, Senior Partner, CultureSync," July 27, 2009, http://www.cmotwo.

com/2009/07/27/cmo-20-influencer-conversation-with-dave-logan-senior-partner-culturesync/.

5. "Whistle but Don't Tweet while You Work," Robert Half Press Release, 2009, http://rht.mediaroom.com/index.php?s=131&item=790.

6. "Freedom to Surf," *University of Melbourne News*, April 2, 2009, http://uninews.unimelb.edu.au/news/5750/.

7. Francois Gossieaux, "CMO 2.0 Influencer Conversation with Alan Webber, Author and Co-Founder of *Fast Company*," October 25, 2009, http://www.cmotwo.com/2009/10/25/cmo-20-influencer-conversation-with-alan-webber-author-and-co-founder-of-fast-company/.

8. Bennis and Biederman, *Organizing Genius*, p. 15.

9. Francois Gossieaux, "CMO 2.0 Influencer Conversation with Dave Logan, Senior Partner, CultureSync," July 27, 2009, http://www.cmotwo.com/2009/07/27/cmo-20-influencer-conversation-with-dave-logan-senior-partner-culturesync/.

10. Bennis and Biederman, *Organizing Genius*, p. 12.

11. Francois Gossieaux, "CMO 2.0 Conversation with Ram Menon, CMO at Tibco," June 8, 2009, http://www.cmotwo.com/2009/06/08/cmo-20-conversation-with-ram-menon-cmo-at-tibco/.

Epilogue

1. Dell, IdeaStorm community, http://www.ideastorm.com/ideaList?lsi=0.

2. Starbucks, My Starbucks Idea community, http://mystarbucksidea.force.com/ideaHome.

3. Francois Gossieaux, "CMO 2.0 Conversation with Rob Spencer, Chief Idea Management Officer at Pfizer," September 22, 2009, http://www.cmotwo.com/2009/09/22/cmo-20-conversation-with-rob-spencer-chief-idea-management-officer-at-pfizer/.

4. Francois Gossieaux, "CMO 2.0 Conversation with Erin Nelson, CMO at Dell, and Manish Mehta, VP of Social Media and Communities," March 4, 2010, http://www.cmotwo.com/2010/03/04/cmo-20-conversation-with-erin-nelson-cmo-at-dell-and-manish-mehta-vp-of-social-media-and-communities/.

5. John Hagel and Marc Singer, "Unbundling the Corporation," *Harvard Business Review*, March 1, 1999, http://harvardbusiness.org/product/unbundling-the-corporation/an/99205-PDF-ENG.

6. Steve Paxhia, "We Are Smarter Than Me Report," Gilbane Group blog, March 21, 2007, http://gilbane.com/blog/2007/03/we_are_smarter_than_me_report.html.

INDEX

ABOUT THE AUTHORS

Francois Gossieaux lives and works in the Boston Area, where he is a cofounder and partner at Human 1.0, formerly Beeline Labs, a boutique marketing innovation consultancy. He is also a board member and senior fellow at the Society for New Communications Research.

Prior to founding Beeline Labs, Francois was the chief marketing officer at eRoom Technology, a collaboration software startup that was acquired by Documentum. He earned a master in science in electronics engineering from the University of Gent (Belgium), and a graduate degree in management and administration from Harvard University.

Edward K. Moran lives and works in New York, where he is Director of Insights and Innovation for the Technology, Media and Telecommunications (TMT) Group at Deloitte Services LP. Ed advises TMT companies in the areas of strategic planning, product innovation, and competitive positioning.

Prior to joining Deloitte Services, Ed was managing partner of a Manhattan law firm, and earned a master in business administration degree in information systems and in management from New York University.